The Symbolist
1870-1910   Generation

The Symbolist Generation

1870-1910

Pierre-Louis Mathieu

SKIRA
RIZZOLI
NEW YORK

To Clotilde

Weinstock

© 1990 by Editions d'Art Albert Skira S.A., Geneva

Reproduction rights reserved by PRO LITTERIS, Zurich, and Cosmopress, Geneva

Published in the United States of America in 1990 by

Rizzoli INTERNATIONAL PUBLICATIONS, INC.
300 Park Avenue South/New York 10010

Translated from the French by Michael Taylor

Library of Congress Cataloging-in-Publication Data

Mathieu, Pierre-Louis.
   [Génération symboliste.   English]
   The Symbolist Generation. 1870-1910/Pierre-Louis Mathieu.
      p.   cm.
   Translation of: La génération symboliste.
   Includes bibliographical references and index.
   ISBN 0-8478-1218-9
   1. Symbolism (Art movement).   2. Arts, Modern—
19th century.
3. Arts, Modern—20th century.   I. Title.
NX600.S95M3813   1990
700—dc20
                                       89-43610
                                          CIP

CONTENTS

INTRODUCTION
TO THE SYMBOLIST GENERATION

Post-Impressionism or Symbolism?

The names of most art movements are coined years, if not generations, after they have flourished. Their members would probably be very surprised to learn how they are labeled today. This is the case with seventeenth-century Baroque art (a strictly twentieth-century term) and, more recently, Expressionism.

Not a few schools of art, Impressionism among them, owe their names to a critic's witticism. But here at least the term Impression corresponds to a group that drew together, in spite of many differences, men and women who agreed to show their works outside official channels—eight group shows organized in Paris between 1874 and 1886 without the term Impressionism ever once being mentioned by any of the interested parties in any of their catalogs. Again, despite the differences that separate landscape painters such as Pissarro and Monet from fellow artists of Degas's or Cézanne's stamp, the same group was given to painting themes springing from the observation of life and nature at first hand. Moreover, around 1890 Impressionism was, in the public eye, as much a synonym for avant-garde art as a description of a distinct school of painting. What shocked the public then was not the Impressionists' subjects, for naturalism was the fashion both in literature and art, but their seemingly loose technique which made visitors and critics at the official art salons regard their pictures as rough sketches—"impressions"—rather than finished paintings. Similarly, Fauvism (1906) and Cubism (1908) were coined by an influential and ironic critic, Louis Vauxcelles.

Art history makes its choices and judgments long after the events it studies have taken place, and it has rightly designated the period spanning the years 1870 to 1886 (the date of the last group exhibit) as the Impressionist period. This was after all the most innovative movement of the time. But it was not the only one, and we tend to

forget too easily that the Impressionists were overshadowed by other contemporary artists who were highly regarded in their day. Until recently these painters were lumped together under the rather derisive label *pompiers*, that is, official artists of little talent. They are now well on the way to being rehabilitated, and at least one art historian, Jacques Thuillier,[1] has suggested that the expression *époque pompier* should be extended to the entire artistic output of the second half of the nineteenth century, a characterization which is going a bit far.

The period following Impressionism—or let us say after 1886, though Monet, Degas, and Renoir were a long way from the end of their prolific careers and, the great painters that they were, would go on to renew their style after that date—is generally called Post-Impressionism. Roughly speaking, it spans the years 1885 to 1905, when it was succeeded by Fauvism and, later, Cubism.

It may be useful to remind the reader of the origin of the term Post-Impressionism. It too was coined by an art critic, the Englishman Roger Fry who gave the perfectly acceptable title "Manet and the Post-Impressionists" to a London art gallery show of French artists active between 1886 and 1910. In addition to works by Manet (wrongly proposed as the "father of Impressionism") this exhibition included canvases by Gauguin, Van Gogh, Cézanne, Seurat, Sérusier, Redon and Denis, as well as the younger artists Marquet, Derain, Rouault, Vlaminck, Matisse, and Picasso. All had one thing in common, in Fry's view, and this was the fact that the "Post-Impressionists consider the Impressionists too naturalistic."[2]

Fry, who was more familiar at the time with classical art than with contemporary painting, was not altogether wrong in describing the fin de siècle painters as artists who had ceased to draw

Gustave Moreau
***Orpheus on the Tomb
of Eurydice***
**1891, oil on canvas,
174 × 128**
Musée Gustave Moreau, Paris
Jealous of his privacy and intent on producing a hermetic work, Moreau nevertheless allowed himself an autobiographical allusion in this picture. Here he identifies himself with Orpheus following the death of the lady friend to whom he had been passionately attached for thirty years. "My soul is alone," he confessed. "It has lost all that made for its radiance, force and sweetness. It weeps over itself, bereft as it is of everything, in its unconsoled solitude."

inspiration from the direct observation of nature. However, his term merely serves to locate these artists in time, lumping together several distinct schools, as they are now viewed—as if the sole quality distinguishing the artists of the London show was the fact that they were active after the Impressionists. On the other hand, there is a word that often crops up in the art criticism of the 1890s, one that several artists of the time used to describe their own work, and that is Symbolism, a term that was at times replaced by the word Idealism. Both these terms define much better the sources of inspiration that moved this generation of painters.

Almost no artist of this period was immune to Symbolism, even if a few would only follow the movement for several years before abandoning it. Moreover, unlike Impressionism, Symbolism was a European, not a specifically French, movement with Paris as its center of attraction. From Helsinki to Barcelona, London to Milan, throughout Belgium, Holland, Poland, Austria, and Switzerland with even a small group in the United States —in all these countries the leading artists of the generation active between 1885 and 1910 shared the same concept of art and can be grouped under the same name.

Seurat (1859-1891) and the French Neo-Impressionists alone escaped its dominion, though critics at the time and some recent art historians have tried not altogether unreasonably to connect Symbolism and the "art-science" Seurat dreamt of inventing and which his disciple Signac (1863-1935) later systematized in his treatise, *D'Eugène Delacroix au néo-impressionnisme* (1899). True, there were Symbolists who borrowed the pointillist technique, but by and large Neo-Impressionism continued, and hoped to give a scientific basis to, the experiments of Impressionism. The Neo-Impressionists, like the Impressionists, were interested mainly in landscape painting and the study of light. But this did not prevent Seurat, who was friendly with several Symbolist artists like Aman-Jean, from admiring Puvis de Chavannes. Nor did it prevent his work from having a Symbolist undercurrent (which Signac discarded after his master's premature death) that was fed by the works of Humbert de Superville, in particular the latter's attempt to give meaning to the direction of lines. As Françoise Cachin has remarked, "Seurat's keen perception of color and line symbolism meant that

he had more in common with the Symbolist poets. Signac's book tends on the contrary to move away from them. Seurat very probably saw in his scientific method a pictorial key to cosmic harmony. The striking thing about the few writings of his that have come down to us is their esoteric vocabulary: the words *harmony* and *rhythm* are the keynotes of a system of laws governing colors and lines, a system that tends at once toward the metaphysical and the scientific."[3]

Like Romanticism, Symbolism offers both the advantage and the disadvantage of also referring to a literary movement. The commonly accepted date of the birth of literary Symbolism is 1886, when Jean Moréas's poetic manifesto appeared in the supplement to the September 18 issue of *Le Figaro*. That very same year—a not altogether fortuitous coincidence—the Impressionists organized their eighth and last group show, minus the presence of painters like Monet, Cézanne, Renoir, Sisley, but instead including works by younger artists such as Seurat and Signac who were giving a new direction to the movement, or others (Gauguin, Odilon Redon) who drew their inspiration from naturalist sources.

Never before or since this period has there been such a marked inclination among writers, artists, and musicians throughout Europe to express certain inner feelings and states of mind common to all. Nor have creators in different fields ever regularly gathered and influenced each other to this extent, in sharp contrast to the previous generation which had concentrated almost exclusively on observing nature and everyday modern life.

Symbol, Symbolism, Allegory

The term Symbolism, which entered French around 1830 and had approximately the same sense in all the European languages, is one of the most difficult of words to define. Its primary meaning is the practice of representing things by symbols, and it is more or less this definition which caused it to be adopted as the name of the literary movement that claimed to spring from Baudelaire and flourished in France and Belgium between 1880 and 1890. It was later extended to the artistic movement then sweeping Europe that was closely connected with literary Symbolism.

One of the very first writers to use the word in this sense, albeit with a pejorative connotation, was Emile Zola, who employed it as early as 1876 in a critical article of Gustave Moreau's painting.

To fully understand the diversity of meanings in the word Symbolism, one must go back to its Greek root, *to sumbolon* (τό σὺμβολον), which originally meant an identifying sign. In the beginning a symbol was a token that was broken in two by a pair of friends or confederates; each kept his own half, handing it down to his children, so that in time the owners of the two halves could establish the connection between their respective families by producing the two fragments and fitting them together. Thus, the words symbol and symbolism contain the basic idea of a message, a thing that is communicated.

What the Symbolist writers and artists indeed had in common was the fact that, by means of words, forms, colors, they sought to communicate to the reader or viewer a personal message of a spiritual, moral, or even religious nature. The Impressionists and Naturalists, on the other hand, had contented themselves with merely reproducing the physical world. Gauguin gives a good description of his creative approach when he says that his purpose was to reach "thought's mysterious center." A Symbolist art work speaks to the viewer's heart, his soul, not to his eyes, those simple receptors.

Symbols are found in every civilization since the dawn of time. They are objects, figures, colors, lines that stand for feelings which cannot be physically perceived. Experts in the interpretation of symbols endeavor to penetrate their deepest, most elementary levels of meaning, notably by studying the civilizations and religions of Mesopotamia, Egypt, the Far East. Christianity, in turn, absorbed many older symbols and included them in its own iconography. The significant role symbols play in Romanesque and Gothic sculpture and stained-glass windows is well known. It was, moreover, precisely around the end of the nineteenth century that historians began to examine this symbolism.

The Symbolist artists gave interpretations of their own to the pre-Christian and Early Christian symbolic conception of life and the universe. Drawing freely on the repertoire of traditional images familiar to every fine arts student, they often gave these symbols an unorthodox interpretation.

Paul Gauguin
Calvary
1889, oil on canvas, 92 × 73.5
Musées Royaux des Beaux-Arts, Brussels
"In this picture there is a disquieting and racy mixture of barbaric splendor, Catholic liturgy, Hindu reverie, Gothic imagery, and obscure and subtle symbolism," wrote in 1891 the novelist and art critic Octave Mirbeau, one of the first to believe in the genius of Gauguin.

9

Under Gustave Moreau's hand, for example, the ancient Egyptian and Greek myth of the Sphinx acquired a uniquely personal moral and sexual dimension. And Gauguin, contrasting his own iconography to Puvis de Chavannes's more classical symbolic imagery, declared, "Puvis calls a painting 'Purity' and elucidates this by painting a young virgin holding a lily in her hand. Gauguin will take the same title and paint a landscape with clear waters, not a sullying trace of civilized man, perhaps a single figure." Edvard Munch went as far as to invent his own symbol of torment, the "blood flower," a reddish plant which appears in several of his pictures. Camille Claudel wrote to her brother Paul that she was working on a sculpture she intended to call *Maturity*; it included a "leaning tree signifying fate."

Many art historians and philologists distinguish between symbols and allegories, which are codified images that stand for abstract ideas, for example a two-faced woman holding a mirror (Prudence) or a woman gripping a sword and scales (Justice). An inventory of such images was published as early as the late sixteenth century: this was Cesare Ripa's often reprinted *Iconologia*, which artists continued to use in the nineteenth century. Gustav Klimt and Franz von Stuck began their careers drawing vignettes for *Allegorien und Embleme*, an album issued by Martin Gerlach in 1882. The Symbolist artists were familiar with these iconographic compendiums, but they often ignored the traditional explanations given in them, preferring interpretations of their own. As a result it is sometimes hard for the contemporary viewer to fathom the symbolic imagery used in these artists' work; understanding this imagery requires knowledge of not only the language of allegory but also the artist's private intentions. Thus, at first glance Paul Sérusier's *The Water Bearers* (c. 1897, Musée des Beaux-Arts, Brest; reproduction p. 12) is a simple scene of daily life in Brittany, whereas the artist's meaning is indeed far from being that straightforward. The young woman carrying the full water jug represents life, the old woman with her spilled jug senility and death. "I needed an allegory, but nothing Greek," the artist stated. "I was in Celtic country —I pictured fairies. Modern fashions change too often; I gave my figures timeless costumes."

One of those to have the clearest perception of the difference between symbol and allegory was the artist Maurice Denis, who was an art historian in his own right. "An allegory speaks to the mind," he states, "a symbol speaks to the eyes; but in addition to simple impressions like joy, terror, mystery, which are experienced universally, it is necessary if you want to give birth to more complex emotions to have an educated background. It is thanks to this background that the symbol reaches the soul without having to go through the rational mind. Allegory, on the other hand, requires an intellectual effort, a reading and a translation."

Precisely because it does not draw on the data of reality the way landscape painting does, Symbolist art expects the viewer to possess a certain level of knowledge, just as religious art requires at least some familiarity with Christian doctrines. The modern viewer is obliged to make an effort to understand the mentality of the Symbolist artists, their aspirations and anxieties—which are not, in the final analysis, all that different from our own. After all, a mere hundred years separate us from these painters, many of whom lived well into the twentieth century, long enough for us in the 1990s to feel that we share some of those mysterious "correspondences" that meant so much to them.

Gustav Klimt
Tragedy
1897, black chalk heightened with white and gold, 41.9 × 30.8
Historisches Museum der Stadt Wien, Vienna
While remaining faithful to the language of classical iconology, in which the artist was perfectly at ease, Klimt adds here a foreign motif, a Chinese dragon representing evil. The female figure on the left abandons herself to the dragon whereas her counterpart on the right fends it off

11

Paul Sérusier
*The Water Bearers
(Weariness)*
**c. 1897, oil on canvas, 111 × 67
Musée des Beaux-Arts, Brest**
These two Breton peasants are
not merely water bearers. The
younger woman represents life
and fecundity; the second woman seated at the foot of the tree
symbolizes old age and death, as
the overturned jug beside her
indicates.

12

Symbolist theorists and critics

The impetus needed to launch an artistic movement based on elective affinities between writers, musicians, and artists has sometimes come from poets or novelists doing double duty as art critics. Such was the part in launching Symbolism played by two very different figures: Georges-Albert Aurier and the propagandist if the Rose + Croix movement (The Order of the Rosy Cross), Sâr Péladan, The Sâr, or magus, whose declared purpose was to organize exhibitions of idealist art, was a personality sufficiently important to merit a chapter of his own. Furthermore, in the early years of this century other art movements following Symbolism so to speak would spring up under similar circumstances: Filippo Tommaso Marinetti and Italian Futurism, André Breton and Surrealism.

Georges-Albert Aurier might have been the André Breton of Symbolism had he not died at the age of 27 in 1892. A mediocre poet, he was one of the founders of the leading Symbolist review, *Le Mercure de France*, to which he contributed art criticism. He was the first and, for a time, only critic to review Van Gogh and Gauguin favorably, and the latter's art inspired his famous theory of "Symbolism in painting." Nothing reflects the artistic sensibilities of this period better than his reviews with their overblown, dated style studded with philosophical terms; what is more, his writing echoes the ideas held by those artists Aurier was personally acquainted with.

Less of a theorist, but nonetheless an attentive observer of the art scene from 1890 to 1900, André Mellerio, a great admirer of Redon and his first biographer, wrote a slender volume called *Le Mouvement idéaliste en peinture* in which he attempted, more dispassionately than Aurier, to examine the birth of the movement. Mellerio pointed out that the term *"idéalisme"* (which he personally preferred) had no more "rational significance" than the words symbolism and impressionism. A knowledgeable and penetrating chronicler of the movement, whose inception he connects with the exhibition of works by Gauguin

and his circle at the Café Volpini in 1889, Mellerio figures prominently in Maurice Denis's well-known group portrait of the Nabis painted in 1900. Finally, there is the *Etudes d'art étrange* (1906) by the Swiss writer William Ritter, an ardent admirer of Böcklin and Wagner. A sweeping survey of European art at the dawn of the twentieth century, Ritter's work devotes equal attention to the Italian artist Giovanni Segantini, and the German Max Klinger; to the Norwegian Edvard Munch, and the Pole Jozef Mehoffer.

But naturally it also fell to the artists themselves to define their art. Maurice Denis, Emile Bernard, Paul Sérusier, and Jean Delville have left us works of the highest interest, outlining their concept of art. Many of the Symbolist artists kept diaries, though not always regularly, and expressed their ideas and beliefs in letters to friends, many of which are still extant and constitute a treasure trove of information about this period. The diaries of Gustave Moreau, Odilon Redon, Maurice Denis, and Edvard Munch are fine examples of intimist literature in their own right. Then too some of the Symbolist artists were genuine poets as well. We might mention in this respect Dante Gabriel Rossetti and Karel de Nerée tot Babberich. As for Alfred Kubin, the Austrian artist wrote a novel which remains a masterpiece of expressionist prose.

"Anywhere out of the world"

The novelist Joris-Karl Huysmans began his career as a disciple of Emile Zola and a champion of Impressionism; later he became one of the leading supporters of Moreau's and Redon's art. The hero of his novel *A rebours* (*Against the Grain*), first published in 1884, is an exhausted young aristocrat. Jaded before he even has much of a chance to experience life, he takes as his personal motto a phrase in English which is the title of a famous prose poem of Baudelaire's, "Anywhere out of the world."

It is a motto that would have fitted any of the Symbolists, so great was their distaste for the world and the period they lived in, so deep went

Odilon Redon
The Stained Glass Window
c. 1895-1903, charcoal and
pastel on cardboard, 87×68
Musée d'Orsay, Paris

"Before the influence of Cézanne," wrote Maurice Denis, "by way of Gauguin and Bernard, it was Redon's line of thought... which in 1890 set art moving in a spiritualist direction." This pastel, at once somber and luminous, inclines the viewer to religious meditation, without, however, laying down any specific subject. Of his drawings, Redon said: "They inspire, they do not designate. They set us down, as music does, in the ambiguous world of the indeterminate." He made this drawing after a visit to Chartres Cathedral.

their rejection of industrial civilization and the modern metropolis (which, in the second half of the nineteenth century, was fast gaining ground on the medieval city). Paris, Vienna, London, Rome were all acquiring their present configuration; ancient quarters were being destroyed, ugly industrial suburbs were pushing into the countryside. The Symbolists hated money, Capitalism, bourgeois democracy; they had no faith in scientific progress, and this led many of them to embrace one form or another of utopian socialism or esoteric brand of mysticism.

Artists like Watts, Moreau, Böcklin, Ryder took refuge in myths and ancient legends, often without moving from the comfort of their homes, and wound up creating purely imaginary worlds sealed off, to varying degrees, from the real world. To the modern metropolis they preferred ancient cities such as Venice and above all Bruges, which still seemed untouched, unchanged since the Middle Ages. In the 1880s, Brittany was the place to escape to if one wanted to get away from what passed for the amenities of modern civilization: the locals still clung to their traditions, their old costumes, their religious faith, their simple ways; the forests seemed untrodden, the coasts wild, and at every crossroads there stood a calvary. Artists from every nation flocked here, stayed a while, and then moved on to landscapes that seemed even less polluted. Gauguin would spend much of his life searching for another Eden, eventually traveling to the edge of the known world to find it. Hodler, Willumsen, and Segantini sought out the clear springs and everlasting snows of high mountains. Others —Munch and Filliger for example—spent months, years tramping from place to place, their thirst for novel sensations never quenched.

If one were to have asked the fin de siècle artists what period they would have preferred to live in, almost all of them would have answered the Middle Ages. Those centuries of ardent faith and cathedral-building fascinated them, as did the deep symbols that scholars everywhere were endeavoring to decipher, and with such earnestness that every detail in a stone-carving or stained glass window seemed to them to have some weighty symbolic meaning. It was precisely in the 1890s that the great decoder of medieval religious art, Emile Mâle, was cataloging the churches of France—and was experiencing some difficulty in persuading his contemporaries that the medieval

artisans did not always have a symbolic intention when they chose to render a flower or legendary beast.

This somewhat romantic perception of a period about which relatively little was known went hand in hand with an idealized view of the medieval "artist's" working conditions. It was their deep faith, the singleness of their inspiration, and their communal living that appealed to the Symbolists and inspired the Pre-Raphaelite and Nabi brotherhoods. The fin de siècle artists regarded manual and artisanal works with enthusiasm, while condemning industrial and mass produced objects. Gauguin, for example, considered himself by turns a painter, a wood carver, a ceramist, an engraver, and a builder (he erected his own house in the Marquesas, *La Maison du Jouir*). William Morris gave up painting to found the Arts and Crafts Movement, whose members attempted to resurrect the life style of the medieval craftsmen; and following in Morris footsteps the Viennese architect Josef Hoffmann established the *Wiener Werkstätte*. Even though such attempts rarely met with commercial success, these workshops (where artists like Burne-Jones and Klimt spent some time) produced some of the finest examples of Art Nouveau.

In their desire to visit the art centers of Europe, many of the Symbolists traveled from country to country like the wandering monks of the Middle Ages—though thanks to the spread of railways they journeyed in relative comfort. Notwithstanding its glorious past, Rome attracted them less than Florence and Venice, cities that held the best collections of works by painters active before the Cinquecento. There the Symbolists could admire artists such as Giotto, Cimabue, and above all Botticelli. Increasingly, however, the hub of the arts, the capital every artist felt obliged to visit, was Paris. Not because of Manet and the Impressionists, who were as yet hardly known, but because of the city's prestigious ateliers, where instruction was dispensed by academic artists whose works were singled out for distinction by the juries of the various Universal Expositions which were held at a steady rate, in 1878, 1889 and 1900, together with the brilliant decennial and centennial retrospectives of works by both French and foreign artists. Almost all the painters of this period were drawn to Paris, a phenomenon that would continue till the outbreak of World War Two. There, in the course

of interminable meetings, they discovered the city's cafés, avant-garde artistic and literary circles, movements that were not, as a rule, those their academic masters had told them about.

Other European capitals played a significant role in the spread of Symbolism, notably Berlin, Munich, and mainly Brussels, whose artists were in touch with the latest developments in both the English- and French-speaking countries. The exhibitions of the *Groupe des XX* and *La Libre Esthétique* gave Belgian and Dutch artists a chance to become acquainted with their counterparts in France. And the Belgians brought Symbolism to the Secession shows in Munich, Berlin, and mainly to the last and most innovative of these exhibitions, the 1898 Vienna *Kunstschau*.

Under the influence of Saturn

The realist and academic artists of the late nineteenth century are not usually credited with having had metaphysical leanings—still less the Impressionists with their often springlike, sun-drenched pictures of nature painted out of doors.

The Symbolist generation, on the other hand, seems to have been born under the influence of Saturn, that pallid, baleful planet which has been associated since the dawn of time with the woes and trials of existence. The Bible of the Symbolist artists and writers was Arthur Schopenhauer's *World as Will and Idea*. Though it was published as early as 1819, Schopenhauer's work became popular in the second half of the century and was

Paul Gauguin
War and Peace
1901, polychrome woodcarving in low relief
Upper panel: 48.5×99.5
Lower panel: 44.5×99.5
Museum of Fine Arts, Boston, Gift of Mr. and Mrs. K. Marshall

A mysterious composition reflecting Gauguin's theological and philosophical speculations at the end of his life. The upper scene represents peace and its benefits, the lower one war and its violence; to the face in the center of the latter, a kind of Christ Pantocrator, he gave his own features, as in several other compositions. Gauguin, especially in periods of depression, liked to identify himself with the redemptive personality of Christ.

16

only translated into French and Italian in the 1880's. It influenced Klinger and Kubin's pessimism; it inspired Segantini, Gustave Moreau, De Chirico. The Parisian artist Moreau, upon being presented with a selection of Schopenhauer's writings by the French translator, thanked the latter with a drawing that represented Helen meditating on the ruins of Troy.

Schopenhauer's view is that happiness is merely an illusion, and passionate love but a travesty of the reproductive urge. The world, as he sees it, is dominated by the *ennui* of the beings who pass through it. Like Schopenhauer himself, a number of Symbolists were drawn to Buddhism and the doctrine of reincarnation.

Considerations of this kind may or may not have anything to do with art. But there is no denying the fact that for the Symbolists the cru-

cial question, one they posed repeatedly in and through their art concerned the meaning of life. Life is pain, happiness and love unattainable, and death the only certainty—this was the disenchanted message they wanted to communicate to the viewer. Some would devote years to expressing their pessimism in elaborate, large scale works, polyptichs and series of related canvases.

In *The Life of Mankind*, for example, Gustave Moreau alternates scenes from the Book of Genesis with episodes from the myth of Orpheus, ending with the murder of Cain, who was redeemed, it is true, by Christ's sacrifice. Rodin labored off and on for thirty years on *The Gates of Hell*, a work steeped in the spirit of Dante's "Abandon all hope, ye who enter here," which remains, however, unrelieved by the Italian poet's grand eschatology. Segantini painted his

Giovanni Segantini
Death (Triptych of Nature)
1898-1899, oil on canvas, 190 × 322
Segantini Museum, St. Moritz
Painted out of doors, at a high altitude in the mountains of the Engadine (Switzerland), this large composition is the artist's final statement of his pantheist faith: he likens the mountain to an altar before which he kneels. Segantini is known to have practiced spiritualism. According to his wife, he had a distinct foreboding, while working on this picture, that he was painting the circumstances of his own death. And so it proved. It was in the mountain shelter pictured here that he died, leaving the canvas unfinished.

17

Triptych of Nature surrounded by alpine glaciers, and died before he was able to complete the last panel—Death. In Tahiti, where he had gone in the hope of finding Eden on earth, Gauguin labored desperately day and night for a whole month on his "testament," *Whence Come We? What Are We? Whither Go We?* The answer to these questions is the goose-like bird in the lower left corner, "a strange, stupid fowl." After completing the painting, the artist swallowed a dose of arsenic. Munch regarded his entire output as one vast "life frieze" illustrating the impossibility of communicating between the sexes and the ubiquity of sorrow and death.

With the exception of Maurice Denis and some of the Nabis who converted to Catholicism, few Symbolists had the traditional Christian faith that might have sustained them through life's hardships. Most of them strove to allay their existential *angst* with spiritism, occultism, or the study of ancient or Far Eastern mysticisms. Almost all of the artists we will encounter in these pages can be linked with one or another of these isms.

Music before all else

Paul Verlaine was proclaiming the tastes of his entire generation when he wrote in his poem "Art poétique" "Music before all else/Music again and forever." Like Verlaine and other writers of the period, the Symbolist artists, many of whom had a good knowledge of music when they were not amateur musicians themselves, were fond of drawing analogies between painting and music. "My drawings inspire, they do not define," wrote Redon. "They do not determine things. Like music itself, they place us in the ambiguous world of the indeterminate." And Watts compared one of his pictures, *Time and Oblivion*, to an "organ chord swelling powerfully but with no modulation."

Robert Schumann and Johannes Brahms were the favorite composers of artists in the German-speaking countries. Max Klinger presented the latter, on his sixtieth birthday, with an album (*Brahmsphantasie*, 1894) containing forty-one etchings which are intended as visual "accompaniments" to the *Lieder*, not mere illustrations. An even greater musical influence on art was Beethoven, whose reputation was then at its peak. At the fourteenth Secession show in Vienna (1902), the great exhibition hall designed by Olbrich had, at its center, a marble statue of the deified composer by Klinger. The Secession artists Alfred Roller, Adolf Böhm, Joseph-Maria Auchentaller, Ferdinand Andri, and mainly Gustav Klimt, had painted a series of wavy friezes as a backdrop to the statue, which the architect Josef Hoffmann had orchestrated to form a sort of voyage of initiation. The high point of this celebration was a performance of the *Ninth Symphony*'s finale conducted by Gustav Mahler.

In France and the English-speaking countries there arose a cult around Richard Wagner. Launched by Baudelaire as early as 1861, it was popularized by *La Revue Wagnérienne* (1885-1888), which was much read in Symbolist circles. One of this journal's leading contributors, the musicologist Teodor de Wyzewa, even went as far as trying to found a "Wagnerian" school of painting as an alternative to the "sensational" and "descriptive" art of Manet and Degas. What he wanted was an "emotional and musical" painting like that of Puvis de Chavannes and Gustave Moreau, a painting that would "pay little heed to the attempt to render objects by lines and colors, treating them merely as signs of emotions and combining them in such a way as to produce in us, through their free interaction, a total impression comparable to the one produced by a symphony."[4]

It was at Bayreuth, regarded as a shrine to Wagner very early on, that Péladan had a revelation in 1888 and decided to found the Rose + Croix Order. And it was after meeting Wagner that Edouard Schuré, the future author of *Les Grands initiés*, decided to devote his life to promoting the German composer's music and *Weltanschauung*.

A number of Symbolist artists took their inspiration from Wagner's musical dramas, with results that varied from the literal illustration to the private interpretation. The best examples of this Wagnerian-derived art were produced by

Fantin-Latour and Redon in France, Burne-Jones and Beardsley in England, Welti in Switzerland, Henry de Groux in Belgium, Ryder and Marcius-Simons in the United States.

Gauguin inscribed a lengthy quote from Wagner on the dining-room walls of the inn where he and his friends were staying in the Breton village of Le Pouldu. He too wanted to establish correspondences between sounds and colors. In an 1895 interview he declared, defending his pink skies and red dogs, "They are absolutely intended! They are necessary, and everything in my work is absolutely calculated, lengthily meditated. Call it music, if you wish! Through arrangements of lines and colors, using an ordinary subject taken from life or nature as a pretext, I obtain symphonies, harmonies that do not represent anything wholly real in the vulgar sense of that word, not directly expressing any idea, but provoking thought, without the aid of ideas or images, simply through mysterious affinities between our brain and certain arrangements of colors and lines."[5]

Wagner wrote his own librettos, composed his own music, designed his own theater at Bayreuth; his idea was to create a total art work, *Gesamtkunstwerk*. A number of artists tried to follow in his footsteps and conceived vast decorative projects designed to be housed in edifices that were a combination of a museum and a sanctuary (Watts in London, Munch and Vigeland in Oslo, Segantini in St. Moritz). In the same spirit, painters like Toorop, Willumsen, Klinger carved and assembled their own picture frames.

Conversely, several musicians were drawn toward literature and the plastic arts, notably

Franz von Lenbach
Richard Wagner
1871, oil on canvas,
55 × 40
Richard Wagner Museum,
Bayreuth

Claude Debussy, until recently considered an "Impressionist" composer, though it is difficult to name a more authentic exponent of Symbolism in music. True, the jury of the Institut de France, when they awarded Debussy the *Grand Prix de Rome* in 1887, admonished him that he had been chosen despite his "Impressionism," meaning his averred lack of precision and his fondness for experimenting with strange tonalities. Debussy's favorite artists at this time were Botticelli and Gustave Moreau and his first score, *La Demoiselle élue*, based on a poem by the Pre-Raphaelite Rossetti, was originally published with illustrations by Maurice Denis. He later composed music for Mallarmé's *Prélude à l'après-midi d'un faune* and Maurice Maeterlinck's *Pelléas et Mélisande*, before suggesting to the poet Victor Segalen, in 1907, that he write the libretto for an opera based on the myth of Orpheus. Segalen agreed and went to the Gustave Moreau Museum for inspiration, however the composer died before writing the music.

The Symbolist dream-world

Symbolism is foremost a gallery of portraits, usually of women depicted full-face with long auburn hair and eyes that are either transfixed or dreamily shut—the stereotype created by Rossetti and Burne-Jones. There is little or no action in these pictures, neither story nor narrative element; one meditates, broods, dreams —never acting—in a melancholy or mournful atmosphere. Oblivious of her surroundings and often draped in jewels and brocade, the typical figure in countless Symbolist pictures from Khnopff to Klimt, Munch to Vrubel, seems a withdrawn, unattainable princess. She could be an idol the way she is covered with precious gems, immersed in flowers.

The choice time for such reveries is twilight or nightfall; the preferred season, autumn or winter with their train of mist; the climate, generally northern, rarely the south. The favorite Symbolist locations are solitary spots, far from the city, or else interiors well insulated from the world outside. Nature, when shown, is frequently hostile, the antithesis of the airy Impressionist scene bathed in warm sunlight.

Water is always present. Not the flowing, living element of springs and streams, but the more opaque water that sleeps in ponds, the canals of Venice and Bruges, whose still surface mirrors the narcissist's gaze.

Swans glide noiselessly over those waters; they are Wagnerian birds, signifying purity when immaculately white, presaging sorrow when black, their necks perfect pretexts for drawing graceful arabesques.

The lily, another symbol of purity, is ubiquitous to the point of becoming a Symbolist cliché.

Such motifs, which the Symbolists never wearied of employing, eventually to the point of exhaustion, crop up in contemporary writing. These texts fed the imagination of painters, whose works in turn inspired the period's men of letters. Stéphane Mallarmé, Joris-Karl Huysmans, Jules Laforgue, Henri de Régnier, Stuart Merril, Albert Samain, Elémir Bourges, Oscar Wilde built their fantasies on Moreau's work, transposing his visions into verse and prose.

Two writers above all were the cornerstones of the Symbolist edifice: Edgar Allan Poe and Charles Baudelaire. The American poet and short-story writer represents the source of Baudelaire's taste for the supernatural. Baudelaire, moreover, translated Poe's tales into French in 1855. Artists throughout Europe and America read and re-read Poe's stories and poems (some of which Mallarmé adapted into French in 1889). James Ensor once observed that it was mainly Poe who inspired his dreams, yet nearly all of the Symbolist painters could have said as much. Redon devoted an album of lithographs to Poe in 1882. With his visionary interpretations of the American writer's uncanny atmosphere, it is difficult at times to tell what springs from Poe's imagination and what from Redon's. Ryder, Gauguin, Degouve de Nuncques, Kubin, Kupka, Martini, all found Poe a source of inspiration and, like Redon, all produced strange pictorial transpositions of Poe's weird tales.

As for Baudelaire, the entire Symbolist generation would meditate on the first two quatrains of his famous "Correspondences" sonnet:

Albert Pinkham Ryder
The Temple of the Mind
c. 1885, oil on panel,
45.1 × 40.6
**Albright-Knox Art Gallery,
Buffalo, N.Y.**
Edgar Allan Poe was one of Ryder's favorite authors, and here the artist records the impression made upon him by one of his poems, "The Haunted Palace," in which Poe draws a comparison between a deranged mind and an old palace whose tenants have been driven out by evil beings. The painter has invented the three graces and the fountain to recreate the wonderful site evoked by the poet, while the little faun stands for the evil which is about to shatter that harmony.

Nature is a temple whose living pillars
Breathe forth confused words from time to time,
A forest of symbols where mankind passes through,
Watched by those familiar eyes.

Like distant, drawn-out echoes intermingling
In a unity that's shadowy, deep,
Vast as the night, broad as daylight,
Sounds, odors, colors echo each other.

Some Symbolist artists, such as Carlos Schwabe and Félicien Rops, devoted the best of their talent to illustrating the works of their literary counterparts. Frequently a deep bond of friendship existed between artists and writers, the latter leading the way and inspiring the former. Among the writers and poets who exercised a certain influence over painters we might mention Ruskin and Swinburne, who inspired Burne-Jones; the forgotten Genevan poet Louis Duchosal and the Swiss painter Hodler; August Strindberg and Munch; Maurice Maeterlinck and Minne; Georges Rodenbach and Lévy-Dhurmer; Stanislaw Przybyszewski, whose work influenced Munch and Weiss.

21

Arabesques

Maurice Denis
April
1892, oil on canvas, 38×61.7
Rijksmuseum Kröller-Müller, Otterlo
In this deftly handled canvas, all in pastel tones, Denis shows how well he has contrived to assimilate the influence of Japanese art: the rising perspective, the use of the arabesque, the cut-out silhouettes of the young women who seem to glide over the lawn, just like the figures of Japanese women in the *ukiyo-e* prints the artist collected.

There is no such thing as a Symbolist style. It is not how the Symbolists painted but what they painted that gives unity to their movement. Their ranks contained artists trained in private studios, like the Académie Julian in Paris, and public academies; they included self-taught artists and practitioners of avant-garde techniques. But whatever their backgrounds, nearly all of them admired the plastic arts of pre-Renaissance Italy, a taste that led some to try and resurrect long-forgotten pictorial practices. This is particularly true of the Pre-Raphaelites and Rose + Croix artists.

The fin de siècle saw a lot of experimenting with novel forms and colors, but its innovations were always subordinated to a message. Though the Symbolists generally did not observe the Impressionists' rule of painting out of doors, a number of them, especially those who emerged from the Pont-Aven group, nonetheless remained attached to physical reality and its representation —even when they sought to transcend reality through Synthetism. Notwithstanding their differences, the Nabis uniformly admired both Cézanne—the Cézanne of the last years—and Japanese prints, which inspired the compositions of many of their own paintings and engravings as well as much of the art of this period. Even Pointillism had its Symbolist adepts: the Dutch artist Jan Toorop, the Italian Gaetano Previati. Gauguin and Georges Lacombe, for their part, pioneered the technique of direct cutting sculpture which they picked up from stonecarvers in Brittany.

Artists with an exceptionally strong personality, Van Gogh and Munch for example, managed to create radically new forms of expression. Others more mystically inclined, like Mondrian and Kupka, wound up embracing non-figurative painting by dint of experimenting with ways of rendering an ideal that appears impossible to express in recognizable forms.

Yet almost all of these artists—even the early Mondrian—shared a passion for arabesques, those wavy, sometimes sensuous lines that delimit figures and objects, embracing them, so to speak, and from time to time leaping into space and twining around themselves.

Baudelaire observed that "The arabesque drawing is the most spiritual of drawings." His contemporary, Gustave Moreau, defined his own aesthetic principles of as "the evocation of thought by means of the line, the arabesque..." Again and again, the word surfaces in the writings of the late nineteenth-century artists. It is hard to say why they were so drawn to this type of line, though etymology offers a clue (one, however, they were almost certainly unaware of). Arabesque signifies a kind of ornament in Islamic art—which bans representations of human figures and animals—and is used in Koranic calligraphy and the decoration of mosques. In this context, it is generally interpreted as an expression of the unseen and the divine. Fin de siècle artists had the example of Japanese prints, too, with their willowy forms and swirling lines; and though there is nothing sacred about these arabesques, they nevertheless have a decorative suppleness that both the Impressionists and the Symbolists found infinitely attractive.

Symbolism and psychoanalysis

The 1899 publication, in Vienna, of a work entitled *Die Traumdeutung* (*The Interpretation of Dreams*) by Dr. Sigmund Freud was an almost predictable event, one reason perhaps why this first printing was relatively small. Scientists around the world had been trying for the two previous decades to unravel the mystery of dreams. The artists of this period too, like their literary counterparts, were, in Mallarmé's famous phrase, "to dreams inured." Gustave Moreau called himself an "assembler of dreams." In his dogged obsession with finding a way to plumb the depths of the self, Odilon Redon titled his first album of lithographs: *Dans le rêve* (*In Dreams*, 1879). "Everything happens," he wrote to one correspondant in 1898, "by tamely surrendering to the unconscious."

More than a few Symbolist works seem outpourings of the artist's inner self, even when their message is explicitly mystical or moral. Many of them obviously sublimate deeply personal repressed material and desires. Unfortunately, in most cases the key to their hidden, intensely private meaning has been lost. Edvard Munch, who regarded his painting as a kind of self-analysis, observes in his diary: "Like Leonardo, who studied the interior of the human anatomy and dissected cadavers, I seek to dissect the soul. He was obliged to write in ciphers, for in his time it was a crime to cut open bodies. Today, it is the dissection of psychic phenomena that people consider immoral and inconsiderate."[6] Certain French artists were pleased to be called "painters of the soul," precisely because they sought to transcribe the various movements of the soul.

It is perhaps a pity that Freud preferred ancient statues to the art of his day. Had he been a regular visitor to the Viennese Secession exhibits, less than a mile from his Berggasse home, he would have discovered the works of Klimt, Khnopff, Klinger, Toorop. A better field of study for his theories concerning the death wish and the sublimation of the life instinct is hard to imagine. In his rare studies of art, he chose instead to investigate Leonardo's childhood memories and only once referred to a modern work, a Rops engraving for Flaubert's *The Temptation of Saint Anthony*, which Freud used to illustrate the concept of suppressed desire among saints and penitents.

We are indebted, however, to one of Freud's closest disciples, Karl Abraham, for what is surely one of the most penetrating psychoanalytic studies ever devoted to an artist. Abraham's long 1911 essay, *Giovanni Segantini*[7], draws on a biography written by a close friend of the Italian painter and attempts to apply Freudian theory to a living artist. Abraham's work remains a model of psychological investigation. More recently, though less persuasively, the French critic Charles Mauron[8] has used psychoanalytic techniques in an effort to understand more fully

Van Gogh's life work, an artist whose personality would seem to lend itself particularly well to this approach. However, interesting as Mauron's psychocriticism undoubtedly is, it does not really seem to probe any deeper than the traditional methods of art history into the creative processes underlying the Dutch genius's painting.

Admittedly, these artists often confided to canvas and paper the kind of secrets that are usually disclosed on a psychoanalysist's couch, however we would subscribe to a remark by Charles Filliger, whose own penchants are revealed clearly enough in his work, "My hands shrink from touching dreams."

Félicien Rops
The Temptation of
St. Anthony
1878, color crayons, 73.8 × 54.3
Print Room, Bibliothèque
royale Albert Ier, Brussels
No better commentary on this drawing than these words of Sigmund Freud: "More suggestively than all the explanations in the world, a well-known print by Félicien Rops illustrates this little noticed fact, one which, however, is worthy of the keenest attention: the artist has represented the type case of repression in saints and penitents."

Salome,
the myth of the femme fatale

Longed for, dreamt of, feared, women haunted the Symbolist imagination. Artists, writers, and musicians traded the theme of the feminine back and forth, mutually enriching it. The pure, unattainable damsel—Millais's Ophelia, Rossetti's Beatrice—was one version of this theme. The Virgin Mary, around whom a veritable cult flowered in the Catholic countries following the miraculous apparition at Lourdes, represented the supreme figure of purity, notably in the works of Carlos Schwabe, Gaetano Previati, Jan Thorn Prikker, and even Gustave Moreau.

But it was the fantasy of the *femme fatale* preying upon men which dominated the art of this period, reflection of an underlying misogyny and fear of woman among the fin de siècle generation. Two mythical figures incarnated this type: the sphinx—the man-eating female sphinx—and Salome, the princess who dances so alluringly before King Herod that he promises her half his kingdom. Counseled by her mother, Herodias, the true culprit in this story, Salome demands the head of St. John the Baptist.

Ever since the Middle Ages, painters and sculptors had freely depicted, with a predilection that belies more than religious motives, the young woman holding a large dish containing the saint's head. By the mid-nineteenth century the religious pretext surrounding this image of martyrdom had disappeared and the scene acquired a totally different meaning which over the years would become weighted with increasingly explicit sexual connotations.[9]

It was the German poet Heinrich Heine in his *Atta Troll* (1847) who first dared to shift the story away from its sacred context towards a meaning that would be further diverted by succeeding artists. Here we see an amorous Herodias doomed for ever to hold the saint's head in her hands covering it with her kisses, for in love with him she had ordered his death to avenge his refusal.

The figure of Herodias was then gradually usurped by that of her daughter. In 1856, Puvis de Chavannes placed Salome in the foreground of one of his paintings, triumphantly brandishing her reward, the grisly platter, while the decapitation itself is relegated to a corner (*The Execution of St. John the Baptist*, Boymans-van Beuningen

Gustave Moreau
Salome at the Column
c. 1885-1890, watercolor and gouache,
35.5 × 17.5
Private Collection, Switzerland

Museum, Rotterdam). But it was really Gustave Moreau, familiar as he was with Heine's poem, who cast the whole episode into a new light with a series of famous oils and watercolors that began to appear in Parisian art shows in 1876.

In Moreau's work, Salome is shown either dancing, a motif that is hardly new, strolling through an enchanted garden bearing her macabre trophy, or recoiling in terror as the saint's head begins to rise above the platter, reproaching her for her crime (*The Apparition*, 1876, Department of Graphic Arts, The Louvre, Paris). "This woman," the artist wrote to his mother, "bored, fantastical, animal-like, giving herself the pleas-

ure, for her a very weak pleasure, of seeing her adversary on the ground, such is her disgust with the satisfaction of her desires... Whenever I wish to render these nuances, I do not go to my subject to find them, but to the very nature of woman seeking unhealthy pleasures; woman who, stupidly, cannot even understand the horror of the most dreadful situations."[10]

The hero of *A rebours* (1884)—Huysmans' fictional alter ego—owns several works by Redon and Moreau, including the latter's two most famous paintings of Salome. In his eyes, the dancer has become "the Symbolic deity of indestructible Luxury, the goddess of immortal Hysteria, the

Julius Klinger
Salome
1909, color zincograph,
19.5×21
Michael Pabst Gallery, Munich

26

accursed Beauty, chosen amongst all her sisters for the catalepsy petrifying her flesh and stiffening her muscles, the monstrous, indifferent, irresponsible, unfeeling Beast who, like Helen of yore, poisons all who see her, all whom she touches."

Oscar Wilde, a great admirer of Moreau and Huysmans, wrote his tragedy *Salome* in 1892, with the idea of giving the leading role to Sarah Bernhardt. Pushing the princess's depravity to new depths, he has her seize the head of the martyred saint in order to kiss him on the lips; Herod himself is so horrified by her behavior that he commands his soldiers to kill her. It was at this disjuncture, as it were, that the young Aubrey Beardsley began to illustrate the tale of Salome as viewed by Oscar Wilde, and in his engravings the story's hitherto latent sexuality blossomed in broad daylight.

Hundreds of poets beginning with Mallarmé, artists, and musicians (like Strauss, who set Wilde's *Salome* to music in 1905) drew on the Salome tradition to the extent that it became a ridiculous cliché. There is a Picasso engraving from 1905 that shows Salome doing splits in front of the platter upon which lies the saint's head, while Gustav Adolf Mossa depicts the grimacing head with the saint's severed hands (*Salome, The Severed Hands*, 1904, Musée J. Chéret, Nice).

The Salome theme inspired several of the Viennese Secession artists too. Klimt superposes images of Salome and her heroic counterpart, Judith. Wilhelm List depicts Salome standing naked, holding the head in her bare hands. But the theme's ultimate expression is a painting by another artist of the review *Ver Sacrum*, Julius Klinger, who depicts Salome, accompanied by a black panther symbolizing lust, escaping from the scene and triumphantly brandishing the saint's genitals—the first illustration of the castration complex which Freud was discovering at precisely this time.

Symbolism and Art Nouveau

At practically the same period that witnessed the growth of the Symbolist movement, which would reach a highpoint of activity in 1900, the decorative arts—or applied arts as they are sometimes called—were thriving too throughout Europe and North America under diverse labels: Art Nouveau in France and Belgium, the Arts and Crafts Movement in England, *Jugendstil* in the German-speaking countries. As Arthur H. Mackmurdo, one of the leaders of the movement in Britain, observed, its goal was "to render all branches of art the sphere no longer of the tradesman, but of the artist. It would restore building, decoration, glass-painting, pottery, wood-carving and metal to their right place beside painting and sculpture." This list could also have included engraving and poster-making, illustrating and book-binding, tapestry-weaving, embroidery, and picture-framing: all these crafts were practiced brilliantly in this period. The late nineteenth century witnessed such a deep interpenetration of the fine arts (painting, sculpture, architecture) and the "minor" arts, as they were still called then, that the turn of the century studies devoted to the decorative arts contain virtually the same names as the present volume. Certain works on Art Nouveau (the generic term for the whole movement), such as those by Stephen Tschudi Madsen, Robert Schmutzler and, more recently, the *Journal de l'Art Nouveau* by J.-P. Bouillon, even devote annexes to painting and sculpture, as if the finest work of the artists of this time lay in the decorative arts. Redon was already leading the way himself by preferring Gauguin's ceramics to his paintings.

True, the Symbolist artists themselves felt strongly drawn toward the applied arts and often set aside their brushes and chisels in order to try their hand at the crafts. The most outstanding examples of this trend are the Pre-Raphaelite William Morris and the French artists Georges de Feure and Armand Point. The Nabis, following Gauguin's example, were keenly interested in engraving and its modern expression, the poster. Franz von Stuck's masterpiece is undoubtedly his villa in Munich, which he himself built and decorated. Gustav Klimt, who was trained as a decorator, entrusted the work on the dining-room mosaics at the Palais Stoclet in Brussels to *Wiener Werkstätte* craftsmen who, like himself, had studied the mosaic technique in Ravenna. To decorate the walls of several Glasgow tearooms, Charles Rennie Mackintosh borrowed motifs from the Symbolist watercolors he had painted when he was twenty. Fusing the arts has never been carried out so extensively and successfully as it was in this period.

From Symbolism to abstract art and Surrealism

Shortly after the deaths of Gauguin, Fantin-Latour and Whistler—an artist who remains difficult to characterize, although his predilection for titles such as *Nocturne* and *Symphony* shows clear affinities with the Symbolists' tastes—the poet and art critic Charles Morice, a close friend of Gauguin and Carrière, published in *Le Mercure de France* in 1905 a survey he had conducted with some fifty young artists on the situation of the fine arts at the time. Most believed that they were working in a kind of void; they had reached an impasse and were unsure whether to follow the "Impressionists, the official [artists], the Symbolists, or the Realists." They declared unanimously that theirs was an age of decline. Not one of them foresaw that within the next couple of years Fauvism and Cubism would shake the art world to its foundations.

In those opening years of the twentieth century, Symbolism, beginning to repeat itself, was running out of steam. Eugène Carrière alone retained enough confidence in the values of the previous decade to state by way of a conclusion to Morice's survey: "Ours is an admirable age. We discuss all the religions, and never has there been such a surge of faith. We have no single style, but we have an abundance of artists. The world's sorrow has never moved mankind's soul as deeply as it does now. Never before has man called out to man so urgently."

Art was about to reach a turning point with the advent of Cubism and Fauvism and would soon take a road radically opposed to Symbolism, at least in the short run. The latter movement was on the point of braking up. Many of its members lacked a strong personality and were incapable of renewing themselves. But before it was to dissolve completely, the Symbolist spirit would penetrate deep into the minds of the succeeding generation's artists and writers. Thus, there would be a historical link between it and those two major twentieth century movements: abstraction and Surrealism.

Officially, abstract art was born around 1910 when Wassily Kandinsky painted his first non-figurative watercolor, even if a number of small oils and watercolors by Moreau that date from the 1890s—and which could be viewed as early

as 1903 in the museum that bears his name—make no reference whatsoever to objective reality. Kandinsky's abstraction was the outcome of a long intellectual process outlined in his famous *On the Spiritual in Art*, published in Munich in 1912. Although his output until then had mainly consisted of landscape painting and Russian folk scenes, which contain few iconographic elements bearing a relation to Symbolism, the very title of this treatise reveals a metaphysical bent having a great deal in common with the Symbolists' spiritual aspirations. Like those painters, Kandinsky wanted to give a spiritual meaning to forms and colors, and, again like them, he was very earnest about theosophical doctrines. Surveying the plastic art of the previous decade or two, he cites several pioneers of what he regards as a spiritual revolution in painting: Rossetti, Burne-Jones, Böcklin, Stuck, and Segantini. "Seekers after immaterial spheres," he calls them. Breaking with Impressionism, he calls for an even more ethereal art, an art somewhat like music, in which "there breathes a spirit organically and intimately connected with the new Reign of the Spirit that is being prepared under our eyes, for this Spirit will be the soul of a period of great Spirituality."[12]

Of the other artists who, around the same time but independently of Kandinsky, were pondering new pictorial ways of expressing their inner self, we will encounter below the Czech artist Franz Kupka and the Dutchman Piet Mondrian. Both were in Paris around the turn of the century, apparently beginning careers as belated Symbolists. Then, between 1910 and 1920, each became absorbed in experiments that eventually led to abstraction. They took this step without rejecting Symbolism, however; on the contrary, they simply pushed its metaphysical requirements further. Little by little, their spiritual thirst (both dabbled in the occult sciences) steered them away from the language of figuration (even when expressed metaphorically through symbols).

In the aftermath of World War One, Surrealism, despite all appearances, would plunge its roots in Symbolism, via the metaphysical painting of Giorgio De Chirico (who made no secret of his debt to Böcklin and Klinger). André

Breton, the central figure of the Surrealist movement, was profoundly marked by Symbolist literature (especially Huysmans and Jarry), which he had read in his youth, and admired Moreau, Gauguin, and Filiger. He later paid tribute to Gauguin and Moreau, calling their œuvres "the two great modern syntheses of magic art." What Breton wanted mainly in a painting was the living presence of symbols and myths; he considered dreams a privileged terrain for the artistic imagination and he welcomed the contribution of psychoanalytic theory which enabled artists to exploit the resources of the unconscious mind more fully.

It was the Surrealists—Breton, Dali, André Masson, Max Ernst—who gradually brought Symbolist art back into fashion and contributed to reintroducing the period, in the sixties, into art history. For though Symbolist literature had been the object of numerous studies and had inspired a memorable exhibit at the Bibliothèque national in 1936, this was far from being the case with pictorial Symbolism. In 1969 the Italian art critic Luigi Carluccio organized a major retrospective at Turin's Galleria Civica d'Arte Moderna, *Il sacro e il profano nell'arte dei Simbolisti*, a sequel moreover to a show he had put together the previous year: *Le muse inquietanti, Maestri del Surrealismo*.

Subsequently, art critics and curators (notably Philippe Jullian, Hans Hofstätter, and Geneviève Lacambre) organized a number of major exhibits which have restored Symbolism to its rightful place in art history (*French Symbolist Painters*, 1972, London, Liverpool, and Barcelona; *Symbolism in Europe*, 1975 and 1976, Rotterdam, Brussels, Baden-Baden, and Paris). Since then, a torrent of theses, articles, and monographs has contributed to our knowledge of this fascinating period.

Notes

[1] J. Thuillier, *Peut-on parler d'une peinture "pompier"?*, Paris, 1984.

[2] See Alan Bowness's introduction to the *Post-Impressionism* exhibition catalogue, Royal Academy of the Arts, London, 1979-1980, pp. 9-12.

[3] See Françoise Cachin's introduction to Paul Signac, *D'Eugène Delacroix au néo-impressionnisme*, Paris, 1978, p. 12.

[4] Teodor de Wyzewa, "*Notes sur la peinture wagnérienne et le Salon de 1886*," in *La Revue Wagnérienne*, 8 June 1886. On Wagner's influence on literature and art in France, see M. Kahane and N. Wild, *Wagner et la France* (exhibit catalog), Bibliothèque Nationale and Théâtre national de l'Opéra de Paris, Paris, 1983.

[5] Gauguin, *Oviri, Ecrits d'un sauvage* (edited and selected by D. Guérin), Paris, 1974, p. 138. The interview was originally published in *L'Echo de Paris*, 13 May 1895.

[6] Edvard Munch, MS T 2734, Munchmuseet Archives, Oslo. Cited by U. M. Schneede, *Edvard Munch. Les chefs-d'œuvre de jeunesse*, Munich and Paris, 1988.

[7] This article is given in Karl Abraham, *Œuvres complètes*, vol. 1 (*Rêve et mythe*), Paris, 1965. (French translation.)

[8] Charles Mauron, *Van Gogh. Etudes psychocritiques*, Paris, 1976.

[9] Good examples of the iconographic development of the Salome theme in French art, notably during the second half of the nineteenth century, were given in *Salomé dans les collections françaises* (exhibit), Musée d'Art et d'Histoire, Saint-Denis, 1988.

[10] G. Moreau, *L'assembleur de rêves* (edited and annotated by P.-L. Mathieu, Fontfroide, 1984, p. 79.

[11] See Ph. Dagen, *La peinture en 1905. "L'enquête sur les tendances actuelles des arts plastiques" de Charles Morice*, Paris, 1986.

[12] W. Kandinsky, *Concerning the Spiritual in Art* (Documents of Modern Art 5), New York, 1947.

Pierre Puvis de Chavannes
The Sacred Wood Dear to the Arts and Muses (detail)
1884-1889, oil on canvas mounted on wood, 93×231 (in full)
The Art Institute of Chicago

To us Puvis de Chavannes may seem a typical example of the official, academic painter, but in the nineteenth century he was considered a renovator, and admired as such by both the Symbolists and the Neo-Impressionists. Of this mural decoration, the artist wrote: "The Arts and the Muses symbolize and beget all the creatures called for in a monument devoted to art." Gauguin was inspired by this picture for his masterpiece, *Whence come we?* So was Seurat, who watched Puvis as he painted this canvas and remembered it when he painted his own figure compositions such as *Bathers at Asnières* and *A Sunday Afternoon on the Island of the Grande-Jatte.*

THE ORIGINATORS OF SYMBOLISM

Determined to break—as is generally the case—with the preceding generation, many young artists who reached adulthood in the years 1885 to 1890 nevertheless regarded several of their immediate precursors as models.

Though not at the center of the main artistic currents marking the end of the century (namely, Realism and Academicism), these precursors, born between 1820 and 1830, had attained notoriety by the end of the century, some after years of working in isolation. The rising generation understood the importance of their message and recognized themselves in these masters, just as their counterparts in music and literature saw themselves in Poe, Baudelaire, Wagner.

The older artists they admired had taken their inspiration from dreams and the imagination. The recurrent words in the titles of their pictures were abstract terms like vision, evocation, hope, death, life. Their academic colleagues tended to depict scenes drawn from history, nature, and daily life; they endeavored either to reproduce the present moment with scrupulous fidelity or to reconstruct historical events with fastidious precision, as if to resurrect them pictorially, the nineteenth century being an age of erudition. The less academically recognized artists, on the other hand, were already inclined to escape into nostalgic evocations of the past—preferably the Middle Ages or ancient mythology—hardly concerning themselves with historical accuracy. The only thing that seemed to matter was creating a misty, factitious alternative to contemporary reality. All of these artists would certainly have subscribed to the aesthetic doctrine of Baudelaire, who observes in his notebook, *Fusées*: "I have found the definition of Beauty—as I see it. It is something ardent and sad, something a bit vague, leaving scope for conjecture."

In a sense, these precursors and originators were a bridge between Romanticism and Symbolism. The Symbolist generation had many things in common with the older Romantic generation. Like the Romantics, they were haunted by the thought of death, obsessed with the idea of love. The difference is that the Symbolists expressed their feelings in laments rather than shouts; they preferred silent contemplation to action, arabesques to color tones.

The Pre-Raphaelites' spiritual angst

The Pre-Raphaelite Brotherhood (or PRB, as its members used to initial their works) was founded in 1848, in London, by seven young artists, three of whom were to attain real distinction later on: William Holman Hunt, Dante Gabriel Rossetti, John Everett Millais, all three students at the Royal Academy, the oldest only 21 years old. In France, this was the age of Realism, the age of Courbet and Millet. British artists too had parted ways with academic eclecticism but were chiefly influenced by the German Nazarenes, who had banded together in an analogous movement around 1810. British artists were also inspired by the writings of John Ruskin (1819-1900), and his idea that England should have a school of painting that would be at once respectful of nature and fired by a lofty ideal. The choice of the name Pre-Raphaelite reflects their main aspiration, to recapture in their works the emotional purity of the Italian artists of the Trecento and Quattrocento, artists as yet unhampered by the pictorial conventions prevailing in fine arts schools and academies after Raphael.

The first "PRB" pictures, many of them inspired by religious feelings, were coldly received, not because of their technique, for each detail in them was rendered with scrupulous precision, but because of their elaborate Christian symbolism in which some critics detected a whiff of popishness. Before long, though, a series of much-noticed articles by Ruskin brought them recognition and a degree of fame, and this at the very moment when the group was about to break apart and each member was beginning to strike out on his own, some of them even deviating from the movement's original principles.

Works by Millais and Hunt were shown at the Paris Universal Exposition of 1855, but they aroused little interest there, either then or later, in 1867. It was only in 1878 that their paintings began to attract notice across the Channel. By then, the Brotherhood had long since ceased to exist; Rossetti, his follower Burne-Jones, and Watts, who had never belonged to the group, were regarded as the leading exponents of the Pre-Raphaelite movement.[1] Hoping to form a similar fraternity with Gauguin, Vincent van Gogh wrote to his brother Theo in June 1888, citing the Pre-Raphaelites as an example: "You know I feel that an association of Impressionists would be something like the association of the twelve English Pre-Raphaelites."

Within the Pre-Raphaelite movement, Rossetti and Burne-Jones began fairly early on to move away from rendering nature realistically (one of the Brotherhood's original tenets) and turned to themes from bygone days having a strong symbolist potential, mostly material from medieval legends. Watts, on the other hand, viewed painting as a means to express his metaphysical fears.

Dante Gabriel Rossetti, poet and painter

Raised to revere Dante by his father, a *Divine Comedy* scholar and political refugee from Naples, the young Dante Gabriel Rossetti (1828-1882) was an exceptionally gifted and precocious child. Equally drawn to poetry and painting, he finally opted for the latter as the more lucrative profession. He had a touch of the angelic as well as the bestial. Women resembling Beatrice, reincarnations of Dante's figure of purity, as well as wanton temptresses fascinated him. He led a gay life and enjoyed flouting the rules of Victorian society. His patron and friend, John Ruskin, once scolded him, not for being evil, for he did not seem to know what evil was, but for doing whatever he felt like doing, "like a lap-dog or pet monkey." Rossetti sought out the company of artists and poets—Whistler, Swinburne—as excentric and tormented as himself; he drank heavily and took drugs. He sank into a kind of paranoia during the last ten years of his prematurely shortened life, torn by remorse at the way he had treated the woman who long hesitated to become his wife and whom he had indirectly driven to suicide, Elizabeth Eleanor Siddal (1829-1862). She had been the model for the Virgin, Beatrice and had even sat for Millais's *Ophelia*, and Rossetti himself had celebrated her beauty in *The House of Life*, the manuscript he had placed in her coffin—only to have it disinterred seven years later and published.

Rossetti often associated a painting and verses he had written before taking up his brushes, a practice that helps us to enter more deeply into the symbolism of his work. A very erudite artist, he was thoroughly familiar with the "symbolic" language of colors, flowers, plants, and planets. He depicted only two types of women: the ethereal beauty, embodied by his wife Elizabeth, and the more sensual, melancholic enchantress, Jane Burden, who was married to his disciple, the decorator and artist William Morris. They were both powerful plastic types; both had sensuous lips, langourous eyes, long thick hair (Elizabeth's was auburn, Jane's was brown). On those occasions when Rossetti was obliged to use other models, he invariably chose young women resembling either Jane or Elizabeth.

Rossetti borrowed many of his themes from Dante and his colors from the Venetian masters. He generally gave his pictures an autobiographical slant, expressing in them his own feelings in a metaphorical guise. In *Beata Beatrix* (1872 The Art Institute of Chicago), the features of Elizabeth on her deathbed are identified with the young girl who inspired Dante's *Vita Nuova*. "The picture," he explained, "must of course be viewed not as a representation of the incident of the death of Beatrice, but as an ideal of the subject, symbolized by a trance or sudden spiritual transfiguration. Beatrice is rapt visibly into Heaven, seeing as it were through her shut lids (...) and in sign of the supreme change, the radiant bird, a messenger of death, drops the white poppy between her open hands. In the background is the City which, as Dante says, 'sat solitary' in mourning for her death; and through whose street Dante himself is seen to pass gazing towards the figure of Love opposite, in whose hand the wavering life of his lady flickers as a flame. On the sundial at her side the shadow falls on the hour of nine, which number Dante connects mystically in many ways with her and with her death." To this long commentary in the artist's own words, one may add the colors of Beatrice's dress (green for hope, purple for death) as well as the doubtlessly unconscious phallic shape of the sundial pointing to the girl's ecstatic face[2].

Dante Gabriel Rossetti
Beata Beatrix
1872, oil on canvas, 85.7×67.3
The Art Institute of Chicago
In this picture, conceived in the manner of a medieval altarpiece, Rossetti associates the Beatrice of Dante with the image of his own wife, who died of an overdose of laudanum at the age of thirty-three. Every detail here conveys some symbolic meaning, often with an autobiographical import.

Dante Gabriel Rossetti
Astarte Syriaca
1877, oil on canvas, 72 × 42
City Art Gallery, Manchester
The woman here is Jane Morris,
who became the central figure
in the artist's life after the death
of his wife. She embodies passion in its fleshly form, represented by a pomegranate, the
symbol of consummated love.
The accompanying poem by
Rossetti ends as follows:
"That face, of Love's all-
⠀⠀⠀⠀⠀⠀[penetrative spell
Amulet, talisman, and
⠀⠀⠀⠀⠀⠀⠀[oracle,—
Betwixt the sun and moon
⠀⠀⠀⠀⠀⠀[a mystery."

Every one of Rossetti's paintings lends itself to a psychoanalytic approach. It would be easy to demonstrate that increasingly, from 1865 on, his symbolic vocabulary expressed private fantasies. The extended series of Proserpines, Astartes, and Pandoras for which Jane Burden posed, surely sublimates a secret sexual fascination which the artist translates into evocations of mythical figures, all of them linked with death.

Whistler had entertained hopes of getting his friend Rossetti included in Fantin-Latour's *Homage to Delacroix* (1864), a kind of canvassing that would have helped to build up the Pre-Raphaelite artist's reputation in France, but Rossetti was unable to come to Paris for the sittings. Oddly enough, Rossetti's name became known on the Continent chiefly for his verse as his poems began to appear in French translation in 1884. In Rome, where he was in residence at the Villa Medicis, Claude Debussy read "The Blessèd Damozel" and set it to music in 1887 and later asked Maurice Denis to illustrate the score. In 1896 another Rossetti poem, "La saulaie" in Pierre Louÿs's translation, inspired the composer to undertake his "last experiments with the chemistry of music," a project that remained unfinished at his death.

Rossetti's true disciple was his friend and pupil Edward Burne-Jones, an extremely prolific artist whose works were displayed throughout continental Europe in the closing years of the nineteenth century.

Dante Gabriel Rossetti
The Blessed Damozel
c. 1875-1878, oil on canvas,
174×94
Fogg Art Museum, Harvard University, Cambridge, Massachusetts
Rossetti drew inspiration from one of his own poems,"The Blessed Damozel," written in 1847, in which the painter-poet, as the new Dante, dreams of the woman who awaits her beloved in the beyond, among couples folded in each other's arms. Translated into French, this poem of Rossetti's was set to music in 1888 by Claude Debussy and published in 1893 with an original lithograph by Maurice Denis.

Edward Burne-Jones
and the metaphysical world
of legends

A divinity student at Oxford, Edward Burne-Jones (1833-1898) was preparing to enter the orders together with his friend William Morris when, in 1854, he discovered the art of the first Pre-Raphaelites. This fired such a passion for painting in him that he gave up his theological studies to become a disciple of both Rossetti and Ruskin, his mentor throughout a tour of Italy they made together. His first models were drawn not only from Rossetti and Watts, but also from the pre-Renaissance Florentine and Venetian masters, Carpaccio, Giorgione, Mantegna, Signorelli and especially Botticelli. Later, he became fascinated with Michelangelo.

The youthful, graceful figure of his wife, a never-ending source of willowy arabesques, appears everywhere in his painting. Even his angels have a feminine lissomeness. His pictures are full of young women with ivory complexions and melancholy eyes. His themes, like Moreau's, are taken entirely from classical mythology, the Bible, and mediaeval legends; his perception of nature is never direct. Critics hailed him as an English Botticelli, and his type of woman shaped the fashion in the 1880s, in Paris as well as London. More attentive than Rossetti to texture, he gave his paintings a tapestry-like feel. He was also a less autobiographical artist than the latter. "I mean by a picture," he declared, "a beautiful romantic dream of something that never was, never will be—in a light better than any light that ever shone—in a land no one can define or remember, only desire—and the forms divinely beautiful." As early as 1861, Burne-Jones extended his search for beauty to new territories by associating himself with William Morris in the endeavor to renew the decorative arts in Britain. He designed cartoons for tapestries, mosaics, stained glass windows, decorated furniture, and so forth. He was, in fact, a major contributor to the birth of Art Nouveau. The *Morris Room*, originally a dining-room done in green dating from 1868 (Victoria and Albert Museum, London), is one example of the two artists's collaboration.

Thanks to his theological and literary background, Burne-Jones was an outstandingly learned artist, skilled at translating ancient myths, biblical stories, and medieval tales into

pictures, though he did so with less emphasis on historical truth than on rendering archetypes.

In England, where he was relatively successful, Burne-Jones had only minor followers, John Roddam Spencer Stanhope (1829-1908), John Melhuish Strudwick (1849-1937). He was also well received in France, where his pictures were exhibited beginning in 1878. Joséphin Péladan asked him (in vain) to contribute works to the Salon de la Rose+Croix, and Puvis de Chavannes invited him to participate in the Salon de la Société Nationale des Beaux-Arts in 1891. But his greatest admirer in Paris seems to have been Gustave Moreau. Moreau hung a reproduction of the *Seven Days of Creation* in his apartment and wrote to Burne-Jones to tell him how highly he regarded his work. The two artists died the same year, 1898, giving critics an opportunity to compare their oeuvres. Burne-Jones' paintings were shown at all the Universal Expositions of the late nineteenth century, and this helped to spread his fame throughout continental Europe. The Belgian artist Fernand Khnopff borrowed heavily from him. Kandinsky cites him as one of the "seekers of immaterial spheres." However, the public became jaded in the end, wearying of his rather repetitious pictorial formulas. The criticism put forth by the novelist and art critic Octave Mirbeau (a champion of Rodin, Gauguin, and Van Gogh), though excessive, nevertheless reflects the public opinion around 1895: "He is becoming increasingly embroiled in the maze of his symbols. He no longer seems to be able to distinguish what is chaste from what is obscene, and he has done a disservice to himself —an unfortunate irony—by inflicting on his paintings successive contradictory commentaries which cancel each other out every two years."[3]

Edward Burne-Jones
The Fifth and Sixth Days of Creation
1875-1876, oil on canvas, each 120.7 X 36.2
Fogg Art Museum, Harvard University, Cambridge, Massachusetts
Each day of the Creation is represented by an angel holding a globe in which the work of God is reflected. On the fifth day the four angels of the previous days are grouped behind the angel who shows the creation of the birds; then, on the sixth day, comes the creation of Adam and Eve. As one critic commented, "It is impossible to imagine a more graceful and less pedantic symbolism."

George Frederic Watts
Hope
1886, oil on canvas, 141 × 110
Tate Gallery, London
The painter himself gave the following explanation of his picture: "All the strings of her
instrument are broken, except one, and she tries to draw as much music as possible out
of this poor instrument." Like so many artists of his time, Watts associated the visual arts
with music.

George Frederic Watts,
or the art of teaching through pictures

George Frederic Watts (1817-1904) was never in good health, yet he lived longer than Queen Victoria. Although he attended the Royal Academy for a few weeks only, at the age of twenty-four he was awarded a prize for his decoration of the House of Parliament. Watts was not a member of the Pre-Raphaelite Brotherhood, even though, like those artists, he was influenced by the early Italian masters, especially Tintoretto and Michelangelo, and wanted to convey a moral message with his paintings. Often depressed, he longed for a protective woman and the security of domestic life. After a first, unconsummated marriage to a sixteen-year-old actress while in his late forties, he remarried at the age of sixty-nine. His second wife, thirty-three years his junior, took care of him in his last years. Shortly before his death, he began to build a gallery in the country to house a substantial part of his oeuvre, which he had bequeathed to the British nation, just as Gustave Moreau had willed his work to the French people a few years earlier.

Watts considered art the best vehicle for metaphysical ideas. He was obsessed with the thought of leaving to posterity a series of paintings that would hang together in a "House of Life"[4] where visitors of all ages and from every walk could absorb a lesson in energy and hope. Once he even proposed to decorate free of charge a railway station, as busy a place as one could wish for, where his work would be viewed by thousands, perhaps millions of travelers. The titles of his paintings are an index of his intentions: *Love and Death*, *The Court of Death*, *Love Guiding the Ship of Humanity*, *Love and Life*, *Hope*, *The Sower of Systems*, and so forth. "All my pictures in the Tate Gallery," he once stated, "are symbolical and for all time... Their symbolism is, however, more suggestive than worked out in any detail. I want to make people think. My idea is really the Book of Ecclesiastes with a higher impulse." One might add that Ecclesiastes is the most pessimistic of the books of the Bible, for it is written there that everything in life, youth, knowledge, wealth, love, is vanity.

Of course, lofty ambitions do not necessarily make for great art. Watts was no innovator. His

George Frederic Watts
The Sower of the Systems
1902, oil on canvas, 66×53
The Watts Gallery, Compton, Surrey
Watts illustrates here, in virtually abstract terms, the creation of the universe, owing something to Michelangelo's famous fresco in the Sistine Chapel, but envisaging God as if he were seen from behind. "The subject," wrote Watts, "was suggested to me by the reflection of a night-light on the ceiling. The artist's imagination saw there a veiled figure, as though projected through space, the trace of planets, suns and stars shooting forth from hand and foot."

painting is derived from the masterpieces of the Venetian school, yet in his last works he produced interesting textures using thick, luminous impasti. Allegory was his favorite mode of expression, and he managed to lend his symbolic vocabulary a certain coloring of originality by stamping it with his own ideas about life. G.K. Chesterton describes his painting *Hope*, which remains one of the most famous in the Tate Gallery, as follows: "Suppose that [the spectator] found himself in the presence of a dim canvas with a bowed and stricken figure cowering over a broken lyre in the twilight. What would he think? His first thought, of course, would be that the picture was called *Despair*; his second (when he discovered his error in the catalogue), that it has been entered under a wrong number; his third, that the painter was mad. But if we imagine that he overcame these preliminary feelings and that as he stared at that queer twilight picture, a dim and powerful sense of meaning began to grow upon him—what would he see? He would see something for which there is neither speech nor language, which has been too vast for any eye to see and too secret for any religion to utter, even in an esoteric doctrine. Standing before that picture he finds himself in the presence of a great truth. He perceives that there is something in man which is always apparently on the eve of disappearing, but never disappears, an assurance which is always apparently saying farewell and yet illimitably lingers, a string which is always stretched to snapping and yet never snaps."[5]

Puvis de Chavannes, a new vision of Arcadia

Notwithstanding his rehabilitation by art historians, buttressed by international exhibitions of his work, the Lyons artist Pierre Puvis de Chavannes (1824-1898) still passes in the eyes of educated people for the typical nineteenth century academic painter. To many, his paintings seem as unfeeling and dull as the walls of the public edifices they decorate. Indeed, his name is still associated with state commissions: the stairs in the provincial museums at Amiens, Marseilles, Lyons, Rouen; the Paris and Poitiers town halls; the life of St. Geneviève at the Panthéon in Paris; the great mural in the Sorbonne's main amphitheater. During one of the insurrectional nights of May 1968, rebel students even voted to remove and auction off the Sorbonne "fresco" (actually the artist hardly ever used the fresco technique; he painted his murals on canvas panels which were then mounted on the wall). Fortunately, they were prevented from carrying out this iconoclastic gesture by the subsequent turn of events.

Yet at the end of the nineteenth century, Puvis de Chavannes represented the leading example of the innovative artist who is misunderstood by critics, rejected by official salon juries, and fervently admired by the young. His supporters saw him as a bridge between a humanism based on classical learning—a successor of the great mid-century decorators Delacroix and Chassériau—and a non-academic painting that heralded the art of the century to come. To young artists, he presented the extra advantage of having resurrected the tradition of the Italian pre-Renaissance painters, whom they associated with purity and religious feeling.

For his seventieth birthday, in 1895, a writers' and artists' banquet, presided by Rodin himself, was held in his honor. The 500 guests invited for the occasion included the likes of Gauguin, Antoine Bourdelle, Monet, Signac, Eugène Carrière, Renoir and Emile Zola. Tributes by Mallarmé, Verlaine, Verhaeren, and others were read during the meal.

Virtually self-taught, Puvis de Chavannes, considered himself primarily a historical painter, an artist practicing what was then regarded as the supreme genre, nobler than landscape or still life painting, or portraiture; an artist who illustrated the great secular and religious episodes marking mankind's history. His idiom, allegory, was fairly conventional (Hope bearing an olive sprig, and so on), but he was often able to breathe new life into these scenes, adapting them to modern concepts. For example, in one of the Boston Library panels, Physics appears in the guise of two muses flying above an aerial electric line.

**Pierre Puvis
de Chavannes**
Hope
**1872, oil on canvas, 70.7 × 82
Musée d'Orsay, Paris**

This fragile-looking girl was painted not long after the Franco-Prussian War (1870-1871); holding a leafy twig in her left hand, she symbolizes hope. But the artist's message goes deeper: Puvis de Chavannes wanted to express his faith in France's rebirth after its defeat—thus the ruins and graves in the background, and the frail flowers between the stones. The painting's severity, the obvious allusions to the art of the Trecento (the figure was inspired by a Lorenzetti fresco in Sienna) reflect the painter's taste for a primitivism synonymous with purity and religious feeling.

Why did his painting seem so innovative at the end of the nineteenth century? Apart from the fact that he had a predilection for light tones and clean forms, his artistic vision drew on neither nature nor any desire to illustrate historical events, but rather on personal inspiration and a profound knowledge of mural art. He conceived his subjects during the daily two hour walks he regularly took for almost forty years between his home on the Place Pigalle in Paris and his studio in the city's outskirts at Neuilly. "A work is born," he would say, "from a sort of indefinite emotion which contains it the way an egg encloses a chick. I roll over in my mind the idea that lies in this emotion; I roll it over until it becomes clear in my eyes and as definite as

possible. Then I search for a spectacle that will translate it accurately... This is Symbolism, if you like."[6]

Compared with Moreau and Redon, Puvis de Chavannes was not a learned artist, although he often gave his works titles in a Latin that is hardly difficult to understand: *Ave Picardia nutrix*, *Ludus pro patria*, *Inter artes et naturam*. But his paintings are replete with meanings that were a good deal clearer to his contemporaries than they are to us. *Hope* makes little sense out of its context, the French defeat in 1870. *The Poor Fisherman* is more than just an allegory of poverty; it expresses a whole period's sensitivity to the theme of poverty, one that inspired many Naturalist writers and artists.

41

Pierre Puvis de Chavannes
Young Girls by the Seaside

1879, oil on canvas, 205 × 154
Musée d'Orsay, Paris

There is no action in this painting, no apparent story—only three female figures by the seaside, one of whom is brushing her hair. To us this canvas seems mainly remarkable for its plastic harmony and soft colors, but the artist's contemporaries were chiefly drawn to its melancholy atmosphere and were often moved to comment about the fragility of the paradisiac world it evokes. One poet, Gustave Kahn, viewed it as an image of Woman, "the same one at three different moments, three acts of her life: young, at the moment of waiting, at the moment of her appeal, at the moment when her throbbing ardor turns back on herself—when she comes to lament the eternal irreconcilability of the sexes." Both Gauguin and Seurat drew inspiration from this painting.

**Pierre Puvis
de Chavannes**
The Poor Fisherman
**1881, oil on canvas,
155.5 × 192.5
Musée d'Orsay, Paris**

The only painting by Puvis de Chavannes to hang in a Paris museum during the artist's lifetime, this picture fascinated the Symbolist generation of 1890 because of its simplified plastic means and minimal subject matter—a resigned fisherman, two children picking flowers on the river bank—which increases its evocative power. As one contemporary critic remarked, "This barely existing painting is singularly expressive: there is something sorrowful in that mist, and something moving about that emptiness. In the middle of the desolate landscape that surrounds him the fisherman is a poignant picture of destitution, dereliction, irremediable poverty."

After his rather allusive fashion, but entirely in tune with the aspirations and nostalgia of the period, Puvis de Chavannes echoed the yearnings of a generation that rejected war, the pauperization of whole classes of capitalist society, the destruction of nature's balance through unregulated industrialization. What these young people longed for was a new Arcadia and his dreamy antique scenes, his ever-burgeoning sacred groves, gave them glimpses of this mythical never-never land.

But beyond the fashions that are inherently a part of every age, the fact is that his art was remarkably modern, and remains so in comparison to much of the production of Second Empire artists. Through his almost excessive stressing of line over color—a technique that has perhaps put his painting out of favor with today's public— Puvis de Chavannes laid the foundations of an authentic artistic revival. He rejected the prevailing Realist and historicist canons, detested pictorial artifices, abolished the classical rules of perspective, and was instead remarkably sensitive to the intrinsic linear rhythms of the pictorial plane. He deliberately eschewed overly precise themes that risked distracting the spectator from the stylistic quality of his work. His art was, in fact, but a step removed from pure painting.

This explains his enormous popularity among the succeeding generation of painters who sought, as he had done, to strike out in a new direction. Intensely admired at the close of the nineteenth century, his oeuvre inspired artists from Boston to Vienna and gave a decisive impetus to their own pictorial experiments, even though many of these turned out to be a far cry from Symbolism. Seurat, Van Gogh, Gauguin, Redon, Maurice Denis and the other Nabis, Hodler, Picasso, Matisse—all were indebted to

43

**Pierre Puvis
de Chavannes**
Ancient Vision
c. 1888-1889, oil on canvas,
105 × 133
**Carnegie Institute, Museum of
Art, Pittsburgh**

The term *vision* which the artist
chose as the title of this picture
is symptomatic of a state of
mind that rejected the modern
world and escaped into dreams
and visions of a vanished world
characterized by a total communion between man and nature, where everything was
tranquil and beautiful. Yet
there is a note of sadness in this
timeless Arcadia—for death is
present even here, as Poussin
had shown earlier in one of his
most famous paintings.

him. His example inspired a large and varied
posterity which carried on the spirit of his innovations far more effectively than the handful of his
disciples and assistants—painters like Alexandre
Séon, Emile-René Ménard, Henri Martin, whose
officially commissioned decorations are but pale
copies of their master's murals.

Rodin, who sculpted a bust of the artist in
1891, is supposed to have exclaimed just before
dying: "And they say that Puvis de Chavannes's
[work] is not beautiful!" This was in 1917, at a
time when the historical painter's renown was
indeed beginning to dim in artistic circles.

Gustave Moreau,
the assembler of dreams

Calling himself a historical painter and thinking that in doing so he was carrying on the great
tradition of Poussin and Delacroix, Gustave
Moreau (1826-1898) gave a personal and rather
strange interpretation of Greek myths and biblical stories. For example, the painting that made
him famous, *Oedipus and the Sphinx* (1864, The
Metropolitan Museum, New York) is clearly no
traditional rendering of the theme. The unmis-
takeably female sphinx is about to kiss Oedipus,
an act that was to be consummated, so to speak,
some thirty years later in Franz von Stuck's *Kiss
of the Sphinx* (1895, Szepmuveszeti Muzeum,
Budapest). It was at this time that Odilon Redon
recalled discovering Moreau's work, "Naturalism was in full swing then. What a comfort his
work was to me! I have long kept the recollection
of that first impression; the force of its impact
on me was perhaps such that it gave me the
strength to follow my road alone, a road that ran
parallel to his, perhaps because of its whole
evocative aspect, dear to men of letters."[7]

Later in his career, Moreau was repeatedly drawn to images of decapitation, whether of Orpheus, "piously gathered up by a Thracian maiden" (*Orpheus*, 1865, Musée d'Orsay, Paris) or John the Baptist, a theme that became an obsession beginning in 1876. Its supreme expression is *The Apparition* (Louvre Museum, Paris), where we see the saint's head floating in mid-air condemning Salome for her crime. Huysmans, Mallarmé, Oscar Wilde, and Aubrey Beardsley were all fascinated by this watercolor and quick to discern its erotic undertones, years before Freud described the castration complex. Moreau's oeuvre is dominated by female figures, both *femmes fatales* whose dire passions are evoked in paintings such as *Messalina* (1874), *Pasiphae* (1876), *Helen* (1880), *The Chimerae* (1884, subtitled *The Satanic Decameron*); and unattainable virgins consumed with desire, such as the *Fairy With Griffins* (1876, Musée Gustave Moreau, Paris), who beguiled André Breton so deeply that he declared he wished he could surprise her in the dark, and *Galatea* (1880, Private Collection). Death and the fate of the male, Orpheus weighed down with all of mankind's sufferings, these too are recurring themes, not only in Moreau's painting, but also in the art of the 1890s generation as a whole.

In striving to give a moral dimension to myths and legends that were by definition subjects for serious art, Moreau wanted to give a new lease on life to a genre increasingly threatened with extinction owing to the shift of public taste toward greater realism. Emile Zola, the champion of Naturalism in art criticism as well as literature, gave a shrewd assessment of Moreau's position when, in 1876 for the first time, he spoke of the artist's "symbolism." Moreau's work bothered him. He saw in it "the most astonishing manifestation of the extravagance that an artist can fall into in his quest for originality and hatred for realism. It is inevitable that contemporary Naturalism and the artistic endeavor to study nature have produced a reaction spawning idealist artists. But with Gustave Moreau this reactionary impulse in the domain of the imagination has acquired a particularly interesting character. Moreau has not found a refuge in romanticism, as one might have expected ... No, he has thrown himself into Symbolism. He paints pictures that consist in part of riddles, rediscovers archaic and primitive forms, models himself upon Mantegna and gives an undue importance to the most trivial objects in his pictures. He has a knack for tackling subjects which other artists have already dealt with, and restating them in a different, more ingenious way. He depicts his own dreams, not the simple artless dreams that we all have, but sophisticated, complicated, enigmatic dreams that cannot be deciphered at first. What can be the value of an art like this today? This is not

Gustave Moreau
Messalina
1874, watercolor, 57 × 33.5
Musée Gustave Moreau, Paris
The artist himself states that he wanted to express here "one of the passions of man and woman, a terrible one: sensual love. The theme is debauchery leading to death." Fascinated by Roman decadence and its manifold excesses, like many artists and writers of this period, Moreau portrays the empress—with just a touch of prurience—as a frigid woman whose only pleasure is to inflame the senses of man.

45

▷ **Gustave Moreau**
*One of the Parcae and
the Angel of Death*
**1890, oil on canvas, 110×67
Musée Gustave Moreau, Paris**
Death is a recurrent theme in
Moreau's oeuvre. Preserved in
the artist's atelier and never
shown during his lifetime, this
painting displays an audacious
brush technique which antici-
pates by fifteen years that of certain Fauve painters, notably
Moreau's favorite student,
Georges Rouault. We will probably never know if the artist
considered this canvas a sketch
or a finished painting. Whatever the case, this canvas is remarkable for its colors and the
way the pigment is set down
here in sweeping juxtaposed
washes and there in thick, heavily worked impasti.

▷▷ **Gustave Moreau**
Galatea
**c. 1896, watercolor and
gouache, 45×34
Thyssen-Bornemisza
Collection, Lugano**
Moreau's fondness for portraying accursed heroines did
not prevent him from painting
dreamlike images of maidens as
pure and beautiful as they are
inaccessible, like this Galatea in
her marine cave, watched by
the lovelorn cyclops Poly-
phemus. It was while visiting
the Musée Gustave Moreau at
the age of fifteen that André
Breton had a revelation of
beauty and love communicated
by "certain female faces, certain
poses" in Moreau's paintings.

an easy question to answer. My view, as I have indicated, is that it is a simple reaction to the modern world. It does not pose much of a threat to science. We shrug and pass on to something else, that is all."[8]

Actually, Zola was not quits yet with Moreau. His attitude to the painter's oeuvre continued to be a combination of attraction and repulsion, and he eventually came around to thinking that the future of painting lay not in Naturalism but in something that revolved around Symbolism. In *L'Oeuvre* (1886), a novel in the Rougon-Macquart series dealing with art, the hero, Claude Lantier—in whom contemporary readers recognized both Manet and Cézanne—is a failed genius who paints, before hanging himself in front of his canvas, a gigantic female nude that seems to have cast a spell over the artist. The nude is none other than Moreau's *Salome*, painted a few years before Zola's novel appeared in print. "Her thighs," writes Zola, "changed into the gilded pillars of a tabernacle; her belly became a planet of dazzling pure yellows and reds, splendid and detached from life. Her nudity, passing strange like the nudity of a censer or that of rare stones, seemed to shine for some religious rite... Who was it then, who had just painted this idol from some unknown religion? Who had fashioned her out of metals, marbles, gems, causing the mystic rose of her sex to blossom between the precious columns of her thighs, under the sacred dome of her belly? Was he the unwitting artisan of this symbol of insatiable desire, this extra-human image of flesh transformed into gold and diamonds by his own fingers in their futile attempt to extract life from it?"

It fell to Zola's erstwhile disciple, Huysmans, to elaborate a definitive version of the "decadent" type in French literature, Des Esseintes, the jaded aesthete who takes off the sting of his Schopenhauerian "spleen" by escaping into preciousness and artificiality. Des Esseintes's favorite modern artists are Moreau and Redon. Many, if not most, of the artists and writers who came of age between 1880 and 1900 recognized something of themselves in Huysmans's hero and shared his tastes. Oscar Wilde, Paul Valéry and André Breton to some extent even modeled themselves on him. To Huysmans, Moreau was "the mystic cloistered in the heart of Paris, in a cell into which the din of contemporary life no longer even penetrated."

True, after 1880, at a time when he enjoyed a solid reputation in artistic and literary circles, Moreau ceased to show his work in the annual salons, secluding himself in his studio at the foot of Montmartre along the rue de La Rochefoucauld, the better to devote himself entirely to an oeuvre he was to bequeathe to the French state in order to create in his own house the museum that bears his name. When Péladan asked him to head the Rose + Croix movement, he declined. Toward the end of his life, he did accept a teaching position at the Ecole des Beaux-Arts and proved a broad-minded teacher who encouraged talents as divers as Rouault, Matisse and Marquet. Although he invariably refused to show his own work to his students, critics regarded him as one of the leading exponents of idealism in art, and several of his students, notably Rouault, exhibited paintings in the salons organized by Péladan.

To Moreau, myths were mysteries handed down from century to century in the collective unconscious of civilizations. "The ancient mysteries and the modern mysteries," he wrote, "the first pertain to the great all-embracing phenomenon of nature, whereas ours belong to the private domain, the subsoil of feeling." A great colorist, his true masters being Delacroix and Chassériau, Moreau produced, particularly towards the end of his life, watercolors and oils that dazzle us with their pure colors, bold textures and brush strokes so free that they seem to cancel out all figurative traits. One hardly hesitates to call such painting abstract, although abstraction would enter art history only in 1910 with Kandinsky.

"One thing predominates in my painting," Moreau noted in a sort of diary he kept: "the drive and feverishness [that propel me] toward abstraction. I am doubtless keenly interested in expressing human feelings, the passions of mankind, but I am less inclined to express these inner motions than to render visible, so to speak, those inner flashes that one is at loss to explain, which have something divine about their seeming insignificance and which, rendered thanks to the wonderful effects of the purely plastic, open up magical, I would even say divine, vistas."[9] Without being acquainted with Moreau's reflections about his own art, Kandinsky too speaks of the imperatives of the "inner necessity" which inspire an artist beyond the data of the external world.

Odilon Redon,
the rule of the unconscious

In 1900, Maurice Denis painted a group portrait of his fellow Nabis, as Fantin-Latour had done for his friends a few decades earlier. He called it *Homage to Cézanne* (Musée d'Orsay, Paris), even though it does not actually include the ageing master himself, who was by then living in seclusion in Aix-en-Provence. Instead, one of Cézanne's still lifes is depicted standing on an easel in Ambroise Vollard's gallery. The figure toward whom the young artists in the portrait (Vuillard, Denis, Sérusier, Ranson, Roussel, Bonnard) are turning is in fact Odilon Redon, whose silhouette could be confused at first glance with Cézanne's.

This gives us the measure of Redon's status among the rising generation of artists. Odilon Redon (1840-1916) was a contemporary of the Impressionists and had taken part in the eighth and last exhibition which the by then dissolving group had organized in 1886.

Yet Redon himself had never been an Impressionist. A self-taught painter and a rebel against the kind of instruction dispensed in academies, he had spent lonely years searching for his own path, studying the old masters—chiefly Rembrandt—and the works of Delacroix and Gustave Moreau. His only mentors had been provincial artists like the bizarre Rodolf Bresdin, who taught him engraving. His first show, in 1881, had gone virtually unnoticed. However, one of the few art connoisseurs to have seen it was none other than Huysmans himself. In *A rebours*, the novelist was the first to write about Redon's "inconceivable apparitions."

Redon had made a name for himself with his charcoals (his "blacks," as he called them) and his albums of lithographs (the first of which was titled *Dans le rêve*) inspired by Goya, Flaubert, Baudelaire, Poe, and the Book of Revelations. He began to work with color around 1890, revealing an extraordinary gift for pastels and decorative painting. His work, like Moreau's, had fervent admirers and collectors—especially in Belgium, Holland and, later, America. Though he himself did not bequeathe his studio to the state, as Moreau had done, Redon's son would accomplish this generous act.

Redon's art focusses entirely on the inner life. Flowing from the artist's unconscious, though

Odilon Redon
The Apparition
1883, charcoal with highlights of white gouache, 58 × 44
Musée des Beaux-Arts, Bordeaux
Redon's apparition was clearly inspired by Gustave Moreau's version, which was exhibited in 1876. But instead of Moreau's teeming details and debauchery of description (reminiscent of Flaubert's in *Salammbô*), Redon gives us a severe geometrical space. In the center, we distinguish John the Baptist's head radiating light—though it is beginning to be eclipsed by a sort of dark disk—while Salome is barely visible on the left. Beyond this subject's obvious level of meaning Redon's message, which concerns the struggle between darkness and light, probably has an esoteric dimension.

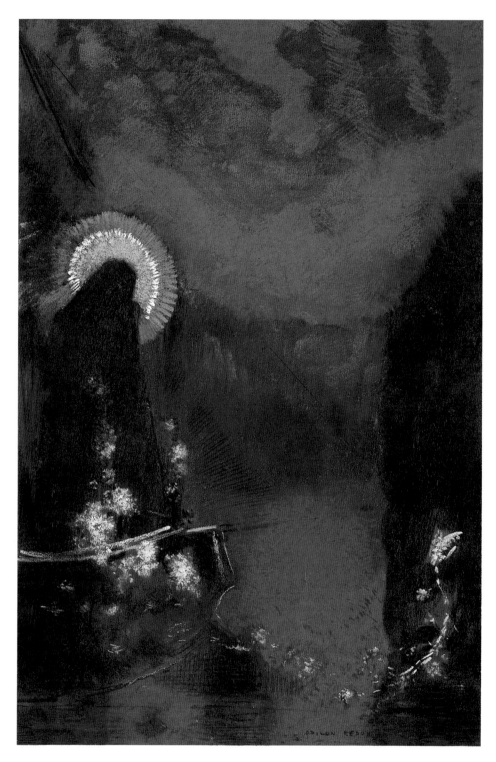

Odilon Redon
Virgin with Corona
c. 1898, pastel, 42.2 × 28
Rijksmuseum Vincent Van Gogh, Amsterdam
The artist, who acknowledged that he had set in his works "a little door opening on mystery," has left us this single comment concerning this pastel: "Dark brown sky, with clouds, violet and red; left, a haloed being on a boat, golden sheaves in the prow, and a kind of blue phosphorescence on the water, like a will-o'-the-wisp." It was the viewer's task, Redon felt, to interpret such fictions, to probe deeper.

never uncontrolled and never completely breaking with external reality (Redon was a marvelous painter of flowers), it reflects on the whole personal aspects of his imagination. The title Redon gave to his diary, *A soi-même* (To Myself), is revealing in this respect. He was acutely conscious of all that separated him from his peers under the sway of the Naturalists' canons of beauty. Recalling the advice of Rodolf Bresdin, who had urged him to meditate on trivial objects ("Do you see that stove pipe? What does it tell you? To me it speaks a legend"), Redon observed in 1913: "Most of the artists of my generation assuredly looked at the stove pipe. And they saw only it. They did not render all the things that the mirage of our own essence is able to give to the wall [behind it]. All the things that transcend, illuminate, or magnify the object and lift the mind into the region of mystery, in the thrill of the unresolved and the delicious anxiety it produces—they were closed to all this. They avoided and feared all that lends itself symbols, all that is unexpected, nebulous, undefinable in my art, all that imparts to it a riddle-like aspect. True parasites of the object, they cultivated art solely in the visual dimension, and in a way they closed art to what transcends it and might be capable of bringing the light of spirituality, I mean a radiance that seizes our spirit and defies all analysis."[10]

Closely acquainted with highly cultivated writers like Mallarmé, Huysmans, Verhaeren, Gide, and something of a music-connoisseur (his favorite composers were Schumann, Berlioz, Debussy and, above all, Wagner, who inspired many of his pictures), Redon set an example for, and was a friend to, young artists in the 1890s, many of whom would have subscribed to Emile Bernard's statement, "Among my contemporaries, I admire only Cézanne and Odilon Redon."

Until 1890, Redon's work was mainly graphic, projecting on to paper nightmares, monstruous apparitions spawned by nocturnal anxieties (curiously enough, the artist's life seems to have been a model of bourgeois respectability), like the "dreadful spider possessing a human face at the center of its body" (Huysmans in *A rebours*), the polyp with its single revulsed eye, or the numerous skeletons and severed heads in his early work, uncommon subjects for contemporary painting, together with a treatment that transgressed the artistic canons of the day.

Odilon Redon
Apollo's Chariot
1905-1914, oil and pastel on canvas, 89 × 70
Musée d'Orsay, Paris

This is Redon's version of Delacroix's decoration for the Galerie d'Apollon at the Louvre (*Apollo Vanquishing the Serpent Python*). The painting represents "the joy of full daylight conquering the sorrows of night and shade," writes the artist, "something like the elation of a sweeter feeling following anguish." We might apply to this canvas what Redon observed concerning Delacroix's ceiling: "This work, so powerful, so striking because it is new, is a whole poem, a symphony. The attribute defining each god becomes superfluous, for the colors have taken on the task of saying everything and saying it perfectly."

After Redon began to use colors, his oeuvre, born in darkness, became increasingly luminous. His nightmares gradually changed into solar visions. The supreme expression of the latter is the series *Apollo's Chariots*, a highly personal interpretation of a theme previously rendered by Delacroix and Moreau. Roseline Bacou rightly compares this turn in Redon's career to what the artist himself says regarding Delacroix's canvas for the Apollo Gallery at the Louvre: "It is the victory of light over darkness. It is the joy of full daylight conquering the sorrows of night and shadows, akin to the joy of a sweeter feeling coming on the heels of anguish." Art therapy? Perhaps not, but one would be hard put to find anything as healthy in another artist of this period.

Reflecting, toward the end of his life, on the meaning of his work, Redon wrote, "I believe I have produced an expressive, suggestive, indeterminate art... Though my art did not immediately strike a response among my rationalist generation, at a time when the rather low-vaulted edifice of Impressionism was built, the present generation (for everything evolves) understands it better. Young people in other countries, very different in their outlook, more sensitive to the supreme waves of music than were their French counterparts in the past, are also necessarily opening up to the fictions and dreams of this art's idealistic plastic." [11]

Arnold Böcklin's Darwinian mythology

The Swiss artist Arnold Böcklin (1827-1901) was unsuccessful in his home town, Basel (where, notwithstanding, most of his work is now on permanent display). Yet at the close of the nineteenth century he was considered one of the greatest of German painters, and was even regarded as a bulwark against the French Realist and Impressionist movements. The fact is that, during his first stay in Paris in 1848, he was horrified by the revolutionary violence he witnessed, and disliked the French ever since. At a time when French art was spreading its influence over the whole of Europe, the Swiss painter stood for—not altogether by design—the values of pan-Germanism; after his death, Böcklin became a favorite

artist of the Nazis, he who had always preferred Gluck to Wagner and had chosen Italy as his second home, spending his last years near Fiesole, where he died and was buried. As a result, and because few of his works can be seen elsewhere, he is still relatively unknown outside Switzerland and Germany.

Although he was trained at Düsseldorf as a landscape artist, Böcklin very early on was drawn to Italy, which he discovered thanks to his compatriot Jakob Burckhardt, the author of the classic *Civilization of the Renaissance in Italy*. After visiting Naples and viewing the frescoes in the Museo Archeologico, after rambling through the Roman countryside immortalized by Poussin and Claude Lorrain, he followed the same road as Puvis de Chavannes and Gustave Moreau, and drew inspiration from ancient mythology. But unlike his French counterparts, with whom he had no contact, Böcklin filled his imaginary landscapes with gods, centaurs, tritons and sirens, as if he had been an eyewitness to the truculent lives of those demigods who, banished from Olympus, had held their sexual jousts and brutal skirmishes in groves and rivers. An Arcadia ruled by Darwinian laws, an ancient earth in the shadow of death and decay Böcklin's world is the opposite of Puvis de Chavannes's idyllic scenes. His choice of fleshy robust figures, his frankly naturalist renderings, his garish colors and grating tonalities all reflect his rejection of the *beau idéal* to which neo-classical artists aspired since the end of the eighteenth century.

Art historians have always found it difficult to classify this original, proud, somewhat eccentric painter who, like da Vinci, experimented in his own garden with human flight. He disliked giving titles to his pictures and declared that he painted in order to make people dream. "Just as it is poetry's task to express feelings, painting must provoke them too. A picture must give the spectator as much food for thought as a poem and must make the same kind of impression as a piece of music." One can hardly imagine a more Symbolist formulation of the fusion of the arts—or the genesis of a painting: "Before you pick up a brush, you must have an idea of what it is you want. You must have in your head the solution to the problem that you are posing yourself, so that all you need do is paint. In this way, you plant the seed of truth in all that takes place [on the canvas]." Böcklin's flight from the contem-

Arnold Böcklin
Vita somnium breve
1888, tempera on wood,
180 × 114.5
Kunstmuseum, Basel
In the heart of nature at springtime, by a fountain inscribed
with the words "Life is but a
dream," three couples are seen
at different times of life: infancy,
maturity, and old age (Death
raising a cudgel behind a seated
old man). Böcklin has been
criticized now and then for his
theatricality, his heavy-handed
effects.

53

Arnold Böcklin
The Plague
**1898, tempera on wood,
149 × 104.5
Kunstmuseum, Basel**
This unfinished painting is one
of the artist's last works.
Throughout his life Böcklin repeatedly depicted the scourges
of mankind: war, the bubonic
plague, cholera, and so on. Six
of his fourteen children died
young; he contracted typhus
several times and suffered a
crippling stroke in 1892. His obsession with death was thus
quite genuine.

54

porary industrial world to a world of myth is in essence Symbolist, as is the expression of private fears (death, war, epidemics that challenge the sanctity of life and the eternity of nature). In the final two decades of his existence, these themes became obsessive: *The Island of the Dead* (1880), *The Sacred Grove* (1882), *Vita somnium breve* (1888, all three at the Kunstmuseum, Basel), *War* (1896, Kunsthaus, Zurich), and *The Plague* (1898, Kunstmuseum , Basel) are prime examples of his last period. After the artist's death, they were criticized for their overly theatrical effects and settings, their too predictably contrasting construction.

Yet the great Swiss historian Heinrich Wölfflin was an unqualified admirer of his fellow Baseler's work, and praised its "simplification and concentration, the clear and decisive expression of its form and color, its aspiration toward a rigorous composition—stylistic tendencies that one cannot designate otherwise than by situating them close to classicism."[12] Léonce Bénédite, the official historian of the Universal Exposition of 1900, compared Böcklin to Gustave Moreau and viewed him as the founder "of a sort of strangely symbolic neo-Romanticism." The Marquis de la Mazelière, in his *Histoire de la peinture allemande au XIXe siècle*, stated that "Arnold Böcklin is the greatest of the German Symbolists."[13] Yet as early as 1905, the German critic Julius Meier-Graefe undertook to demonstrate in *Der Fall Böcklin* (*The Böcklin Case*) that the kind of philosophical painting the Swiss artist had practiced ran counter to the modernist trend exemplified by Impressionism. Böcklin's reputation has only recently recovered from this devastating attack.[14]

His message nevertheless left a mark on a number of young artists steeped in German culture. Munch regarded him highly. Kandinsky included him in his list of "seekers of immaterial spheres" (together with Rossetti, Burne-Jones, and Franz von Stuck), but noted that Böcklin "has clothed his abstract figures in powerfully emphatic material forms." Undoubtedly, the artists who were most influenced by Böcklin were Salvador Dali, Ernst Fuchs, and above all Giorgio De Chirico, the inventor of *la pittura metafisica*, that bridge between Symbolism and Surrealism.

Notes

1 See J . Lethève, "La connaissance des peintres préraphaélites anglais en France (1865-1900)," *Gazette des Beaux-Arts*, May-June 1959, pp. 316-328.

2 See *The Pre-Raphaelites* (catalog), The Tate Gallery, London, 1984, p. 209.

3 Octave Mirbeau, "*Toujours des lys!*" (article dated 28 April 1895), reprinted in Octave Mirbeau, *Des artistes*, Paris, 1986.

4 See *G. F. Watts, A Nineteenth Century Phenomenon* (catalog), The Whitechapel Art Gallery, London, 1974.

5 G. K. Chesterton, *G. F. Watts*, London, 1904; cited in *Great Victorian Painters* (catalog), Arts Council of Great Britain, Leeds-Leicester-Bristol-London, 1978, p. 88.

6 Quoted in L. Hautecœur, *Littérature et peinture en France du XVIIe au XXe siècle*, Paris, 1942, p. 192.

7 *Lettres d'Odilon Redon (1878-1916)*, Paris-Brussels, 1923, p. 38 (letter dated 29 January 1900).

8 E. Zola, "*Deux expositions d'art au mois de mai,*" reprinted in E. Zola, *Le bon combat. De Courbet aux impressionnistes* (selected writings on art edited by J.-P. Bouillon), Paris, 1974, pp. 180-181.

9 G. Moreau, *L'assembleur de rêves*, op. cit., p. 29.

10 O. Redon, *A soi-même*, Paris, 1961, p. 132.

11 *Ibidem*, p. 116.

12 H. Wölfflin, "*Classical*" *Böcklin (Ulysses and Calypso)*, in *Reflections on Art History*.

13 Marquis de La Mazelière, *La peinture allemande au XIXe siècle*, Paris, 1900, p. 353.

14 J. Meier-Graefe, *Der Fall Böcklin*, Stuttgart, 1905. See also W. Ranke, "Le cas Böcklin. Un épisode toujours actuel de l'art en Allemagne," *Revue de l'Art*, n° 45, Paris, 1979, pp. 37-49.

Henri Fantin-Latour
Scene One from
Wagner's Das Rheingold
1888, oil on canvas, 165×79
Kunsthalle, Hamburg

Fantin-Latour's later oeuvre
centers mainly on imaginary
subjects, inspired notably by
Wagner's operas. Contemporary critics praised this painting
shown at the Salon of 1888,
pointing out that it manifested
the artist's determination "to
make a complete break with
Naturalism in art, with the
faithful copy of real life which
was long the great ambition of
painting, and to lead the latter
to the loftiest peaks of Symbolism, already occupied by music
and poetry."

SYMBOLISM IN FRANCE

1

From Naturalism to Symbolism

Fantin-Latour: from the Batignolles studio to Wagnerian fantasies

An isolated artist because he is so difficult to classify, a retiring yet extraordinarily gifted painter who refined his skill by copying masterpieces of the Venetian school, Henri Fantin-Latour (1836-1904) reinvented the group portrait, a genre that had been one of the crowning achievements of eighteenth-century Dutch painting. He strove to catch the likeness of his contemporaries with utmost realism. Under a variety of pretexts, and with an unerring instinct for depicting future celebrities, he brought together and portrayed his friends Manet, Whistler, and the Impressionists; a music-lover, he immortalized the boldest composers of his day—Schumann, Berlioz, and mainly Wagner; and he portrayed Baudelaire, Verlaine and Rimbaud, long before any of them were recognized as literary giants.

His unconscious eclecticism and shyness long prevented him from committing himself to one or another contemporary art trend. Raised to respect Delacroix and the late Romantics—indeed, it was his *Homage to Delacroix* (1864, Musée d'Orsay, Paris) that first brought him acclaim—champion of Manet and, briefly, standard-bearer of the rising Naturalist school (*Studio in Batignolles*, 1870, also at the Musée d'Orsay), before long Fantin-Latour would condemn the evolution of young artists such as Renoir and Monet who had sat for his *Studio*.

His true inclination lay toward a more visionary art. His first original painting is titled *The Dream*. As early as 1862 he came under the spell of Wagner's operas and, with a series of lithographs inspired by them, was one of the very first to encourage the spread of the German composer's music in France. He flirted with Symbolism but was never able to contribute a really novel vision to it, nor was he ever a model for the succeeding generation. Although Fantin-Latour proved a certified Wagnerian from the very start, even going as far as to postpone his wedding in order to attend the first Bayreuth Festival in 1876, the pictures he painted under Wagner's influence, despite their fashionable fin de siècle mistiness and convolutedness, just barely transcend the level of libretto illustrations. Basically, they never rise above the conventional language of allegory. Odilon Redon, with his indifference to academic canons, was able to capture the mythical aura of Wagner's heroes far more suggestively. Notwithstanding two decades of Symbolist inspiration, Fantin-Latour is much less convincing representing scenes from *Das Rheingold* and *Tannhäuser* than painting group portraits or pictures of flowers. Obviously, the latter satisfied his need to stay in touch with reality in ways the former could not.

57

Eugène Carrière
Suffering
1891, oil on canvas, 78.7 × 63.5
National Museum of Wales,
Cardiff

With his wife and children as
practically his only models,
Carrière expressed, through
their joys and sorrows, their
faces and poses, the leading
themes of the Symbolist poets:
reverie, meditation, birth, suffering, death. The artist's indefinite forms and sfumato are pictorial equivalents of the kind of
poetry defined by Verlaine, who
preferred allusiveness to description, nuances to forthright
colors.

Eugène Carrière's humanitarian symbolism

A fairly neglected artist today, owing perhaps to the repetitive and somewhat old-fashioned sentimentality of his favorite subjects, Eugène Carrière (1849-1906) was very highly regarded at the close of the nineteenth century, not only by the masses but also by critics and the upperclasses. Motherhood—nearly always modeled by his wife and five children—was his dominant, indeed almost his only theme. The cares and joys of family life as seen through the eyes of a devoted husband and father, this was his one great topic. One automatically contrasts the shadowy scenes he painted to the radiant, albeit rather superficial, view of motherhood in the work of the unmarried Impressionist, Mary Cassatt.

Carrière had started out doing naturalistic sentimental genre scenes, one of the most popular types of painting in the last quarter of the nineteenth century. Living in the working-class district of Belleville in Paris, he was a militant socialist and might easily have made a career illustrating affecting scenes from the novels of Zola. If many of his works have a maudlin quality—yet we forget how often illness and death intruded on family life in those days—he nevertheless managed, in the words of one contemporary, "to lend the enchantment of dreams to reality."

Carrière's technique is unique. His palette is largely limited to umbers. His paintings are brown or rust-colored monochromes, with a few

Eugène Carrière
The Young Mothers
c. 1906, oil on canvas, 279×357
Musée du Petit Palais, Paris
Typical of the artist's fluid technique and predilection for alternating areas of shadow and light creating a low-relief effect, this canvas belongs to an ensemble of four panels intended as a decoration for the banquet hall of one of Paris's *mairies*. The series' theme was to be *The Ages of Mankind*, but the artist died before completing it. His idea was to show, through four paintings entitled *The Young Mothers*, *The Betrothed*, *The Old Ones*, the cycle of human existence, with an emphasis on woman's paramount role in giving life.

59

sparing touches of color on the hands and faces of his figures. His fluid brush strokes model thin, sinuous arabesques that dissolve in luminous patches and sink into shadow, creating effects that remind one of sculpture, particularly the statues of Carrière's close friend and admirer, Rodin, a fervent collector of Carrière's paintings, as any visitor to the Rodin Museum in Paris can see for himself. The deep affinity between the two artists did not go unnoticed by contemporary critics, who frequently compared their respective talents. "The man whom Rodin resembles the most and who is the most profoundly marked by his influence," wrote a friend of both, "is undoubtedly Eugène Carrière. He has admired Rodin for many years. He is a refined intellectual, gruff in appearance and taciturn like Rodin himself, speaking only to deliver terse, infinitely sensible remarks. In pure intelligence he is superior to Rodin, who knows it and who, with the progressive intensity of expression of his groups, has relied heavily on his [Carrière's] judgements [...]. Carrière's canvases at the recent Salons are an amazing combination of the mysterious and the sculptural. They are bas-reliefs bathed in shadows. These two great artists interpenetrate and influence each other; both combine the art of shadows with stone, supremely harmonizing painting and sculpture in the abstract study of values, that fundamental element, impassive to the beguiling variations of color."[1]

The sfumato that invariably surrounds a Carrière figure—a technique picked up from the French artist Jean-Jacques Henner—inspired Degas to quip, "One should not smoke in a child's room." A better indication of how Carrière's contemporaries viewed his work is the remark by Gauguin, an artist Carrière never ceased to encourage, "Beautiful colors exist, though one is unaware of them, and can be sensed behind the sheer curtain that modesty has drawn. Conceived in love, little girls elicit tenderness; hands clutch and stroke. Without hesitation, I say it's Carrière."[2]

By focussing on the little world of his own family, Carrière was able to reach the universal. His goal was to paint a history of mankind; his images of motherhood are secular versions of Christianity's Virgin with Child. A firm believer in scientific as well as artistic progress who wrote the preface to the catalog of the first Art Nouveau show at the Galerie Bing in 1898 and presided at the 1904 Salon d'Automne, Carrière undertook in 1897 to paint, elaborating on a project commissioned by the City of Paris, four large-scale canvases representing *The Ages of Man* (Petit Palais, Paris). His early death prevented him from completing this series, in which he wanted to illustrate continuity of life as given and transmitted by women.

Well-known as a portrait painter—notably for his likeness of the key Symbolist figure, Verlaine—Carrière was remarkably warm and encouraging toward the young artists he befriended. He began a portrait of Gauguin before the latter left for Tahiti in 1891. He had a fairly durable influence on some of the Nabis, such as Vuillard and Denis, whose predilection for intimist scenes surely owes something to him. Carrière's example can even be glimpsed in some of the melancholy monochrome motherhood scenes of Picasso's blue period.

Auguste Rodin
The Gates of Hell
1880-1917, bronze, 680 × 400 × 85
Musée Rodin, Paris
This monumental door which Rodin left unfinished at his death was meant to adorn the entrance of what is now the Musée d'Orsay in Paris, but bears little resemblance to the work Rodin was originally commissioned to execute on the theme of *The Divine Comedy*. Instead, the sculptor turned it into a huge poem on life, love, and death, closely inspired by Baudelaire's *Les Fleurs du Mal*. The left pillar illustrates the successive stages in woman's existence: birth, childhood, the disappointments of maturity, old age. The right pillar depicts the relations between the sexes, and the pediment represents the Last Judgement dominated by the sculptor's celebrated *Thinker*, who belongs here because he is pondering the meaning of existence. The central part, its rather confused composition more than compensated for by the powerful plasticity of the figures, shows a swirling avalanche of naked figures, their exhausted bodies "vanquished in the eternal struggle between the human beast and the deadly, unappeasable ideal" (Octave Mirbeau).

Auguste Rodin and Camille Claudel

"Michelangelo's dreams refracted through the soul and brain of Gustave Doré." This is how Gustave Moreau unflatteringly describes Auguste Rodin (1840-1917). One wonders if Moreau knew that Antony Roux, his most ardent admirer, the man who eagerly awaited each new work to come out of his studio, was also an enthusiastic collector of Rodin, taking pride in being the first to show an interest in the sculptor.

Obviously, Rodin *was* fascinated with Michelangelo, but to compare him to Doré, who had

Camille Claudel
Maturity
(Fate or Life's Path)
1894-1900, bronze, 114 × 163 × 72
Musée d'Orsay, Paris

Its dynamics entirely concentrated in expressing flight, this bronze is a private confession: Camille Claudel, on her knees, is trying to retain a male figure —Rodin—who is being lured away from her by a soaring female figure representing Fate —as well as the sculptor's steadfast companion, Rose Beuret. In the initial, more realistic version of this group, the latter is depicted as an ageing woman sheltering in the man's arms. As for the young girl, this is how her brother Paul Claudel describes her: "Supplicating, humiliated, on her knees, and naked! It is the end! This is what she has left for us to gaze upon forever! And do you know what is being torn from her, this very moment, under our eyes? Her soul! Everything in one fell swoop: the soul, her genius, her mind, her beauty, life, her very name!"

illustrated *The Divine Comedy*, is to seriously underestimate the creative power of a sculptor whose works struck a special chord among the Symbolist generation. "The poignant thing about Rodin's figures," wrote Octave Mirbeau, "is that we recognize ourselves in them, we project our own disenchantment onto them; they are, to borrow Monsieur Stéphane Mallarmé's fine phrase, our painful comrades."[3]

In 1880 Rodin, whose talent had only begun to be recognized when the sculptor was in his forties, was commissioned to create a bas-relief based on *The Divine Comedy. The Gates of Hell* was to attain proportions that no one would have imagined at the work's inception. Indeed, Rodin worked on it sporadically right up to the end of his life and left this important project incomplete at his death. The plaster maquette of the piece is now at the Musée d'Orsay in Paris. As this work progressed, Rodin—a keen reader of poetry, though virtually illiterate at the age of twenty —gradually forgot that his monumental portal was to have *The Divine Comedy* as its theme and began to draw his inspiration from what was his favorite book, a work that Rodin illustrated with numerous drawings, Baudelaire's *Les Fleurs du mal*. One might even say that this masterpiece's main source of inspiration was not Dante but Baudelaire, *the* reference of the Symbolist generation. Nearly each of the monument's figures can be seen as a plastic equivalent of a poem by Baudelaire. The principle themes of *Les Fleurs du mal* are all there: the accursed or impossible couplings, the torment that is the lot of man who pursues beauty and woman, the inevitable presence of death in the throes of pleasure, all this contained in a broad fresco of human existence steeped in a pessimism that no glimmer of hope alleviates. The only part of Dante's poem that Rodin seems to have retained is *The Inferno*; neither Purgatory nor, *a fortiori*, Paradise nor God apprently fits into the sculptor's world view, though we know that as a young man he had toyed with the notion of entering a monastery. In point of fact, Rodin was occasionally criticized for burdening his art with too much literature. "But if my figures are correct and alive, what right have they to take me to task?" he once replied. "What right have they to forbid me to infuse them with certain intentions? Why should they complain if, on top of my professional work, I give them ideas?"[4]

Let us listen to a contemporary critic, who followed the genesis of Rodin's oeuvre very closely, explain why his works were so perfectly in tune with the atmosphere of the time while transcending it with their universality: "By registering passions in symbols, he touches all sensibilities, and all his dreams are materialized in his marbles and bronzes, there being no limit to his subjects, and his subjects being ethical, abstract, emotive, never anecdotal, and therefore instilled with great lyric poetry [...]. He fascinates all contemporary poets because he is able to make the most finite of the arts radiate the infinite."[5]

To an even greater extent than Rodin's oeuvre, the work of his pupil Camille Claudel (1864-1943) expresses an inner world and her passionate feelings toward her master, a passion that eventually drove her over the brink of madness to the psychiatric institution where she spent the last thirty years of her life. She was Rodin's assistant and model at first, lending her features to the fine regular face of *La Pensée* (1886-1889, Musée d'Orsay, Paris), then his mistress for a decade. However, she never recovered after he broke off their relationship and gradually sank into delusions of persecution which crippled her.

Though her manner reflects Rodin's influence, her powerful personality led her to create works that are filled with pathos and to which she devoted herself body and soul. *Cacountala* or *The Surrender* (1888, Musée Bertrand, Chateauroux) is more than just a feminine version of Rodin's *Eternal Idol*; it is the concrete expression of the moment when a woman yields to a man's desire, "even to the most secret palpitations of the soul and flesh," as her brother Paul Claudel put it.[6] *The Waltz* (1891-1905, Musée Rodin, Paris), that tottering vortex showing a couple embracing, reflects the intoxicated feelings of the artist who shaped it. In *Maturity* or *Fate* (1894-1900, Musée d'Orsay, Paris), on the other hand, we witness the drama of her separation from Rodin; the beseeching figure is Camille Claudel herself reaching out desperately to catch the hand of her departing lover. Rarely in art history do we find an oeuvre so intimately connected with the artist's personal drama. "What makes my sister's work so uniquely interesting," observed her brother Paul, "is the fact that it is entirely the story of her life."[7]

Paul Gauguin, an Impressionist in search of the soul's colors

Paul Gauguin (1848-1903) began as a Sunday painter and early collector of Impressionist art. At the age of thirty-one, he decided to become a full-time artist, a choice made partly under the pressure of a financial crisis that threatened his future as broker at the Paris stock exchange.

Encouraged by Degas and, mainly, Pissarro, he showed his pictures at the Impressionist exhibitions as early as 1879: landscapes after the manner of Pissarro and Cézanne and sculptures —it was Gauguin the sculptor that Redon, his senior by eight years, was later to admire. A

self-taught painter "tormented by art," as he liked to describe himself, he began, around 1885, to move away from straightforward landscape painting and to search for the *sensation*. He proclaimed that a "great artist" consists of "an intelligence of the highest order, receiving the brain's most delicate and consequently most invisible feelings and translations."[8]

As an example he cited the "misunderstood Cézanne," and was probably the first to understand that reclusive artist's struggle to transcend strictly physical reality.

Poverty and a desire to seek inspiration in as primitive an environment as possible, one untouched by industrialization and still filled with a mythic sense of nature, drove him first to Brittany and later to even more remote spots. Whereas his first paintings at Pont-Aven were in the Impressionist vein, their compositions were already beginning to reflect the influence of Japanese prints, and their subjects, many of them suggested by the very young Emile Bernard, were new. Indeed, it was after the encounter with Bernard that Gauguin's genius suddenly blossomed, notably in *The Vision After the Sermon* (1888, National Gallery of Scotland, Edinburgh), based on the famous passage in Genesis relating Jacob's stuggle with the angel. The break with Impressionism was total, starting with the title, which Gauguin explained as follows in a letter to Vincent Van Gogh, whom he was soon to join in Arles, "To me, the landscape and the struggle in this picture exist only in the imagination of the people praying after the sermon. That is why there is a contrast between the unsophisticated people and the struggle in the mannered and disproportionate landscape."[9] To a friend who expressed surprise about the savage "mysticism" that was leading Gauguin in a direction opposite to the one he had followed until then, the artist declared, "Of course, this symbolic road is full of pitfalls, and so far I have only touched it with my fingertips, but it is there, deep down inside me, and one must always obey one's temperament. I know very well that people will understand me less and less. Does it matter if I move away from the others? I will be a puzzle to the crowd, a poet to the few, and sooner or later reason will prevail."[10] Indeed, his Impressionist friends soon regarded him as a renegade.

Paul Gauguin
The Vision After the Sermon (Jacob Wrestling with the Angel)
1888, oil on canvas, 74 × 93
National Gallery of Scotland, Edinburgh

With this pictorial manifesto Gauguin is announcing his break with the Impressionism of his beginnings, a break in subject matter, technique, and composition which owes a good deal to Emile Bernard's paintings. The artist has depicted a mystical vision of praying women who were painted from life, whereas the apparition is set in an imaginary landscape constructed in complete defiance of the laws of perspective.

Paul Gauguin
Be Amorous,
You Will Be Happy
**1890, bas-relief on carved and
painted wood panel, 97×75
Museum of Fine Arts, Boston**
Autobiographical in content
and abstruse, this bas-relief, its
title unrelated to the scene it
depicts, represents a man with
Gauguin's features attempting
to beat a woman. According to
the artist, the fox in the lower
right corner symbolizes perversity—a key to the meaning of
the overall composition where,
to quote Georges-Albert Aurier,
"all lewdness, all the struggle
between flesh and mind, all the
pain of sexual bliss writhe and
gnash their teeth, as it were."

Gauguin left Brittany just as a number of young artists were beginning to flock to him, and went to join Van Gogh in the south of France —among other reasons, because he had run out of funds. At Arles, he continued to experiment with his new manner. Van Gogh "sees this as a place to do Daumiers," he explained, but "I see it as a place to paint a mixture of colored Puvis and Japan." Van Gogh, in fact, found one of the few canvases that Gauguin painted there, *Man's Trials* (or *The Grape Harvest in Arles*), "very strange." This painting depicts several peasant women in traditional Breton costumes—a sign of nostalgia for Gauguin, who preferred Pont-Aven to the Provence—their bright colors and poses totally unrelated to the scene being rendered. "Do you see a poor wretch among the grape-pickers? She is not," Gauguin explained, "a soul deprived of intelligence, gracefulness, and all nature's gifts. She is a woman. With her two hands under her chin, she is thinking about trifles but feels consoled to be on that earth (nothing but earth) flooded by the sun with its red triangle among the grape vines. And a woman dressed in black is walking by, gazing at her like a sister. To explain by means of painting is not the same thing as to describe. That is why I prefer forms to have a suggestive color, and the composition

to be a parable rather than a painted novel. For many, I'm wrong and perhaps all this is in my imagination, yet if I succeed in giving you a feeling of the beyond, it is perhaps owing to this magnetic current of thought whose absolute progress one divines even if one has ceased to understand it. In painting, a hand clutching a handkerchief can express the feeling that galvanizes it, an entire past life or a life to come. Since all is convention and in French happiness and unhappiness are words that express a state of affairs while black expresses mourning, why can't we come around to creating divers harmonies corresponding to the state of our soul? Too bad for those who are unable to read; we must not explain to them."[11]

Gauguin had a genius for assimilating influences. Cézanne, Pissarro, and Bernard accused him by turns of having imitated, even pillaged, and eventually disowned their work. After 1889, Gauguin was a diligent member of the circle of Parisian Symbolist poets, many of whom, like their mentor Baudelaire, wrote art criticism. And they gradually came to see him as the quintessential Symbolist artist. He began to be considered the head of a new school of painting and believed, for a while, that long-awaited commercial success was his. An auction of his paintings

Paul Gauguin
Whence Come We?
What Are We?
Whither Go We?
1897, oil on canvas, 139×375
Museum of Fine Arts, Boston
A pictorial testament and an artistic summation, this vast canvas is the response of Gauguin *"le Sauvage"* to Puvis de Chavannes "the Greek." The mysteries of man's fate from birth to death are evoked in a landscape untouched by European civilization. "Close to the death of an old woman, a strange, stupid bird concludes (the allegory)," writes the artist who, completely disillusioned, would shortly make an attempt on his life.

67

in February 1891, well publicized in the press, even brought him, after years of hardship, enough money to pay for his passage to Tahiti. He left Paris after a farewell banquet in his honor, presided by the greatest of the Symbolist poets, Mallarmé. Poetry, says Mallarmé, is "the expression, by means of human language restored to its essential rhythm, of the mysterious sense of existence." Replace the words "human language" with "the plastic arts" and you have a good definition of Gauguin's art.

It was at this juncture that, after a series of conversations with the artist, the young Symbolist poet Georges-Albert Aurier made Gauguin's painting the cornerstone of his history of pictorial Symbolism, "Symbolism in Painting," published in the March 1891 issue of *Le Mercure de France*.

"Symbolism in Painting—Paul Gauguin"

A document of major importance today because it frames the doctrine of Symbolist art, "Symbolism in Art" did not have the kind of impact when first published that critics have lent it retrospectively.[12] Written in the affected, flowery style fashionable at the time, it starts out with a lengthy description of *The Vision After the Sermon*. This gives the author a pretext to point out the difference between Gauguin's painting and Impressionism, which he views as a "mere variation of Realism, a refined, spiritualized, dilettantish Realism, but Realism all the same." Aurier saw the new trend in art as an idealist, even mystical, reaction and thought it would lead to a development in the plastic arts parallel to what was taking place in literature. The label "Impressionism" was not adequate to express this new trend in taste and it therefore seemed necessary to coin a new term for the "newcomers led by Gauguin. Call them Synthetists, *idéistes*, Symbolists, whatever you please, but above all abandon that inept generic term 'Impressionists.' Let that title be reserved strictly for those painters who view art as nothing more than a translation of the artist's sensations and impressions."

Aurier goes on to say that he considers Gauguin a "sublime visionary. I see him as the founder of a new art, if not in history then at least in our own time. Let us therefore analyse this art from the viewpoint of aesthetics in general." In paragraph after paragraph, he draws a certain number of principles from Gauguin's painting, and it is sometimes hard to separate the artist's ideas from the critic's theories. Aurier draws up a virtual manifesto at the end of the article: "To sum up… the work of art such as I have been pleased to describe it logically here will be:

1° *Ideaist*, in that its unique ideal will be to express the Idea;

2° *Symbolist*, in that it will express this Idea by means of forms;

3° *Synthetist*, in that it will set forth these forms, these signs, in a generally understandable manner;

4° *Subjective*, in that the object will never be viewed merely as an object, but as the sign of an idea perceived by the subject;

5° (and consequently) *decorative*, in that decorative painting properly speaking, such as it was understood by the Egyptians, the Greeks in all probability, and the Primitives, is nothing more than a manifestation of art that is at once subjective, synthetic, symbolist, and ideaist."

To Aurier, the highest art was mural decoration and, except for Puvis de Chavannes, he could think of no contemporary artist capable of measuring up to it. No one, that is, save Gauguin: "Walls! walls! give him walls!" Unfortunately, the latter was never commissioned to do a mural, though he was to respond to Aurier's call a few years later by painting his masterpiece, *Whence Come We? What Are We? Whither Go We?*

After reading Aurier's article, Gauguin's first mentor, Pissarro, who had been so encouraging at the start of Gauguin's career, disapproved heartily of the turn his art was taking and even accused him of betraying the Impressionist cause in order to follow fashion and enjoy easy success. "I do not reproach Gauguin for painting a vermilion background," he wrote to his son regarding *The Vision After the Sermon*, "nor for his two fighting warriors and the Breton peasant-woman in the foreground; I take exception to the fact that he has stolen from the Japanese, the Byzantine artists, and others; I reproach him for not applying his synthesis to our modern philosophy which is absolutely social, anti-authoritarian, and anti-mystical. That is where the gravity of the issue lies. It is a step backward. Gauguin is not a seer, he is a shrewd operator who has sensed the bourgeoisie's regressiveness. It is the same

Paul Gauguin
Barbarian Tales
1902, oil on canvas, 131.5 × 90.5
Folkwang Museum, Essen

Two youths (one of whom, the figure seen full-face, is androgynous) are shown daydreaming, their poses inspired by Buddhist statues, in the midst of the natural paradise of the Marquises Islands where Gauguin spent his last years. Though "barbarian," they nevertheless incarnate a primordial beauty and purity, in contrast to the ugly features of the voyeuristic figure eyeing the pair lustfully, who represents Western civilization, a figure modeled in fact on a painter Gauguin had known at Pont-Aven and whose unlucky rival in love he had been. To emphasize his message, the artist has replaced one of the white man's feet with a fox paw, the fox being a symbol of lewdness.

thing with the Symbolists! What do you think? That is why we must fight them like the plague!"[13]

Another avant-garde critic of the time, Félix Fénéon, who wanted an evolution in Impressionism but in a scientific direction and championed Seurat's Neo-Impressionism, deplored the new turn in Gauguin's art too. Fénéon blamed this change on the artist's friendly relations with the Symbolist literary circles, who, he thought, had gulled Gauguin into believing that it was his mission to enrich the modern soul. True, the painter had not had much of an education—a fact that did not prevent him from being a great correspondent—and was no doubt rather impressed by his new acquaintances and felt honored to be invited to Mallarmé's "Tuesdays." But Gauguin evolved in this manner because he was already inclined toward the spiritual; his thirst for higher things had declared itself several years earlier and had been strengthened by endless conversations with his young artist friends in Brittany, Emile Bernard and Paul Sérusier. Probably too much emphasis has been given to Charles Chassé's report that, after a Symbolist soirée in a Paris café, Gauguin remarked to Sérusier: "So now we're Symbolists! Did you understand a single word of their doctrines?" And when Sérusier replied "Not a word," Gauguin is supposed to have said, "Me neither. But Symbolism's alright by me."[14]

Certain works of this period, for example, *The Loss of Virginity* (1891, Chrysler Museum, Norfolk), do in fact contain poetic allusions that clearly owe something to his literary friendships, but they are not his strongest paintings. Several others, on the contrary, equally permeated with Symbolist influences, figure among his masterpieces, notably the polychrome wood bas-relief, *Be Amorous, You Will be Happy* (1890, Museum of Fine Arts, Boston). This is one of the first examples in Western art of an artist borrowing from a non-Western primitive culture, a source of inspiration that would play a leading role in twentieth century art and would become increasingly important in the output of Gauguin's last decade. The artist himself described the panel to Emile Bernard in the following terms: "I did a large, size thirty panel in sculpture in order to be able to do it in wood later. . . As sculpture it is the best and most powerful thing I've done. Gauguin (like a monster) taking the hand of a resisting woman,

telling her Be amorous and you will be happy. The fox, an Indian symbol for perversity; then, in the intervals, little figures."[15] It is, in fact, the fox that gives this work its meaning for, despite its euphoric title, the carving creates an impression of sadness, uneasiness. The woman on the right, clutching her head woefully between her hands, is a figure of grief and death, derived from a Peruvian mummy Gauguin had seen in a museum. Far from being "literary," the Symbolism here is private. The panel is a confession whose meaning would surely escape the viewer —the artist's contemporaries regarded it as the work of a sex maniac—were it not for Gauguin's personal explanation and what we know about his private life.[16]

Gauguin did not find the happiness he had hoped for in the South Pacific, far from it, but at least the physical beauty of the natives and the splendor of the scenery boosted his pictorial genius to new heights. The landscapes he painted there seem real views of a paradise on earth. His symbolism was refined and became more private. Though it is present in all of his works, it reveals itself mainly in pictures painted in moments of depression, such as his masterpiece and most ambitious composition, *Whence Come We? What Are We? Whither Go We?* (1897, Museum of Fine Arts, Boston).

Gauguin's pictorial testament

Whence Come We? is Gauguin's pictorial testament. It recapitulates the poses and colors of Gauguin's oeuvre and sums up his aesthetic and philosophical, even theological message. Around the time that he was working on this canvas, Gauguin put into writing a series of religious thoughts—he had received a very strong religious education in a Catholic school as a child—accusing the Catholic clergy of having suppressed the Bible's true meaning. With the help of several recently published books, he tried to frame a synthesis that would reconcile science and the Scriptures.[17] Formally, his large canvas (almost a mural in size) restates the theme of the sacred grove somewhat in the manner of Puvis de Chavannes, the supreme reference for Gauguin, who kept several reproductions of the great mural painter's work in his Tahitian hut. However, if the painting's pictorial qualities and flawless composition set this canvas apart as a masterpiece, one cannot really appreciate its significance without taking into account what the artist himself has to say about it: "At the bottom, to the right, a sleeping baby, then three crouching women. Two figures dressed in purple are confiding their thoughts to each other; a deliberately enormous figure, flouting perspective, raises his arms in the air and looks on wonderingly. The figure in the middle is picking a fruit. Two cats next to a child. A white goat. The idol, its twin arms raised mysteriously, rhythmically, seems to point the way to the other world. The crouching figure seems to be listening to the idol. And, finally, an old woman close to death seems to be accepting, to be resigned to what she is thinking, and ends the legend. A strange bird at her feet, holding a lizard in its claws, stands for the futility of idle words... If, for the Prix de Rome competition, Beaux-Arts students were told: The picture that you will paint must represent Whence come we? What are we? Whither go we? What would they do? I have completed a philosophical work on this theme as compared to the Gospel. I think it's good; if I have the strength to copy it, I will send it to you."[18]

These lines reflect the combination of syncretism and agnosticism that Gauguin, battered by life, had reached in 1897. After signing his name to the canvas he tried to kill himself.

Gauguin died at the age of fifty-five in his "House of Bliss," whose wooden entrance was sculpted by the artist himself and is now found in the Musée d'Orsay, Paris. His works were beginning to sell in Paris by then, where the few young artists who had known him at Pont-Aven and fallen under the spell of his personality, his innovative technique, his world view, banded together to form the Nabis group following his departure for the South Pacific. Critics had proclaimed Gauguin the originator of Symbolist painting, but a rival artist, Emile Bernard, claimed this title as well, and continued to clamor for it until the end of his life, which was considerably longer than Gauguin's. It is worth pausing to take a closer look at the facts.

Notes

1 Camille Mauclair, quoted in R. J. Bantens, *Eugène Carrière. His Work and Influence*, Ann Arbor, Michigan, 1983, p. 236.

2 P. Gauguin, *Avant et après* (c. 1903), reprinted in *Oviri. Ecrits d'un sauvage*, p. 305.

3 O. Mirbeau, *Des artistes*, Paris, 1986, pp. 100-101. (This article originally appeared in 1889).

4 A. Rodin, *L'art. Entretiens réunis par P. Gsell*, Paris, 1911, p. 114.

5 A. Le Normand-Romain, "Le symbolisme," in *La sculpture française au XIXe siècle* (catalog), Le Grand Palais, Paris, 1986, p. 380.

6 P. Claudel, in *Camille Claudel* (catalog), Musée Rodin, Paris, 1951, p. 6.

7 *Ibidem*, p. 11.

8 Letter to E. Schuffenecker, 14 January 1885, quoted in *Correspondance de Paul Gauguin (1873-1888)*, edited by V. Merlhès, Paris, 1984, pp. 87-88.

9 *Ibidem*, letter written around 25-27 September 1888, p. 232.

10 *Ibidem*, letter dated 18 October 1888, p. 255.

11 *Ibidem*, letter written around 20 December 1888, p. 306.

12 See the article published in *Le Mercure de France*, March 1891, pp. 155-166.

13 *Lettres de Camille Pissarro à son fils Lucien*, Paris, 1950, letter dated 20 April 1891, pp. 234-235.

14 C. Chassé, *Gauguin et son temps*, Paris, 1955, p. 125.

15 P. Gauguin, *Oviri. Ecrits d'un sauvage*, letter to E. Bernard, early September 1889, p. 54.

16 For more about this complex work, see C. Grey, *Sculpture and Ceramics of Paul Gauguin*, Baltimore, 1963, pp. 42-47.

17 Generous excerpts from these notes are given in P. Gauguin, *Oviri. Ecrits d'un sauvage*, pp. 196-216.

18 See all of Gauguin's writings relating to this painting in G. Wildenstein, *Gauguin*, Paris, 1964, pp. 232-234.

Paul Sérusier
The Talisman
1888, oil on panel, 27 × 22
Musée d'Orsay, Paris
Painted by the young Sérusier under Gauguin's direction, this little painting was the starting point of the Nabi movement. An almost abstract rendering of a view of the Pont-Aven river, it signals a break with the Impressionists' realist vision and presents itself instead as the transposition of a personal sensation. Calling it "the talisman," Sérusier showed it to his fellow students at the Académie Julian, several of whom were soon to band together under the name *Les Nabis*, meaning the prophets of a new school of painting.

2

The Symbolism of the Pont-Aven Group

The "Pont-Aven School," as it is called a trifle solemnly, was essentially a group of three or four painters gathered by chance, at least in the beginning, around Gauguin. The latter, when funds were low, would move from Pont-Aven, which was already becoming colonized by artists, to take up residence at the *Buvette de la plage*, an extremely modest inn near the village of Le Pouldu, a dozen miles to the south-east. It was there that the young André Gide, who was touring Brittany on foot, happened to meet them one autumn evening in 1889. This is how the encounter is described in Gide's novel, *Si le grain ne meurt*: "A servant girl ushered me into a white-washed room and left me there, before a glass of cider. The sparse furniture and absence of wallpaper made a large number of canvases and artists' stretchers stacked on the floor, facing the wall, all the more noticeable. No sooner was I alone than I scuttled over to these canvases; I turned them around one by one and viewed them with growing amazement; they were merely childish daubings, it seemed to me, but their colors were so bright, so unusual, so joyful that I no longer thought about leaving. I wanted to meet the artists who had been capable of those amusing vagaries; I gave up my initial plan of reaching Pont-Aven that evening, took a room in the inn, and inquired when dinner would be served.

"'Do you wish to be served separately, or will you dine in the same room as the Gentlemen?' asked the servant.

"The 'Gentlemen' were the authors of the canvases. They were a trio, and soon they showed up with their easels and paint boxes. It goes without saying that I asked to have my dinner served with them, provided they didn't mind. They made it clear, as a matter of fact, that I was not disturbing them at all, that is to say they were completely free and easy. They were all three barefoot, superbly untidy, and loud. I was on the edge of my chair during the entire meal, drinking in their words, tormented by a desire to talk to them, to make myself known, to get to know them, and to tell the tall bright-eyed one that the theme he was singing at the top of his lungs, and which the others were repeating in chorus, was not, as he seemed to think, by Massenet but by Bizet [. . .]. I met one of them later at Mallarmé's —it was Gauguin. The other was Sérusier. I haven't been able to identify the third (it was Filigier [sic], I think)."

Gide's account gives a good idea of the atmosphere surrounding Gauguin, who, with his friends, decorated the inn's dining-room with paintings and inscriptions, including a rather free rendering of a statement of Wagner's they had adopted as their creed: "I believe in a Last

Judgement when to all those in this world who dare to falsify chaste and sublime art, all those who sully and degrade it with their base feelings and their vile avidness for material satisfactions, will be meted out a terrible sentence..."[1] These brash young artists, who painted out of doors, had other ambitions than merely to reproduce the scenes and peasants before their easels. They had heated discussions about religion and philosophy (Plato, Schopenhauer, Swedenborg) and, when in Paris, regularly attended concerts, proving themselves to be solid admirers of Wagner. They were avid readers too: Carlyle's *Sartor Resartus* and Milton's *Paradise Lost* appear in Gauguin's portrait of his Dutch disciple, Jacob Meyer de Haan, another Le Pouldu regular. However, they did not content themselves with giving a moral or intellectual message to their painting. They also sought to express their ideas through new pictorial means, and that is what shocked Gide's unaccustomed eye, whose sole modern references were hanging in the Musée du Luxembourg, the period's contemporary art museum.

During the 1889 Universal Exposition, Gauguin and his circle decided to show their works outside the official exhibition halls (where they were not admitted), just as Manet and Courbet had done during previous expositions. They managed to get permission to hang their paintings in a *café-concert* owned by a certain Monsieur Volpini and located near the entrance of the Palace of Fine Arts. Except for the enthusiastic response of a few young artists whom Sérusier brought, the show, whose catalog bore the title *Groupe impressionniste et synthétiste*, was a flop: not a single painting sold.

Paul Sérusier (1864-1927) had met Gauguin at Pont-Aven a year earlier. He had been entranced by the older artist's revolutionary message, and had come back from his stay in Brittany with a small painting done in a single afternoon: a rough view of the banks of the Aven. Sérusier showed it to his fellow students at the Académie Julian. Like him, they were preparing to enter the Ecole des Beaux-Arts under the guidance of established artists who were teaching a kind of painting that was far removed from what Gauguin was doing. Sérusier's picture, not much larger than a cigar box top, circulated among these young artists like a *Talisman*, hence its name (1888, Musée d'Orsay, Paris).

Maurice Denis has recorded, and embellished perhaps, Gauguin's advice to Sérusier as the latter was painting this picture under his aegis: "A landscape communicates by dint of being formulated synthetically, in purple, vermilion, Veronese green, and other pure colors, straight from the tube, with almost no white mixed in. 'How do you see that tree?' Gauguin said as they were facing a corner of the Bois d'Amour. 'Isn't it green? Well, then make it green, the finest green on your palette. And what about that shadow, bluish isn't it? Don't hesitate to make it as blue as you can.' It was in these paradoxical and unforgetable terms that, for the first time, the fertile concept of the 'flat surface covered with colors arranged in a certain order' was presented to us. And thus it was that we learned that every work of art is a translation, a caricature, an impassioned equivalent of a received sensation."[2] This famous definition has sometimes been regarded as a foreshadowing of abstraction; actually, it simply describes a painting that lies at the turning point between Impressionism (for it is, after all, painted out of doors) and a new pictorial art that attempted to go beyond description. As for "sensation," the word means here a message received from the exterior (the landscape before the artist's eyes), but perhaps it also designates a feeling in the artist's consciousness —a shade of meaning that explains the immense success Gauguin's formula has enjoyed.

One of the young artists enthralled by the paintings Gauguin exhibited at the Café Volpini was Armand Seguin (1869-1903). Seguin soon became Gauguin's favorite follower. The latter even wrote a preface for the catalog of the only show that Seguin had during his life, at the Le Barc de Boutteville gallery in 1895. It is in an article devoted to this exhibit that Maurice Denis proclaimed the following profession of faith, "I still believe in Symbolism, in a theory that affirms the possible expression of human emotions and thoughts through aesthetic correspondences, through equivalences in Beauty." A shy, moody artist who suffered from tuberculosis, Seguin lived with Sérusier after an abortive suicide attempt. He died young. There are about a dozen of his canvases known to exist (and often mistaken for Gauguins, so completely did Seguin assimilate the older artist's manner) and some ninety engravings, mostly of Breton landscapes. His *Fleurs du mal* (Josefowitz Collection), admit-

Armand Seguin
Les Fleurs du Mal
c. 1893, oil on canvas, 53×35
Josefowitz Collection
In the preface to the catalog of
Seguin's exhibition in 1895,
Gauguin wrote this: "He knows
how to read in the mysterious
Book and he knows how to
speak that Book's language. I
need only warn the visitor that
Seguin is above all a cerebral
—to be sure, I am not saying a
'literary'—artist who does not
express what he sees but what he
thinks, with an original linear
harmony, a drawing curiously
included in the arabesque."

75

tedly an isolated example in his oeuvre, is a sensitive and mysterious tribute to a poet whom all the Symbolists revered.

Emile Bernard and his quarrel with Gauguin over who fathered pictorial Symbolism

It was during his first stay at Pont-Aven, in 1886, that Gauguin had met—paying little attention to their acquaintance at first—an artist young enough to have been his son, Emile Bernard (1868-1941), twenty years Gauguin's junior. The older painter always called him "*le petit Bernard*," the *young* Bernard, with just a touch of condescension. Bernard had fled the established Parisian ateliers to come to Brittany in search of non-academic sources of inspiration. He was both knowledgeable about the latest developments in the art world and familiar with the paintings of the Impressionists, Cézanne, Seurat, Redon, and the Japanese print makers. Curiosity was one of the main traits of his character; it led him constantly toward new horizons and, as a result, he never developed nor gave depth to his truly personal style. When he encountered Gauguin at Pont-Aven once again, in 1888 following the older artist's journey to Martinique, Bernard had in the meantime associated with Van Gogh and carried out, with friends like Louis Anquetin, new pictorial experiments, elaborating the style he first called "*cloisonnisme*" and later "*synthétisme*." This was a manner of painting by setting down colors in flat areas, with no modeling, and surrounding them with thick black contours, as in stained glass windows and medieval enamels. Classical perspective was abolished and, instead, a three-dimensional effect was obtained by superposing figures of decreasing size.

Bernard's experiments interested Gauguin, who promptly absorbed the younger artist's "inventions" and, only a few weeks later, painted his first masterpiece, *The Vision After the Sermon*, extending the scope of Bernard's discoveries. The two painters were seeing each other daily at this time. Bernard had just completed *The Breton Peasant Women in the Green Meadow* (1888, Denis Collection, France), a canvas that plainly inspired Gauguin, for he took it to Arles a few weeks later to show to Van Gogh, who made a copy of it in watercolors—a good indication of the inter-est Bernard's work raised. A deeply religious young man, Bernard was fond of visiting churches and primitive calvaries in Brittany, and talked endlessly about religion. He claimed to have gotten the idea of Synthetism while reading the neo-Platonic writings of St. Denys the Areopagite. It was precisely at this time that Gauguin was painting his most deeply religious works, *The Yellow Christ* (1889, Albright-Knox Art Gallery, Buffalo), the *Breton Calvary* (1889, Musées Royaux des Beaux-Arts, Brussels), and others. Oddly enough, Bernard continued to paint and engrave mainly secular themes, "*bretonneries*," rural Breton scenes. Much inclined to speculate about aesthetic matters, he attached an overall, "synthetic" meaning to colors, lines, geometric compositions. He wanted to communicate this meaning to the viewer naturally and without resorting to any artifice. "Color and style are the foundation," he would write later, "but color is handled the way it is in Oriental rugs and medieval illuminations. It is applied pure or with only minimal alterations. As its role is to determine the feeling or state of mind of the painting, it is adapted to the subject—that is, its symbolic character. As for style, which deforms in keeping with what it is intended to mean, it is engendered by the memory of the object—for the artist must never copy the latter. It is a painting that takes memory as its origin and repeats within the mind what it has perceived externally. Hence the errors in taste, the unacceptable warpings in the drawing, when the artist is clumsy and his emotion is not sufficiently aesthetic. In short, Symbolism does not paint things, but the idea of things outside those things."[3] It is left to the viewer to discover the content of the artist's message—it is not always obvious—and clearly the artist must have a gift for communicating his own perceptions. Bernard, as a matter of fact, would soon reach an impasse and tap other sources of inspiration, notably religious themes (*Pietà*, 1890, Private Collection, Paris). Gauguin summed up the two artists' theories more simply: "Don't do too much copying from nature. Art is an abstraction; glean it from nature by dreaming in front of her, and think of the creating rather than the outcome, it is the only way to rise toward God, doing what our divine master does—creating."[4]

Bernard's masterpiece dating from this period, *Madeleine au Bois d'Amour* (1888, Musée d'Orsay, Paris), is a canvas of rather large dimensions; the

Emile Bernard
Madeleine in the Bois d'Amour
1888, oil on canvas, 137×164
Musée d'Orsay, Paris
In this canvas painted at Pont-Aven, the artist who was undoubtedly inspired, for the
overall composition, by a Max Klinger engraving, combines a pictorial concept that
derives from Puvis de Chavannes (a supine figure—a tomb figure, as the artist called her
—in a sacred wood) with a *cloisonniste* manner that led him to outline forms with a heavy
black contour.

77

Vincent Van Gogh
The Starry Night
1889, oil on canvas, 73.7 × 92.1
The Museum of Modern Art,
New York
This nocturnal scene is really a cosmic vision, not just a night view of Saint-Rémy (whose church steeple the artist has oddly transformed into a Dutch village steeple). Georges-Albert Aurier, who was the only critic to write an article on Van Gogh during the artist's lifetime, ranged him among the Symbolists, observing correctly that his "brilliant and dazzling symphonies of colors and lines, whatever their importance is to the painter, are only simple expressive means, mere symbolic procedures."

artist painted the work at Pont-Aven, using his sister as a model. He depicts her "in the recumbent pose of a tomb figure," lying in a beech wood on the hill overlooking the river upstream from the village. The dreamy-eyed young girl reminds us of Puvis de Chavannes's *The Dream* (Musée d'Orsay, Paris), a painting that had been exhibited in Paris a short while earlier.[5]

Bernard has gone back to Puvis de Chavannes's favorite theme of the sacred grove, but here the background is a landscape painted from nature, from a point on the hill's slope looking down toward the river. The composition is harmonious, cunningly constructed, with vertical tree trunks connecting the horizontals of the girl and the river. The color areas, which are mostly flat planes on the river and the sunny spots in the foreground, and the black contours, especially around the figure, help to make this portrait a timeless image of the experience of being one with nature.

Bernard painted few pictures of this level. One room in the Musée d'Orsay in Paris contains several Gauguins and Bernards painted around the same time. The latter are remarkable for their formal and technical innovations, though more often than not they are inspired by Cézanne, Seurat, Puvis de Chavannes; the former show an equal control and mastery of technique. Bernard, who was inclined to have mystical crises and whose plans to get married never seemed to work out, wound up becoming acutely jealous of Gauguin. The break between the two came when Georges-Albert Aurier proclaimed Gauguin the originator and leader of pictorial Symbolism and Bernard, very unfairly, his disciple.

A prolific writer and historian of the Symbolist movement, Bernard wrote lengthy articles describing the beginnings of the Pont-Aven group and stressing the importance of his own role in its inception. His work unfortunately began to lose some of its originality. At the 1892 Rose + Croix Salon, he showed three canvases depicting scenes from the life of Christ. They caught the eye of a benefactor who gave him a substantial grant to study the Italian Pre-Raphaelites. Bernard moved to Cairo in 1894 and spent ten years there, an erstwhile avant-garde artist turned painter of Oriental genre scenes. What, then, was his contribution to Symbolism? It is to Redon, who followed the careers of both artists closely, and was admired by both, that we must turn for the final

word about the birth of pictorial Symbolism in France: "I think that Bernard, who is a theorist, must have contributed a great deal to the Pont-Aven experiments. And Gauguin, spontaneous and quick to assimilate, constantly working, lost no time in rivaling these first innovations. This was the starting point, but what difference does it make anyway? The works are there, and Bernard has done fine things, in sculpture as well; of course, he is no Gauguin."[6]

The unstudied Symbolism of Vincent Van Gogh

In the course of his pathetic existence, Vincent Van Gogh (1853-1890) was mentioned but once in print. In January 1890, Georges-Albert Aurier wrote a highly favorable article about him for *Le Mercure de France*, singling out his remarkable gifts as a colorist ("...he is the only painter to perceive the chromatic nature of things with this intensity, this metallic, gemlike quality..."), as well as his characteristic impasti ("...which lend to certain of his canvases the solid appearance of dazzling walls of sunlight and crystals").[7] We know that, after discovering French painting (Delacroix, Millet, Monticelli, the Impressionists) during his stay in Paris between 1886 and 1888, Van Gogh enjoyed close ties with Bernard and Gauguin. He considered himself an Impressionist, continued to draw inspiration chiefly from nature and was quite surprised to find himself called a Symbolist by Aurier, albeit flattered by the journalist's enthusiastic study of his work. "I hope to keep on thinking that I do not paint like that," he wrote to his brother Theo, "but I see instead how I should be painting. For the article is perfectly right inasmuch as it points out a gap that needs to be filled."[8]

A mystic by temperament who, steeped in the Bible, had dreamed of becoming a minister and delivering a spiritual message, Van Gogh nevertheless refused the logic of Gauguin and Bernard's arguments in favor of drawing inspiration from outside of nature. He even had harsh words to say about Bernard's *Christ on the Mount of Olives* and cited one of his own canvases, *The Park of the Hospital at Saint-Rémy* (1889, Folkwang Museum, Essen), as a counterexample: "You will understand that this combination of a red ochre, of a sad

green, of gray, of black lines defining contours, creates some of the anguish that afflicts a few of my companions in misfortune—they call it the "red blues" [literally *le noir rouge*]—and besides, the motif of the large tree struck by lightning, the sickly greenish-pink smile of the last-blooming flowers of autumn, help to confirm this idea. Another canvas depicts a sunrise behind a yellow wheat field, lines receding into the distance, furrows that climb high in the picture, rising toward a wall. Here, in contrast to the other canvas, I have endeavored to express tranquility, a great peacefulness."[9] Thus, Van Gogh offers a masterly lesson in the Symbolist conception of art, written with splendid clarity, in which he attempts to show his reader that the intrinsic meaning of an art work does not lie in the choice of the subject, but in its colors, lines, composition.

There is then in Van Gogh's work, particularly in the paintings of the last period, a sort of instinctive, unstudied Symbolism, a *symbolisme brut* in the sense of Dubuffet's *art brut*, a painting that is spontaneous, powerfully inventive, owes nothing to academic or literary criteria. To an even greater extent than his "pals" Gauguin and Bernard, Van Gogh has outlined in his wonderful letters a thoroughly personal Symbolist theory of color as the expression of innermost feelings, even in pictures that, given their subject, seem far removed from any spiritual concern as, for example, *The Café at Night* (1888, Yale University Gallery, New Haven), in which the artist claims

Vincent Van Gogh
The Park of the Hospital at Saint-Rémy
1889, oil on canvas, 73 × 92
Folkwang Museum, Essen

Van Gogh seeks to show here that woeful and anguished feelings can be expressed as clearly in a garden view as in a scene from the Gospels, for example the *Christ in the Garden of Olives* which his "pal" Emile Bernard had just painted.

that he "tried to express the terrible human passions with red and green." In *The Wheat Field With Reaper* (1889, Rijksmuseum Vincent Van Gogh, Amsterdam), he goes beyond the simple Millet-style scene that offered itself to his eyes and perceives in the small peasant figure toiling in the vast yellow field an "image of death in the sense that mankind is like the wheat being reaped [...], an image of death such as we are told of in the great book of nature, but what I looked for was the nearly smiling." *The Starry Night* (1889, The Museum of Modern Art, New York) is a veritable transfiguration of the landscape. The Provençal village of Saint-Rémy has been turned into a Dutch village; the cypress trees are tormented arabesques against a sky lit by eleven enormous stars and a crescent moon, which have

inspired a lot of scholarly exegesis, though Van Gogh himself had almost nothing to say about this picture, except to remark that in feeling it seemed to be very close to that expressed by Bernard's and Gauguin's pictures.

Under the "very substantial substance" of Van Gogh's paintings, Georges-Albert Aurier discerned thought, ideas, symbols. Too powerful a genius to be limited to any single trend, Van Gogh was indeed an "isolated figure," as the critic wrote, but one whose unstudied Symbolism, unrelated to the ideas of his artist and writer friends, was clearly understood by the most perspicacious among the latter. It was Emile Bernard who initiated the first Van Gogh exhibit in Paris, at the Le Barc de Boutteville Gallery, whose doors were always open to the Nabis.

Vincent Van Gogh
Wheat Field with Reaper
1889, oil on canvas, 74×92
Rijksmuseum Vincent Van Gogh, Amsterdam

Referring to this painting, Van Gogh wrote to his brother Theo: "I live then in that reaper—a vague figure toiling like a devil in the heat to finish his task—I live then the image of death in the sense that mankind is like the wheat being reaped [...]. But there is no sadness in that death, it takes place out in the open with the sun flooding everything with fine gold light [...], it is an image of death such as we are told of in the great book of nature, but what I sought was the almost smiling."

Gauguin's mystical disciple, Charles Filiger

Charles Filiger
Christ Entombed
c. 1895, gouache with silver highlights, 19×35
Musée du Prieuré, Saint-Germain-en-Laye

Drawing inspiration from Holbein's famous *Dead Christ*, Filiger sought to create an impression of naïveté synonymous with purity. His technique here is a blend of folk art and the Pont-Aven artistic approach (flat colored forms delimited by black contours, a window in the rear wall of the tomb opening on to a typical Breton coast landscape).

Some of Gauguin's followers in Brittany ended up becoming militant Catholics. Gauguin himself, as we have said, was inclined to meditate over scriptural matters, a trait that did not prevent him from swearing like a navvy; in moments of stress he even tended to identify with Christ, lending Him his own features in several pictures representing the Mount of Olives. A number of artists in his circle were converts. Jan Verkade, a Dutchman who was an important influence on Sérusier, became a monk. The Danish artist, Mogens Ballin, abjured his Jewish faith and joined the lay order of St. Francis. Charles Filiger (1863-1928), an Alsatian, was a Christian mystic. A regular visitor at Pont-Aven and Le Pouldu, he spent most of his unhappy life roaming around Brittany, his health undermined by

alcohol and nervous ailments. From 1890 to 1900 he lived on the munificence of the Count de La Rochefoucauld, one of the key figures in the Rose+Croix movement, who payed him an annuity in exchange for his paintings. Totally forgotten after the turn of the century, Filiger was only rediscovered long after his death by the Surrealist André Breton.

Filiger summed up his own creative approach as follows: "My hands are almost afraid of touching Dreams, yet one cannot refuse to reach down, out of charity toward one's fellow-creatures, and do one's utmost to attain the reality of Dreams." He was torn between deep religious feelings and a latent homosexuality that led him to include emaciated adolescents and young Breton sailors in many of his pictures. His quest for purity

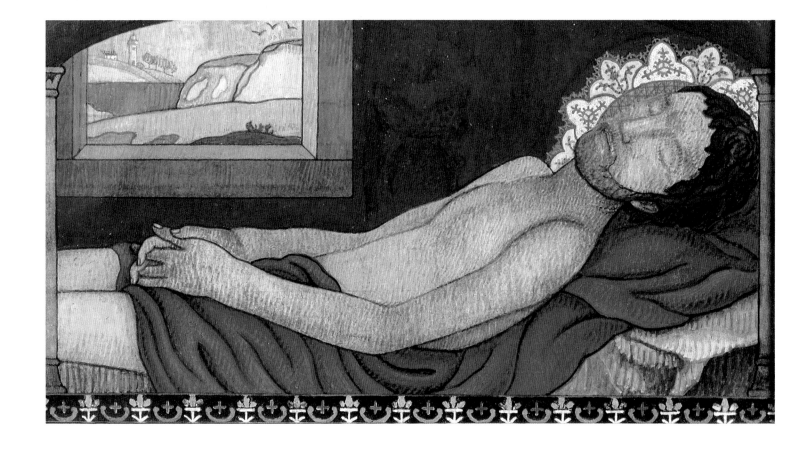

inspired him to paint in a very simple manner that draws at once upon popular prints and the Italian primitives using the golds and silvers of early masters like Cimabue and Duccio. His patient illuminator's technique, plainly marked by the desire to return to medieval artistic practices, made him prefer small pictures, often watercolors, many of them virtual miniatures illustrating scenes from the Gospels. His art also bears the stamp of Gauguin's and Bernard's pictorial theories, the stylized forms defined by means of black contours, the almost perfectly oval and impassive faces rendered without modeling, the few simple colors, the entire artistic process viewed as a kind of spiritual discipline. Even in his various Pietà, the background is nearly always a deserted Breton landscape.

Filiger believed that art, like metaphysics and theology, is able to communicate an eschatology. On a humbler level, that of the "chromatic notations" which he usually built around a saint's face by means of scales of colors kaleidoscopically juxtaposed by the artist, Filiger created beautiful harmonic effects that would delight André Breton with the variety and refinement of their tones. His experiments reveal a predilection for the kind of aesthetic theorizing that many of the Symbolist artists went in for; it crops up in Sérusier's pictures and, again, in the early twentieth century, in the work of some of the leading Bauhaus artists, Feininger and Itten for example, who both wanted to create a spiritual conception of art based on the relationships between colors and geometric shapes.

Charles Filiger
Landscape of Le Pouldu
c. 1890, gouache on paper, 26 × 38.5
Musée des Beaux-Arts, Quimper
In addition to his religious scenes, Filiger has left us a few views of Breton landscapes, principally at Le Pouldu, in which, skillfully using the principles of Synthetism set down by Bernard and Gauguin, he sought to render the essence of the desolate, wind-swept solitude of the Breton coast.

Charles Filiger
The Last Judgement
**c. 1889, gouache with silver
and gold highlights, 41 × 24
Josefowitz Collection**

Immersing himself in a mystical
past, like many other Symbolists, the artist employed both
the Synthetist technique and
decorative elements drawn from
medieval art, such as gold backgrounds, embroidery designs,
and triptych compositions. The
central panel of this work was to
be devoted to Christ, but was
never completed. The panel on
the left, which depicts the Elect,
is airy and open to the sky, in
contrast to the right panel, representing the Damned.

Notes

1 For more about Wagner's statement, see H. Dorra, "'Le texte Wagner' de Gauguin," in *Bulletin de la Société de l'Art Français (1984)*, Paris, 1986, pp. 281-288.

2 M. Denis, *Du symbolisme au classicisme. Théories*, edited by O. Revault d'Allonnes, Paris, 1964, p. 51.

3 *Notes inédites d'Emile Bernard sur le Symbolisme*. Undated notes quoted in *Emile Bernard* (catalog), Musée des Beaux-Arts, Lille, 1967, p. 10.

4 *Correspondance de Paul Gauguin. 1873-1888, op. cit.*, letter dated 14 August 1888, p. 210.

5 See E. Walter, "Madeleine au Bois d'Amour par Emile Bernard," in *La Revue du Louvre*, 4-1978, pp. 286-291.

The author compares the composition of Bernard's paint-ing to yet another visual source, Max Klinger's engraving, *Début de printemps*, 1879.

6 *Lettres d'Odilon Redon (1878-1916)*, Paris and Brussels, 1923, letter dated 5 February 1904, p. 55.

7 G.-A. Aurier, "Les isolés: Vincent Van Gogh," in *Le Mercure de France*, January, 1890.

8 *Correspondance complète de Vincent Van Gogh*, Paris, 1960, 3 vols., letter dated 1 February 1890, vol. 3, p. 434.

9 *Lettres de Van Gogh à Emile Bernard*, Paris, 1911, p. 143.

10 See M.-A. Anquetil, *Filiger. Dessins. Gouaches. Aquarelles* (catalog), Musée du Prieuré, Saint-Germain-en-Laye, 1981.

3

The Nabis

The birth of the Nabi group

Paul Sérusier was the *massier* (treasurer and student-representative) of one of the ateliers at the Académie Julian in Paris. A *bachelier*, in other words, he had passed the state baccalaureate examinations, he was fascinated by philosophy, especially Plato and Plotinus, which he interested Maurice Denis in as well. Both were exceptionally well-educated young artists. Sérusier, like several other members of the future Nabi group, had attended the Lycée Condorcet in what was then Paris's art gallery district. A persuasive advocate of Gauguin's artistic theories, always ready to show *The Talisman* to anyone who would listen to him, he converted many of his fellow students at the Académie Julian to the new painting.

Late in 1888 or early 1889, these budding artists began to meet regularly to question the teachings of their instructors at the Académie, several of whom were members of the prestigious Institut de France and pillars of official art.[1] Thus, between 1889 and 1891, there formed around Sérusier a group including Denis, Edouard Vuillard, Pierre Bonnard, Paul Ranson, Ker Xavier Roussel, Henri Gabriel Ibels, Jan Verkade and George Lacombe. All were around twenty years old and eager to renew painting; most had had a classical schooling, were fond of debating philosophical and religious issues and

had acquired a taste for drama and music—especially Wagner's. Most of them had well-off bourgeois parents and were not under pressure, at least in the beginning, to produce marketable pictures.

They founded a sort of brotherhood, calling themselves *les Nabis*. A *nabi* (*nabis* or *nebiim* in the plural) is a prophet in Hebrew; in the Old Testament it is the term for the inspired ones, the messengers who proclaim the Word of God. Sérusier and his friends probably picked it up from Edouard Schuré's *Les grands initiés*, published in 1889. The chapter on Jesus begins with a few lines about "the Nebiim, those schools of prophets in the face of the emerging monarchy and the already decayed priesthood. He (the prophet Samuel, the founder of the kingship in Israel) appointed them the stern guardians of the esoteric tradition and the universal teachings of Moses, as opposed to the kings, in whom the political ideal and the goal of nationhood predominated. These fraternities indeed preserved what remained of Moses's teachings, the sacred music with its modes and powers, the occult art of healing and, lastly, the art of divination that the great prophets unfolded with a truly magisterial authority, elevation, and abnegation."

The young men in Sérusier's circle had no program; they did not even proclaim the founding of their group. Indeed, the name Nabi was unknown to their contemporaries, who called them "Symbolists," "*Idéalistes*," or "neo-traditionalists" (Maurice Denis preferred the latter, because of the parallel with neo-Impressionism). With the fervor of proselytes, they addressed each other as "Brother," baptized the apartment they held their meetings in "the Temple," and organized ceremonies which were, incidentally, far from being humorless. They adopted a sort of esoteric code based on words borrowed from the ancient religions of the Orient that a friend and Hebrew scholar, Auguste Cazalis, furnished them: a studio was an *ergastère*, a painting an "icon," a priest a *cohène*; philistines and bourgeois were *pelitchim*, Friday was "the day of Venus," and so forth. When signing their letters they appended the initials ETPMVEMP, for *En Ta Paume Mon Verbe et Ma Pensée* (In Thy Palm My Word and Thought), a ritual salutation of the Neoplatonists.

Sérusier has left us a portrait of his friend Ranson in Nabi attire (Private Collection, Paris). Ranson is wearing a chasuble, holding a crosier adorned with cabalistic signs, and his finger is on a sort of missel lying open before him. There is no saying whether these ritual attributes actually existed, but the fact that Ranson is depicted with them shows us the atmosphere of the group, which was permeated with the spirit of Schuré's history of mankind elucidated by theosophical doctrines derived from the real or apocryphal teachings of Krishna, Buddha, Zoroaster, Hermes Trismegistus, Orpheus, Moses, Pythagorus, and Jesus.

Each of the Nabis had a nickname that alluded to either his physical appearance or a particular propensity. Bonnard, who was especially interested in Japanese prints, was the "arch Jap Nabi" and Paul Ranson the "arch-arch Jap Nabi." Maurice Denis, a fervent Catholic and lover of religious art, was the "Nabi of the beautiful icons," and Paul Lacombe, who was drawn to sculpture, was the "sculptor Nabi." The bearded, red-haired Paul Sérusier was the "Nabi with the dazzling beard"; Vuillard was nicknamed the "Zouave" because he had considered making a career in the army; Félix Vallotton, a native of Switzerland who joined the group later on, was the "foreign Nabi"; and the tall, slender Dutchman, Jan Verkade, was the "obeliscal Nabi." There was a spirit of student horseplay in the

group and no doubt its members behaved less solemnly than the German Nazarenes or the Pre-Raphaelites whose example they followed. Sérusier and Denis were more sedate and theory-minded than Bonnard and Vallotton.

Their weekly gatherings, extending into lively dinners, were occasions for exchanging ideas as well as pictorial experiences. Mindful of the fact that they had been brought together by their mutual fervor for Gauguin, who had by then removed himself to distant shores, and always eager to view the daring paintings of Cézanne and Van Gogh, they exhibited together fairly often at the Le Barc de Boutteville gallery, which advertised "Impressionist and Symbolist Paintings." All told, ten exhibitions were organized under this slogan between 1891 and 1896. The renowned Ambroise Vollard opened his premises on the Rue Lafitte to the Nabis from 1897 on. But by then the movement was losing its momentum and was beginning to disintegrate; its members were each about to strike out on his own, albeit without rejecting the group's initial experiments or breaking off the friendships that had united them.

Although a number of them—Denis, Sérusier, Verkade (who eventually became a monk)—were absorbed by religious questions and others, like Ranson and Lacombe, were drawn toward esoteric doctrines, still others, such as Bonnard and Vuillard, gave priority to pictorial research and their works soon took a radically different turn. In fact, one would be hard put to find even a trace of Symbolism in the paintings of the latter pair; and for this reason, though both kept in touch with their former comrades, we must regretfully part company with them. Notwithstanding their diverging inclinations, all of the erstwhile Nabis remained interested in the decorative arts (book illustrations, posters, stage designs) and enjoyed close ties with poets and dramatists, who generally bore the Symbolist stamp. The early plays of Alfred Jarry, Oscar Wilde, and Maurice Maeterlinck were thus performed in decors conceived by Bonnard or Sérusier. Then too, the ex-Nabis were all familiar with the theory of correspondences so dear to Baudelaire and all of them dreamed, like Wagner, of creating *Gesamtkunstwerke*, total art works encompassing every sphere of artistic creation.

It is appropriate that this survey of the Nabis painters should begin with Sérusier. Not only had

Paul Sérusier
***Portrait of Paul Ranson
in Nabi Attire***
1890, oil on canvas, 60 × 45
Private Collection

This costume was doubtless never worn by any of the Nabis, but was probably imagined by Paul Sérusier who liked to design theater costumes and decors. The portrait itself, however, is quite real: the sitter is Paul Ranson who usually hosted the Nabis meetings and was the high priest of their ceremonies. Ranson and Sérusier were the two members of the group most deeply versed in matters occult.

he received the teachings embodied in *The Talisman* directly from Gauguin himself, but he was filled with a desire to communicate a message. He was a kind of Moses for the other Nabis, a gifted teacher imbued with a quasi religious certainty.

Sérusier the theorist

Paul Sérusier (1864-1927) was drawn by temperament to experimenting and teaching. His encounter with Gauguin cured him of the diligent naturalism of his first period, and thereafter he devoted his existence to both developing the revelation he had received at Pont-Aven and searching for the fundamental principles that underlie a painting's composition and determine its relationship to the viewer.[2] He felt that art must speak to the soul and suggest an essentially spiritual message, not only through its subject matter but also through its rhythms, lines, colors. Without ever foregoing a figurative underpinning—he continued to depict the landscape and people of Brittany, while gradually purging his work of anecdotal elements—Sérusier elaborated a theory of color and, after 1896, began to be influenced by the ideas of Father Desiderius Lenz, whom he became acquainted with through his former Nabi comrade Jan Verkade, by now a Benedictine monk. At the Benedictine monastery of Beuron in Upper Swabia, Father Desiderius, building on certain ideas of the early nineteenth century Nazarene artists, had framed a new code for Christian art based on simple geometric proportions which he dubbed the "Sacred Measurements" and, he believed, had already inspired ancient Egyptian art. Sérusier translated Father Desiderius writings into French and drew on them in his own treatise, *ABC de la peinture* (1921). His doctrines are exemplified in a series of extremely hieratic, Egyptian-inspired frescos decorating his house and private chapel at Châteauneuf-du-Faou, near Quimper in Brittany.

After the turn of the century Sérusier's technique evolved toward increasingly simplified forms and attained such a degree of austerity that his later paintings create an effect of coldness and stiffness that is surely unintended. It is his Nabi works, painted prior to 1900, that attract the most attention, with their aura of Symbolism and their barely discernible debt to Gauguin and Puvis de Chavannes. They are severe and melancholic, these pictures of Sérusier's best years, filled with a pervasive feeling of weariness, even discouragement, further heightened by the mysterious, expressionless faces of the figures depicted in them, as if the men and women in the artist's world were all locked in their own thoughts with no hope of release.

tals—a choice subject for an esoteric painter like Sérusier. The artist transposes this eminently classical scene to a forest in Brittany: through a colonnade of trees we glimpse three women engaging in a secret ritual at the foot of a dolmen shaped like a bear's head. This painting may have been inspired by a Breton legend, or perhaps, as George L. Mauner has suggested, by one of Baudelaire's poems. It is deeply mysterious, even though what our eye tends to linger on most is the plastic and decorative qualities of the composition.

The Pont-Aven Triptych (1892-1893, Private Collection, Paris) seems at first glance to be a depiction of Breton women picking apples—it is sometimes called *The Apple-Pickers*—by the edge of a cliff overhanging the sea. Gauguin's influence, particularly in the colors and the way they are applied in flat areas, is unmistakable; the placing of the figures and the overall organization of the planes, on the other hand, owe a great deal to Puvis de Chavannes's *Inter Artes et Naturam* (1890, Musée des Beaux-Arts, Rouen), completed two years earlier. But beyond the picture's apparent subject, the artist has chosen to represent the three ages of man *and*, through the Biblical allegory of the original sin, the loss of innocence. One of the side panels shows the innocence and candor of childhood (the figures are wearing white coifs); the other depicts old age and sin (the women have black bonnets). And the apples in the middle scene are of course the forbidden fruit. The Symbolism of *The Water Bearers* (around 1896, Musée des Beaux-Arts, Brest) is equally elaborate and it too requires a reading on two levels. The younger of the two Breton peasant women is life—her water jug is full; the other, an old crone stretched out at the foot of a tree, her upturned jug beside her, represents death.

Admittedly, the strictly plastic means in the above examples are not sufficient in themselves to carry a work of art's meaning, which requires a more philosophical reading. Sérusier's weakness is that he subordinates the pictorial to the theoretical; and thoughout his life he pursued the chimerical goal of expressing abstract ideas with brushes and paint. His best period remains the years immediately following his encounter with Gauguin, doubtless because the latter gave him not only a new vision of pictorial art, but also the technical means to express that vision.

Paul Sérusier
Solitude
c. 1892, oil on canvas, 75 × 60
Musée des Beaux-Arts, Rennes
The impression of isolation and sadness emanating from this simplified tableau painted on the spot in Brittany is accentuated by the painting's asymmetrical composition, the absence of a sky, the cold tones, and (for Sérusier) the unusual lack of any literary or esoteric allusion.

A canvas like *Solitude* (around 1892, Musée des Beaux-Arts, Rennes) expresses, by means of a technique closely related to Gauguin's, the unfathomable sadness of a Breton peasant girl sitting amid a rocky landscape, her moral and social isolation made more poignant still by her natural pose and the somewhat threatening granite boulders beside her. *The Incantation in the Sacred Wood* (1891, Musée des Beaux-Arts, Quimper) elaborates on the favorite Symbolist theme of the sacred grove, where the gods appear before mor-

Paul Sérusier
The Incantation
(The Sacred Wood)
1891, oil on canvas, 93×72
Musée des Beaux-Arts,
Quimper

The art historian George Mauner has suggested that this scene—a magic rite of some sort in the heart of a Breton forest —is a pictorial equivalent of Baudelaire's famous *Correspondances* sonnet:

La nature est un temple où de
[vivants piliers
Laissent parfois sortir de confuses
[paroles.
L'homme y passe à travers des forêts
[de symboles
Qui l'observent avec des regards
[familiers.

89

Maurice Denis's beautiful icons

On the eve of the year 1889, an eighteen year old student who had just passed his *baccalauréat* examinations and, knowing that he would become a painter, had begun to frequent the studios at the Académie Julian, wrote as follows in his diary: "Lord, we're just a few Young artists, devotees of the Symbol, misjudged by the world, which jeeringly calls us Mystics! Lord, I cry unto Thee, let our reign begin! And recall to Thy memory the glory of Paul Sérusier, who has guided me toward superior art."[3] Maurice Denis (1870-1943), the author of these lines, had just met Sérusier and the latter had showed him *The Talisman*. And he had pored over the works of Joséphin Péladan and, through him, had discovered the greatness of Fra Angelico; and so, he too wanted to become a Christian artist.

Sérusier was the founder of the Nabi movement; Denis, a remarkably gifted writer, was its theorist and historian. He had only just turned twenty when he wrote a manifesto which begins with these words: "Remember that a painting —before being a charger, a nude woman, or one anecdote or another—is essentially a flat surface covered with colors assembled in a certain order."[4] With this often quoted and variously interpreted statement, the young artist was simply asserting the supremacy of the art work over the subject it represents and boldly declaring that a picture must stand on its pictorial merits. He proposed to call this new painting "neo-traditionalism" (in contrast to Seurat's "neo-Impressionism") to show that, far from breaking with the past, this movement on the contrary had to build upon examples drawn from the history of art. He did not reject Impressionism out of hand, but thought one should go beyond it. He felt that, notwithstanding their gifts, the artists of that school had merely sought to reproduce the landscape or model before their eyes. But now, he decreed, nature must be represented by means of colored or plastic correlatives. Invoking Gauguin's authority he pointed out that, "Our superior impression, which is of a moral order when we behold the *Calvary* or the *Be Amorous* bas-relief, derives in no way from the motif or natural motifs that are represented there, but from the representation itself, from its form and coloring. From the canvas itself, that flat surface coated with colors, springs the bitter or comfort-ing "literary" emotion (as artists call it) without requiring the mediation of some remembered sensation (like that of the natural motif being employed)."[5] Denis fairly soon dropped the word neo-traditionalism and instead began using Symbolism. In 1912, he published a collection of his writings on art under the title *Théories (1890-1910): du symbolisme et de Gauguin vers un nouvel ordre classique*. Though used by musicians and writers, who moreover adhered to the same values as their counterparts in the plastic arts, the term Symbolism adequately expresses the search for equivalences which defines an art work in Denis's view. "The expressive synthesis, the symbol of a physical perception was to be an eloquent transcription and at the same time an object composed to give pleasure to the eye."[6]

Like his Nabi friends, Denis investigated the broad field of pictorial experiences that offered itself to him in past as well as contemporary art. By turns he pondered Egyptian art and Japanese art, the art of the Italian primitives (which held his interest longest) and great masters such as Poussin and Ingres, as well as the contemporary art of Gauguin, Redon, Cézanne, Puvis de Chavannes. It is probably with this last artist that he can best be compared, for like Puvis de Chavannes he was given opportunities—opportunites all the other Nabis envied—to decorate both secular buildings (the Théâtre des Champs-Elysées in Paris, the Assembly Hall in the Palace of the League of Nations in Geneva) and—this was his greatest wish—religious architecture, a genre he had always dreamed of undertaking. Perhaps the finest of his many church decorations are his frescoes in the chapel of his home at Saint-Germain-en-Laye near Paris, which was recently turned into a museum, le Musée du Prieuré, where a significant portion of his oeuvre is on permanent display along with works by his Nabi comrades.

Intensely fond of the curves and arabesques so dear to the Art Nouveau artists, Denis worked with a light-toned palette where pinks, mauves, oranges, soft greens, and pale blues predominated. It seemed as if, in his search for harmony, he felt obliged to avoid overly bright tones. A devout Christian, he used his brush to praise God. In 1919, he founded, with the artist Georges Desvallières, the Ateliers d'Art Sacré, hoping

Maurice Denis
The Muses
1893, oil on canvas, 168 × 135
Musée d'Orsay, Paris
Denis has modernized the theme of the sacred wood by setting this classically inspired
scene in the Luxembourg Gardens in Paris. The modern muses are young women preparing for exams.

thereby to rescue Catholic art from the sentimental stereotypes of pious imagery. He endeavored to find plastic equivalents for the deep faith that sustained him in his daily life. His wife, his numerous children, his ordinary experience as a Christian, were his favorite sources of inspiration, and he translated them into key scenes from the Gospels. A prolific illustrator, always in tune with the literature of his time, he drew on the works of the leading Symbolist authors: Rossetti (*The Blessed Damosel*, which Debussy set to music), Verlaine (*Sagesse*), Gide (*Le Voyage d'Urien*), Francis Jammes (*Ma fille Bernadette*), Claudel (*L'annonce faite à Marie*), and so forth.

Maurice Denis
Procession Under
the Trees
1892, oil on canvas, 56×81
Mr and Mrs Arthur
G. Altschul Collection,
New York

Maurice Denis
Jacob Wrestling with the Angel
1893, oil on canvas, 48×36
Josefowitz Collection
Painted at Perros-Guirec, the small Breton fishing port one glimpses in the background,
this canvas is a faithful expression of Gauguin's technique of setting down flat color areas
delimited by dark outlines. It subject is of course the same as that of Gauguin's first
Symbolist canvas.

93

Georges Lacombe, the Nabi sculptor

Georges Lacombe
Yellow Sea at Camaret
**c. 1892, egg-based paint
on canvas, 60.7 × 81.3
Musée de Brest**
Lacombe liked to use nature's
"accidents"—such as these weird
rocks with human silhouettes
—to create a strange, somewhat
uncanny atmosphere. His
strong, often unnatural colors
reflect Gauguin's technical influence on the Nabis.

Like Maurice Denis, Georges Lacombe (1868-
1916) was brought into the Nabi fraternity by
Sérusier. The son of well-off parents who were
amateur artists (his mother was a painter, his
father a cabinetmaker), Lacombe was known as
the *Nabi sculpteur*, however he also produced a
pictorial oeuvre that is still by and large ignored.
Most of his works remained in the hands of his
family and have only recently found their way
into museums.[7] Drawn to esoteric speculation
—like Sérusier—Lacombe was an avid reader of
Péladan and Schuré. His pictures and sculptures
are hermetic, but are clearly the works of a gifted
and singularly original artist.

Stylistically Lacombe's paintings remind us of
Sérusier's work and, from 1892, on, Lacombe was
in fact the latter's disciple. The same Breton land-

scapes, the same underlying Symbolism in scenes
apparently drawn from daily life, appear in both
artists' production. There is even a similarity in
the way both apply the technique handed down
by Gauguin, though Lacombe's taste for the eerie
and strange warpings of natural forms gives his
style a look of its own.

Gauguin, by this time in Oceania, learned of
the existence of this student of Sérusier's "who,
like me, carves wood." Indeed, Lacombe too
sculpted wood straight from the tree, a primitive
medium he was careful to avoid refining, leaving
his chisel marks clearly visible. The most striking
examples of his sculpture are the four bas-reliefs
for *Bed* (Musée d'Orsay, Paris). These panels for
a bed which was surely never slept in are meant
to symbolize the true mysteries of human exis-

tence—after all, it is in bed that life's fundamental events, conception, birth, death, ordinarily take place. Lacombe gravitated more to the creeds and religions of the Orient than to Christianity. Hence the wood-carving *Isis* (Musée d'Orsay, Paris) which depicts the Egyptian goddess of fertility lying on a bed of flowers, a work that impresses us through both its plastic force and its aura of strangeness.

Deciphering works like these sometimes requires an encyclopedia of religions, yet Gauguin hardly proceeded differently when drawing on ancient Maori religious beliefs for the paintings and sculptures he was executing during this same period in the distant South Seas. The curators of the Musée d'Orsay in Paris have hung the latter's "wild" works and those of his Nabi disciple in the same space, and this is no arbitrary choice. Lacombe does not suffer from the comparison.

Georges Lacombe
The Ages of Man
**c. 1894, egg-based paint
on canvas, 151 × 240
Petit Palais, Geneva**
On a lane beneath powerful trees whose boughs intertwine overhead, a group of figures in Breton peasant costumes evoke the cycle of man's life, which is linked here to the springtime rebirth in nature's cycle. The style reflects the influence of Lacombe's master, Sérusier.

Georges Lacombe

Isis
**c. 1894-1895, polychrome wood
carving, 111 × 60
Musée d'Orsay, Paris**

Isis, the supreme goddess in ancient Egyptian religion, was
viewed in theosophical circles as
the incarnation of the feminine
principle, the source of all fertility. Hence the two streams of
red—the blood of life—spurting
from her breasts and the five-
petalled flowers which recall the
pentagram symbolizing the
unity of male and female.

Bed
**c. 1894-1896, wood bas-reliefs
consisting of four panels:
Existence, 41 × 69,
Conception, 49 × 194,
Birth, 41 × 69,
Death, 49 × 194.**

Three of these panels represent
life's principal phases. The
treatment is at once primitive,
reminiscent of folk decorations
of rural furniture, and realist (in
Birth a woman is actually in the
throes of giving birth). The
fourth panel is more abstract; it
combines the serpent Ourobo-
ros biting its own tail—a double
symbol of the eternal return and
of self-fecundation—with a huge
mouth (the female sexual or-
gans) surrounded by filaments
representing sperm cells.

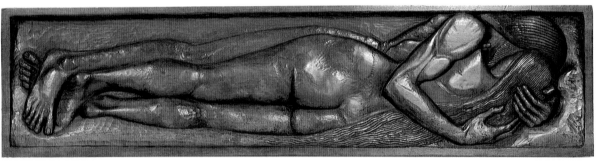

Paul Ranson, the Occulist Nabi

To an even greater extent than Lacombe, Paul Elie Ranson (1861-1909) turned to syncretism as a source of inspiration. Sérusier painted a portrait of Ranson in what may be imaginary Nabi garb, but the model's pince-nez, pointed goatee, and crew cut give away the eminently Third Republic bourgeois lying beneath the disguise of this son of a well-known anti-clerical politician. One of the early Nabis, he let the small group use his large family home on the Boulevard Montparnasse in Paris for their meetings; his studio was their "Temple" and his wife, a warm and generous hostess, was the "Light of the Temple." It was undoubtedly Ranson who gave the members of the circle their nicknames; he himself shared with Bonnard the sobriquet "arch-arch Jap Nabi," though he might well have been called the "Occultist Nabi," for he was as partial to esoteric studies as his friend Lacombe. His correspondence with the other Nabis, in particular Verkade, is studded with the group's arcane ex-

Paul Ranson
Princesses on a Terrace
1894, oil on canvas, 73 × 92
Josefowitz Collection
The enigmatic message of this curious dialogue on a magic terrace pales beside the composition's decorative elegance. The painter's very Art Nouveau style harmonizes the sinuous arabesques of the dogs, the flowers, the trees, and the gowns.

Paul Ranson
Nabi Landscape
1890, oil on canvas, 91 × 118
Josefowitz Collection
Against a very Japanese horizon, the artist has imagined the dream of a prophet dozing in a bizarre desert filled with stylized shrubs and birdlike apparitions. G.-A. Aurier once observed that Ranson's brain teems with "teratological inventions, like that of a Chinaman."

pressions[8], and his personal library, one of the few Nabi book collections known to us, contained numerous esoteric works by Eliphas Lévi, Papus, Jules Bois, Edouard Schuré, and others of that ilk.

Ranson's colorful background gave rise to a strange artistic production, whose essentially syncretic meaning is far from obvious. His *Christ and Buddha* (around 1890, Altschul Collection, New York), for example, combines a crucifixion inspired by Gauguin's *Yellow Christ* with silhouetted buddhas interspersed with wavy lotus flowers. In other, even more hermetic paintings, he depicts conversing figures attired in long oriental-looking robes covered with cabalistic signs and heraldic beasts, or stages Nabi dreams in deserts inhabited by imaginary creatures. Maurice Denis remarked that Ranson touches on the domain of the fantastic, the satanic, the enchanted; he slips witches with black cats into his pictures, ox heads, trees whose forked branches are writhing monsters. They may have shocked the pious Denis, these motifs which Ranson (who was fond of writing mordant and, as often as not, savagely anti-clerical little plays for a puppet theater) elaborated according to his fancy, making it extremely difficult to decipher some of his pictures.

His imagery might have served to illustrate works of esoteric literature had it not been for his manifest decorative talent, his ability to construct personal arrangements of form and color, notably with ornamental arabesques and flat areas of color combined with chiaroscuro lighting effects in which his often nocturnal scenes are bathed, a fitting technique for an adept of the occult sciences. Like the other Nabis, Ranson was influenced by a number of sources, Gauguin's *synthétisme*, Japanese print making, medieval miniatures, formal experiments based on the direct observation of nature. His penchant for the applied arts (which he shared with many of the Symbolists hostile to the increasing mechanization in industrial society) led him to design stage sets, cartoons for tapestries (which his wife, France Ranson, usually executed) and stained glass windows, as well as bookbindings, for Tiffany and Bing. In 1908, Ranson opened an art academy where his friends Sérusier and Maurice Denis came to teach; and France Ranson continued to run it after his death.

Paul Ranson
Christ and Buddha
c. 1895, oil on canvas, 72.8 × 51.5
**Mr and Mrs Arthur
G. Altschul Collection,
New York**

Combining Christ and the Buddha, Ranson illustrates here the syncretism in vogue at the turn of the century, as set forth notably in Edouard Schuré's *Les grands initiés* (1889). The obscure inscription in arabic writing at the bottom of the painting reads "Seigniory of the Nabis." Gauguin's influence is discernible in the yellow tones of the Crucifixion, but the viewer's eye is mainly caught by the very elegant arabesques of the lotus stems in the foreground. (The lotus is a symbol of spiritual plenitude.)

99

Félix Vallotton
Summer Evening
Bathers
1892, oil on canvas, 97 × 131
Kunsthaus, Zurich

At the time he painted this canvas, Vallotton was heavily influenced by Puvis de Chavannes and Hodler, but his inborn naturalism nevertheless led him to depict these naiads as very real women, some young, some old. One Symbolist critic especially admired "in the transparency and fresh limpidity of the water... [the] young women in pure and swooning poses, twisted in pleasure."

The Nabi Artistic Canon

In his preface to the ninth exhibition of "Impressionist and Symbolist Painters" at the Le Barc de Boutteville gallery in 1895, Maurice Denis reviewed the achievements of the Nabi artists over the previous five to six years. Their average age was now twenty-five, and critics were beginning to take them seriously. "They have popularized the loathing for naturalism," he observed, "It is vastly to their credit that they scorned the witless notion, taught everywhere and so injurious to yesterday's artists, that it is enough for a painter to copy what he sees, the way he sees it; that a painting is a window on nature; and that Art consists of rendering things exactly... In their own works, they chose to create expression with ornamentation, the harmony of forms and colors, and texture, rather than draw it from the subject itself. They felt that every emotion, every human thought, has a plastic decorative equivalent, a reciprocating beauty."[9]

The artists we have just surveyed may not all have been equally skillful in privileging beauty over what they believed or thought. But, whatever their pictorial gifts, they voiced the literary Symbolism and the doctrines that were in fashion when they were twenty, and in this respect they bore witness to the times.

They were not all equally drawn to the unseen and the supernatural. There is not a trace of anything metaphysical in the works of the greatest of the Nabis, Pierre Bonnard. He was more interested in the technical and ornamental experiments of his comrades; and he strove to render the joy of being alive in the midst of light and nature, in contrast to the more metaphysical concerns of the other Nabis. Almost the same could be said about Edouard Vuillard. He delighted in depicting the simple pleasures of family intimacy among the bourgeoisie. His brother-in-law, Ker Xavier Roussel did not burden himself much with spiritual preoccupations either, though his large decorative compositions are modeled on those of Puvis de Chavannes, and like the latter he preferred mythological subjects. His world is a world of springtime landscapes, leaping fauns pursuing willing nymphs through flowering groves. With him, we are far from Böcklin's disquieting scenes under the cruel Mediterranean sun.

The Swiss artist Félix Vallotton (1865-1925), who joined the group toward 1892 and showed several paintings at the first Rose + Croix Salon, was by nature too caught up in ordinary reality to ever become very deeply imbued with the Symbolist spirit. Though he attended Mallarmé's "Tuesdays," and has left us a gallery of splendid wood-cut portraits of Symbolist writers and composers, he was never comfortable with ethereal themes. His *Summer Evening Bath* (1892, Kunsthaus, Zurich), despite its obvious debt to Puvis de Chavannes and Hodler, displays more irony than Symbolism; and it is like nothing else in his oeuvre.

Each Nabi had his own distinct personality and, as we have seen, the members of the group were by no means all inclined toward the mystical and the occult. But all took part in the intellectual trends of the fin de siècle and all were profoundly interested in poetry and the theater. *La Revue blanche*, the foremost organ of the Symbolist movement between 1889 and 1903, carried texts by writers such as Mallarmé, Gide, Proust, as well as contributions by composers like Debussy and engravings by Nabis artists.[10]

Like the Pre-Raphaelites, who were very much in fashion in the 1890s, the Nabis rejected anything that smacked of the mechanical or the industrial, and were drawn instead to the crafts, with a marked preference for primitive techniques such as wood engraving and tapestry-weaving—there was Gauguin's example to follow, after all. In the closing years of the nineteenth century, each of the Nabis began to go his own way, often in a direction very different from the group's initial path, as Sérusier (who at-tempted after 1895 to convert his comrades to the ideas of Father Desiderius) observed with some bitterness. "For years I have been reflecting on those proportions based on simple numbers. A man cannot single-handedly reconstruct all that; it is a job for several men, it calls for a concerted effort. This should have been the task of the Nabis, as I used to call them proudly. But the quest for personality, that invention of journalists, has scattered all that beautiful energy."[11]

The fact remains that, between the end of Impressionism and the beginning of the twentieth century, the Nabis were the foremost school of painting in France (in opposition to neo-Impressionism, which sought to give landscape painting a new lease on life by providing it with a scientific basis). Before long, this school would be dissolved in Art Nouveau and, in 1905, would be succeeded, as a pictorial movement, by Fauvism. There is thus good reason to speak of a Nabi artistic canon, that penchant for arabesques and color synthetism combined with a refusal to break with the data of reality. Indeed, most of the Nabis remained true, after a fashion, to the Breton landscapes and scenes of everyday life that had revealed the new pictorial potential to them —as if, in homage to Gauguin, they wanted to keep in touch with the ultimate reality of the earth. In contrast, the Rose + Croix exhibitions, which were perfectly contemporary with the Nabis and in which some members of the group even took part, reflected only a single source of inspiration and evinced no unity of style. The paintings they showed were characterized by a return to the predominance of subject matter and, in many cases, a rejection of nature.

Notes

[1] The most recent book on this subject is: G.L. Mauner, *The Nabis. Their History and their Art. 1888-1896*, New York and London, 1978.

[2] See M. Guicheteau, *Paul Sérusier*, Paris, 1976; and, mainly, C. Boyle-Turner, *Paul Sérusier*, Ann Arbor, Michigan, 1983.

[3] M. Denis, *Journal*, vol. 1 (1884-1904), Paris, 1957, p. 73.

[4] M. Denis, *Définition du néo-traditionnisme*, 1890, reprinted in M. Denis, *Du symbolisme au classicisme. Théories, op. cit.*, p. 33.

[5] M. Denis, *ibidem*, p. 43.

[6] *Ibidem*, p. 119.

[7] J. Ansieau has excerpted the following articles from his unpublished thesis (for the Ecole du Louvre) on Lacombe's oeuvre: "*Georges Lacombe*," in *Bulletin des Amis du Musée de Rennes*, N° 2, Summer 1978, pp. 81-87; "*Deux sculptures de Georges Lacombe: Isis et le Christ*," in *La Revue du Louvre*, 4-1983, pp. 287-295.

[8] Some of these letters are given in: G.L. Mauner, *op. cit.*.

[9] M. Denis, *Du symbolisme au classicisme. Théories, op. cit.*, pp. 47-48.

[10] See G. Bernier, *La Revue blanche. Paris in the days of Post-Impressionism and Symbolism* (catalog), Wildenstein Gallery, New York, Nov.-Dec., 1983.

[11] Letter from Sérusier to Verkade, Spring 1986, quoted in G.L. Mauner, *op. cit.*, p. 187.

Alexandre Séon
Portrait of
Joséphin Péladan
1891, oil on canvas, 132.5 × 80
Musée des Beaux-Arts, Lyons
Péladan thought very highly of
this portrait: "You have conceived the Nabi of fearless ideal-
ity in his purple robe confronting his riotous and insulting
epoch," he wrote to the artist;
"calm and fearless, for his word
is the word of faith... You have
not only painted him through
your grasp of the Chaldean features that characterize me. You
have painted the soul of the
Sâr."

4

The esoteric symbolism of the Rose+Croix Salons

Joséphin Péladan,
the paladin of idealist art

Joséphin Péladan (1858-1918) was a prominent figure in the art world during the last two
decades of the nineteenth century, not only in
France, where he organized six Rose+Croix
exhibits between 1892 and 1897, but also in
Belgium, the Netherlands, Switzerland, even
Scandinavia. In all of these countries, he had a
large following among artists.

A man of immense though rather muddled
erudition, he had taught himself art history, aesthetics (he considered himself an opponent of
Taine's determinism), and the occult sciences. In
1889, he helped to launch the Ordre Kabba-
listique de la Rose+Croix, founded by Stanislas
de Guaïta as a revival of the secret societies of the
Rosicrucians in seventeenth century Germany. A
novelist and dramatist, Péladan produced a vast
body of work which now seems unreadable,
though it was popular in the years 1880 to 1890.
He posed as a kind of anti-Zola, Péladan's *bête
noire*. As an art critic, he published, beginning in
1882, reviews of the annual Paris art salons in
which he vigorously attacked Naturalism. In
1890, following a schism within Guaïta's own
group, he founded the Ordre de la Rose+Croix
du Temple et du Graal and proclaimed himself
its Grand Master, adopting the title of Sâr
Péladan.

The aspirations of this new society were aesthetic rather than occult. "Artist, you are a
priest," Péladan declared. "Art is the supreme
mystery. When your efforts result in a masterpiece, a divine ray beams down as onto an altar.
O real presence of the divinity shining forth
under these sovereign names: da Vinci, Raphael,
Michelangelo, Beethoven, Wagner." Péladan
wanted to create something broader than a secret
society—he wanted as many followers as possible.
He issued no directives regarding technique
properly speaking, other than to point to the
example of Italian painting from Giotto and Fra
Angelico on. His god was Leonardo da Vinci,
whose *Treatise on Painting* he translated into
French (rather approximately, for his knowledge
of Italian was sketchy). What he admired most
was Leonardo's androgynous bodies and *sfumato*.
His ambition was to be for the artists of the
eighties and nineties what Ruskin had been to the
Pre-Raphaelites. Still more ambitiously, he was
fond of comparing himself to Pico della Miran-
dola and Marsilio Ficino, the two humanists who
had contributed to the flowering of Renaissance
art in Florence by giving it the underpinning of
neo-Platonic theory.

Péladan prescribed painting subjects that
celebrated, even when imperfectly executed,

"dreams instead of reality, the ideal instead of the ugly." He rejected historical and military themes, seascapes and landscapes (except after the manner of Poussin)—which left out the Impressionists—and categorically forbade all representations of contemporary or rural life, still lifes, and so on. He would have liked to have placed his movement under the aegis of one of the late nineteenth century masters of idealist art—Gustave Moreau, Puvis de Chavannes, Burne-Jones, Watts, Böcklin—but all those he approached declined his invitation. It was not Péladan's ideas which put them off, it seems, but his extravagant attire and histrionic manner.

The first Salon de la Rose + Croix, held in March 1892 at the Durand-Ruel gallery in Paris, was an enormous success. 225 paintings by sixty-nine artists were exhibited in an atmospher of ceremoniousness inspired by the Bayreuth Festival, with trumpet flourishes composed by Eric Satie. The participants were in many cases young and little known—though this Salon would reveal many of them to the public. Their ranks included Edmond Aman-Jean, Emile Bernard, the future sculptor Antoine Bourdelle, Rupert Carabin (who designed extraordinary anthropomorphic furniture), Maurice Chabas, Charles Filiger, Henri Martin, Charles Maurin, Alphonse Osbert, Armand Point, Alexandre Séon; the Belgian artists Albert Ciamberlani, Jean Delville, George Minne, Fernand Khnopff; the Dutch painter Jan Toorop; the Swiss artists Eugène Grasset, Ferdinand Hodler, Carlos Schwabe, Albert Trachsel, Félix Vallotton; the Italian Gaetano Previati, and others who are now forgotten.

The works exhibited at the Salon tended to be filled with thought and fraught with an intellectual content. This prompted the caustic art critic Félix Fénéon to observe, "a painting must first of all beguile us with its rhythms; a painter shows too much humility when he chooses a subject that is already rich in literary meaning; three pears on a table cloth by Paul Cézanne are moving, sometimes even mystic, and Wagner's Valhalla, when they paint it, is altogether as uninteresting as the Chamber of Deputies when they paint that."[1] Five other Rose + Croix exhibits followed the first. They were all equally successful, even though many critics remained unconvinced by Péladan's extravagance and enthusiasm prompted by the subjects of the art works he showed rather than by any real pictorial qualities. It was Péladan himself who decided suddenly after the 1897 Salon to discontinue these exhibitions, for reasons that have never been clear. It may be that he had simply realized he was becoming a mere organizer of art shows, he who had dreamt of founding an aesthetic fraternity that would sweep the world. True, he had gained fresh recruits since the first Salon, artists like Gaston Bussière, Georges de Feure, Emile Fabry, Xavier Mellery, Louis Welden Hawkins, Pinckney Marcius-Simons, and several of Gustave Moreau's students at the Ecole des Beaux-Arts: Antonin Bourbon, Edgar Maxence, Charles Milcendeau, Pierre-Marcel Béronneau, and Georges Rouault. Perhaps the ageing "Assembler of Dreams" had finally discovered a certain number of points in common between his own artistic outlook and Péladan's, and had been persuaded to let some of his favorite students exhibit their works at the latter's Salons. But in a sense Péladan was a victim of his own success. The Symbolist vogue between 1890 and 1900 had spread to the official salons which were held annually in Paris, where works by many of the artists who had exhibited in the Rose + Croix shows could now be seen. Then, too, as we have already seen, the art dealer Le Barc de Boutteville was by this time regularly organizing exhibits of "Impressionist and Symbolist" art, especially Nabi paintings, and other galleries were following suite. In short, the "artists of the soul," as they were sometimes called, had become altogether too ubiquitous. "Lilies, always lilies," complained Octave Mirbeau, deriding Schwabe, Séon, Osbert, Point, Denis, Bernard, and Burne-Jones. In an article dating from 1896, Mirbeau imagines the following little scenario: Walking in a cemetary, he meets a desolate old man who, after being questioned at length, confesses to being Sandro Botticelli, returned from the hereafter to protest about the way the Symbolists have been claiming him as their patron. "Why do they, says the Italian master, all those daubers, those paint-smearers, those weepy Symbolists, why do the cabalists and Pre-Raphaelites and demonists and embryogeneticists, and all those painters of putrid virgins, pining princesses, sexless lovers, why do they all proclaim themselves to be my followers?"[2]

Péladan did not significantly shape the painting of his era nor, despite his claims to the contrary, invent a new school of art. Nevertheless, he brought together, with his exhibitions and writings, some of the trends that arose between 1885 and 1900. With a good deal more talent than he had, critics like Huysmans and Fénéon castigated the mediocrity of the official Salons, while clearly discerning the limits of Impressionism's contribution. The fashion at this time was for the British Pre-Raphaelites, the Italian primitives, the great Renaissance masters like da Vinci. Péladan's followers would go to the Louvre to copy the old masters and would then produce pastiches of them, more or less, in their own paintings. "Go to da Vinci for drawing," Péladan would advise them, "and to Michelangelo for the rhetoric of forms, to Raphael for composition, Rembrandt for chiaroscuro, Velázquez for technical painting, Mantegna for masculine gracefulnes, Botticelli and Melozzo da Forlì for feminine gracefulness, Signorelli for androgynous gracefulness."

The living artists under whose patronage Péladan had hoped to place his "aesthetic gesture" already exercised a kind of ministry over the younger generation of artists. Puvis de Chavannes was president of the Société Nationale des Beaux-Arts. Gustave Moreau's classes at the Ecole des Beaux-Arts were famous for their liberal and uplifting approach. Many of the young painters who flocked to Péladan had already begun to paint in the Symbolist vein. The success they enjoyed at the Rose + Croix Salons probably encouraged them to persevere and, at the same time, helped to turn them away from landscapes and scenes drawn from contemporary life. Péladan's writings gave some of them ideas for subjects, a taste for Wagnerian themes, certain aesthetic stereotypes, for example the androgynous figure (which the neo-Platonist that Péladan wanted to be characterized as the essence of the human shape), or an interest in pictorial languages based on flowers, birds, or objects possessing esoteric meanings incomprehensible to the uninitiated.

Péladan claimed to be a Catholic, an Idealist, and a mystic. But he also gave credence to the Devil, evil, human perversity. He admired artists like Félicien Rops, who engraved a frontispiece for his best-known novel, *Le Vice suprême*. "Between the harmonious Puvis de Chavannes and the subtle Gustave Moreau," Péladan declared, "the intense Félicien Rops closes the cabalistic triangle of great Art." The demands of the arduous uphill struggle to attain chastity and the Ideal, which Péladan extolled in his writings, apparently did not prevent him from lingering over, if not wallowing in, descriptions of macabre-erotic aspects of late nineteenth century mores—doubtlessly with the intention of decrying them more effectively.

Carlos Schwabe
Poster for the First Rose+Croix Salon
1892, lithograph, 199 × 80
Musée d'Art et d'Histoire, Geneva
Mankind crouches in the foreground, mired in materialism, looking up at two female figures ascending the steps leading to the Ideal. The first personifies Faith who, having snapped the chain tethering her to earth, is reaching out to Purity, who stands one degree closer to Heaven. The geometry of the rising steps reinforces the impression of mystical longing that the artist clearly meant to convey here.

105

The disciples of Puvis de Chavannes

Alexandre Séon (1855-1917) was Puvis de Chavannes's pupil and assistant for the latter's work on the Panthéon murals when, in 1890, he met Péladan. He very soon became the chief illustrator of the "Sâr's" works, designing the frontispieces for most of his numerous novels and painting the official portrait of the magus wearing a violet tunic (1891, Musée des Beaux-Arts, Lyons). Séon was a prolific contributor to the Rose + Croix Salons. His pictorial style resembles that of Puvis de Chavannes, whose linear treatment of forms and pallid colors he copied. His was a somewhat systematic approach, however ; he invented a system, based on the color symbolism of the Catholic clergy's liturgical vestments, whereby blue and purple expressed melancholy, orange stood for sadness, white for purity, and so forth. His favorite themes were states of being (*Rêverie, Sadness, Grief, Thought, The Return of the Native*), but it was with subjects derived from Gustave Moreau and rendered with a considerable economy of means (*The Poet, The Chimaera's Despair, The Lyre of Orpheus*, Musée d'Art et d'Histoire, Saint-Etienne; or *The Lamentation of Orpheus*, Musée d'Orsay, Paris) that he expressed his thirst for the ideal most convincingly.

Alphonse Osbert (1857-1939), another regular of the Rose + Croix shows, had a more artificial approach. He too was heavily influenced by Puvis de Chavannes's serene art. Idyllic forest clearings and sea coasts under blue and mauve twilight, with slender, contemplative figures of timeless muses holding a lyre and silhouetted against the dying light, are his characteristic themes. The titles of his oils and pastels—*Antique Evening, Hymn to the Sea, Poem to Evening, Vision, Solitude, Serenity, Lyricism in the Forest*—are entirely in keeping with the fin de siècle sensibility in the poetry of this era.

There comes a delicious moment when twilight falls
And the sky is filled with rosy processions
Scattering their rose petals and souls,
Wafting sweet smells from invisible censers

wrote the Belgian poet, Georges Rodenbach. Which of us has not felt the magic of such twilight moments when time itself seems suspended? Osbert had a fine touch—and a weakness: he end-

Alexandre Séon
The Lyre of Orpheus
1898, oil on canvas, 27 × 46
Musée d'Art et d'Industrie,
Saint-Etienne

The theme of Orpheus, that figure of the poet suffering for mankind's sake and sacrificing his life in order to appease man and beast, is a recurring one in the work of this artist who was fond of repeating subjects dear to Puvis de Chavannes and Gustave Moreau. But the clean severe lines, the subdued palette, the pared down composition lend qualities to this and other Séon canvases that go beyond those of a mere imitator.

lessly repeated the same landscapes, which were reproduced so often on postal calenders that they lost what force they had originally possessed.

Osbert's style and predilections recall those of another follower of Puvis de Chavannes, Emile-René Ménard (1862-1930). Ménard, who never exhibited at the Rose + Croix Salons, was raised in an atmosphere of quasi-religious fervor for all that belonged to ancient Greece. His uncle authored a book that was popular in Symbolist circles: *Rêveries d'un païen mystique* (1876). Ménard spent his life evoking the golden age of Greek civilization, as he saw it, and traveling to Greece and Sicily to absorb what remained of its genius. Particularly attentive to the vibration of light at dawn or dusk, he was able to express the feelings that arise when one contemplates a beautiful classical landscape, both in his very sensitive pastels and his large decorative compositions like *The Dream of Antiquity* or *The Golden Age* (1908-1909) which once decorated the Salle des Actes at the old Faculty of Law in Paris, opposite the Panthéon where Puvis de Chavannes's murals are still seen.

Alphonse Osbert
Ancient Evening
1908, canvas curved upper edge, 150.5 × 135.5
Musée du Petit Palais, Paris

Emile-René Ménard
The Judgement of Paris
c. 1907, pastel on canvas, 43.5 × 74.8
Musée du Petit Palais, Paris

Edmond Aman-Jean
Confiding Secrets
1898, oil on canvas, 197 × 104
Musée des Arts décoratifs, Paris
Between 1890 and 1900 the artist frequently painted languid, dreamy-eyed maidens seated or walking in gardens, reminding us of the young girls in Marcel Proust's novels. The pastel tones and interweaving arabesques and curves are characteristic of the art in fashion around the turn of the century.

Edmond Aman-Jean (1859-1936) was Georges Seurat's closest friend, and shared his admiration for Puvis de Chavannes. Both artists, moreover, were briefly the latter's assistants. But while Seurat was carrying on his solitary research based on Impressionism and Chevreul's color theory, developing "chromo-luminism" (better known as Pointillism), Aman-Jean was studying the art of the fresco in Italy. He fell under Péladan's spell a little later, and executed the poster for the second Rose+Croix Salon, in 1893, drawing on Rossetti's Beatrice. But Aman-Jean's Symbolism was only briefly influenced by Rosicrucianism. He had a delicate touch, was fond of arabesques, half-tones, and pastel hues. His most successful works are portraits of dreamy young girls posing in the midst of flowering gardens in a misty atmosphere that corresponds perfectly to the intimist spirit of the poems of Albert Samain and Paul Verlaine. The latter's lines might have been written for him:

> *For it is more nuance that we want,*
> *Not color. Nothing but nuance!*
> *Ah! only nuance weds*
> *Dream to dream, flute to horn.*

Until quite recently, such works, with titles like *The Young Girl and the Peacock* (1895) or *Private Affairs* (Musée des Arts décoratifs, Paris), were considered vapid and artificial. We now view them more indulgently, as reflections of an era that also witnessed Marcel Proust's budding young girls.

The Toulouse artist, Henri Martin (1860-1943), another regular exhibitor at the Rose+Croix Salons, regarded himself as one of Puvis de Chavannes's heirs. He decorated a good number of public buildings, including the Paris and Toulouse town halls, and made no secret of his debt to the older artist. His canvas *Serenity* (1899, Musée d'Orsay, Paris) takes its inspiration directly from Puvis de Chavannes. However, thanks to his friendship with Aman-Jean, Martin was well acquainted with Neo-Expressionist experiments, and the often pleasant luminosity of his canvases owes a lot to the Pointillist technique. With some justification, Signac accused him, in his book *D'Eugène Delacroix au néo-impressionnisme*, of cultivating an eclectic genre and obtaining the popularity the pure Pointillists were denied: "Monsieur Henri Martin's paintings, whose technique is totally borrowed from Neo-Impressionism, appeal to the public, the critics, municipal committees, and the State. The dot does not shock in his work, yet remains useless—and therefore awkward—since, having a gray, ashen, flattened color, it does not supply the benefits of luminosity or coloring needed to offset the possible disadvantages of the technique. In his hands, Pointillism is acceptable... whereas the great Seurat, the inventor of Divisionism and author of so many grand calm works, is still ignored."[3] Degas had already complained about artists who borrowed the most superficial aspects of Impressionism in order to look modern: "They're not only shooting us down, they're emptying our pockets."

The art of the handsome Armand Point (1860-1932) was undoubtedly the one that corresponded most closely to Péladan's conception of art. Point, who had begun his career as a painter of Oriental scenes, followed the magus's prescription and went to Italy to study Botticelli and da Vinci, even going so far as to attempt to recon-struct their respective palettes and revive their techniques. The themes that inspired him, often derived from mythology, were those that had haunted Moreau; he was particularly drawn to figures of indeterminate sex (*Narcissus, Apollo and Daphne, The Death of Narcissus, The Siren, Orpheus, Eros*), in keeping with the precepts of the neo-Platonist that Péladan aspired to be. A very learned artist, Point founded in 1896 an artists' community at Marlotte in the country south-east of Paris, a community much like the one William Morris had established in England. The Atelier de Haute-Claire, as it was called, produced art objects inspired by the techniques of medieval and Renaissance goldsmiths. Although Péladan hailed him as a new Benvenuto Cellini, Point was a derivative craftsman who combined pastiches of Florentine gold and silver work with a pinch of Art Nouveau, as in his jewel cases at the Musée d'Orsay in Paris.

Armand Point
Siren
1897, pastel, 88 × 67.5
Barry Friedman Ltd.
Collection, New York

The rustic Charles Maurin (1856-1914), a native of the Auvergne, seemed out of place among the ethereal crowd that exhibited their paintings at the Rose + Croix Salon. This extremely inventive painter was mainly known as a companion of Toulouse-Lautrec in the cabarets of Montmartre, with whom, moreover, Maurin exhibited. Notwithstanding his anarchist leanings, Maurin shared the reverence of his fellow-painters at the Salon for Wagner, Burne-Jones, and the Italian primitives; like them, he also read Poe, Baudelaire, Huysmans. His triptych, *Dawn* (Musée d'Art et d'Industrie, Saint-Etienne) recalls a medieval altarpiece. In three panels, Maurin unfolds the cycle of human existence: *The Dawn of Dreams* is dedicated to Baudelaire, *The Dawn of Work* celebrates a workers' uprising, and *The Dawn of Love* depicts heroically nude lovers, under the aegis of Rimbaud. Geneviève Lacambre has rightly compared this Socialist-inspired Symbolism to that of the Belgian poet Emile Verhaeren, some of whose works Maurin in fact illustrated. Maurin's presence at the Rose + Croix Salon was no accident: he exhibited there several times, contributing paintings such as *Material Love*, *Soul Love*, *Spiritual Love* and *The Prelude to Lohengrin* (1892, Musée Crozatier, Le Puy), the title of which is in itself an indication of the convergence of ideas between the artist and Péladan. In another canvas, *Maternity* (1893, Musée Crozatier, Le Puy), Maurin endeavored to express the joys and sorrows of woman's lot —as well as the psychological burden of sterility. An artist who tried his hand at a variety of genres and exhausted his energies in fruitless technical research ("He has spoiled one of the finest talents I know of," Degas once said of him), Maurin is represented in only a few museums in central France. His manner, consisting of flat colors surrounded by very linear contours has great originality, both similar to and quite different from the Synthetism of Gauguin and Emile Bernard.

Charles Maurin
The Dawn of the Dream
or Les Fleurs du Mal
1891, oil on canvas, 81 × 100
Musée d'Art et d'Industrie,
Saint-Etienne

Charles Maurin
Motherhood
1893, oil on canvas, 80 × 100
Musée Crozatier, Le Puy

Louis Welden Hawkins
Halos
1894, oil on canvas, 61 × 50
Private Collection, Paris
These two saints with their sensuous shapes recall the type of woman Rossetti liked to depict. The original frame bore the following inscription: "They sing the angels' hymns with lips still stained with earth." The artist's ambiguous view of woman—saint or sinner?—was bound to appeal to Péladan, who invited him to show his work at the Salon de la Rose + Croix.

Louis Welden Hawkins (1849-1910) was born in England and became a French citizen in 1895. He received an academic training and began to make a name for himself as a genre painter with pictures like *The Orphans*. He dreamt of working with Puvis de Chavannes and, in 1890 or thereabouts, became acquainted with a number of Symbolist writers, in particular the most famous of them, Mallarmé, who sent him one of his brilliant pieces of occasional verse to thank him for the gift of a painting: "Talisman of the long hours that no gaze can exhaust." Hawkins, who admired the art of the Trecento and was influenced by the British Pre-Raphaelites, often placed his figures against a golden background, after the precious manner of the medieval masters. Thus, he gave the features of a Byzantine saint to the feminist journalist who sat for his portrait, *Séverine* (1895, Musée d'Orsay, Paris).

Ma Patronne (1903, Petit Palais, Paris) inevitably recalls William Holman Hunt's famous *The Light of the World* (Keble College, Oxford). After the turn of the century, Hawkins specialized in nocturnal landscapes akin to those of the Belgian artist, William Degouve de Nuncques.

Georges de Feure, from Symbolism to Art Nouveau

The art of the Dutch painter Georges Joseph Van Sluÿters (1868-1943), known in France under the pseudonym de Feure, renewed itself entirely after outgrowing the Rose + Croix influence. De Feure was first noticed for his caricatures and posters for the cafés-concerts of Montmartre, done in a style resembling that of Jules Chéret. He then exhibited oils and watercolors

Georges de Feure
The Voice of Evil
1895, oil on wood, 65 × 59
Robert Walker Collection
De Feure drew his inspiration
mainly from Baudelaire, especially the poems on lesbian
amours. All forms of "parallel"
sexuality held a deep fascination
for the writers and artists of the
Symbolist generation, as did the
theme of androgyny in all its
possible variations.

with the Nabis at the Le Barc de Boutteville gallery and at Péladan's salons. Ian Millman's recent work[4] on this artist suggests that it was
the engraver Marcelin Desboutin, an active propagandist in artistic circles for the magus' ideas
and one of his "official" portraitists, who encouraged de Feure to submit his work to these shows.

Péladan, in his novels, described in detail the
temptations and vices of the decadent civilization
he claimed to reform. Baudelaire, too, in his quest
for the ideal, had written with delectation about
the secret rooms in the gallery of love and sexual
deviations. De Feure's paintings often depict the
kind of *femmes damnées* engaging in Sapphic em-
braces described by the poet in the verses that
landed him in court. For instance, *The Voice of
Evil* (Robert Walker Collection, Great Britain)
shows a woman absorbed in a daydream that appears to be a lesbian fantasy. Like every Symbol-

ist, de Feure toyed with the notion of doing a
series of illustrations combining, in the spirit of
Wagner, women and flowers. Though unable to
realize this project which de Feure tentatively
called *Féminiflores*, he often associated in his paintings female figures and obscure vegetal forms. His
very personal style combined the Synthetism of
the Nabis with highly decorative arabesques and
"the most disparate tones cunningly disposed in
bizarre harmonies," as one contemporary critic
put it. Such refinements of color and precious
ornamentation are found in a series of watercolors on the deadly sins; the most spectacular of
them, *Swan Lake*, would seem to be an illustration
of pride.

The development of Georges de Feure's art
offers a prime example of the transition from
Symbolism to Art Nouveau. In 1893, the dealer
Siegfried Bing, who had started out popularizing

Georges de Feure
Swan Lake
c. 1897, watercolor, 32.4×51.5
Private Collection
Surrounded by flowers and
birds, a woman on a boat gazes
at her reflection in the water,
unable to tear herself away from
it. The figure of the peacock, a
symbol of vanity, lends meaning
to a composition remarkable for
its fluid lines and transparent
hues.

Japanese art in France, had discovered, during
a trip to the United States, the vases and stained
glass windows of Louis Comfort Tiffany and had
opened his Galerie de l'Art Nouveau toward the
end of 1895 as a showcase for Tiffany's techniques. He invited French artists to submit designs for furniture and art objects. Maurice
Denis, Bonnard, Sérusier, Ranson, Lacombe,
Schwabe, and Khnopff were among the first to
do so. De Feure became one of the pillars of
Bing's exhibits, which soon gained an international standing with the Art Nouveau pavilion
at the Universal Exposition of 1900. De Feure
designed the pavilion's façade and the decorations and furniture of the interior, ornamenting
them with the female forms and floral motifs
of his earlier work, now divested of their Symbol-

ist message and treated solely as decorative
elements.

Moreau's students at
the Rose+Croix Salons

In 1895, one of the most perspicacious of the
turn-of-the-century critics, the man who as organizer of the retrospectives of French nineteenth
century art at the Universal Expositions of 1889
and 1900 opened these prestigious exhibitions to
the Impressionists, Roger Marx wrote: "Historians tomorrow will all regard Gustave Moreau
as an inspired pioneer and the artist foreordained
to serve as a link between the Romantic school
and the new Symbolism. Because it transports us

far from nauseous banality, to the enchanted land of whimsey and dreams, Gustave Moreau's visionary art answers the private terrors of contemporary [artists], satisfies the fierce desire for infinity that torments them."

At the Ecole des Beaux-Arts, where he was viewed as an innovator and attracted to his studio young artists who wanted something more than a strictly academic approach to art, Moreau taught his students to respect the Renaissance masters and preached that painting, like poetry, must have a message. It is not surprising, therefore, that about ten of his students were drawn to exhibit at the Salon de la Rose + Croix, notably those whose style and sources of inspiration seemed closest to their master's, even though the latter carefully avoided showing them his own work.

Edgard Maxence (1871-1954) showed paintings with mythological or medieval themes at Péladan's last three salons. More remarkable for their plastic qualities than for their spiritual content, they reflected the influence of Rossetti, Burne-Jones and Moreau, and their technique was clearly inspired by the Italian primitives. The artist used gold backgrounds, for instance, and experimented with painting on slightly modeled plaster. A good example of his art is the "sculpto-painting" *Two Haloed Heads* (Alain Lesieutre Collection, Paris), with its icon-like appearance. Maxence made a career as a portraitist, but continued to paint scenes of prayer and contemplation showing saints or angels in brocade gowns in a medieval atmosphere (*The Soul of the Forest*, 1898, Musée des Beaux-Arts, Nantes).

Edgard Maxence
The Soul of the Forest
1898, oil on canvas, 88 × 83
Musée des Beaux-Arts, Nantes   115

Georges Rouault
Stella matutina
(Daytime Vision)
1895, oil on canvas, 274 × 182
Musée de l'Avallonais, Avallon

Most monographs on Georges Rouault (1871-1958) make no mention of the substantial contribution to the Rose + Croix shows (thirteen works in the last salon) of the painter who was to become the greatest religious artist of the twentieth century. Moreau's favorite pupil, "his spiritual heir," Rouault from the very first concentrated almost exclusively on religious subjects pervaded with influences of both his master and Rembrandt (*The Infant Jesus Among the Theologians*, 1894, Musée d'Unterlinden, Colmar; *Nativity*, 1900, Private Collection, Paris). His presence at the Salon de la Rose + Croix (like that of many other artists who showed their work there—Péladan did not require them to subscribe to the Rosicrucian doctrine) mainly reflected his desire to have his paintings viewed by the public, but the fact is that his manner at this time coincided perfectly with the magus' conception of art. Among the works he exhibited in 1897, a pair of large paintings deserves particular notice: *Stella matutina* (or *The Diurnal Vision*, 1895, Musée de l'Avallonais, Avallon) and *Stella vespertina* (or *The Nocturnal Vision, ibidem*). They have remarkable decorative qualities and are infused with the spirit of this period of Symbolism. As early as 1900, Rouault would begin to turn toward a somber Expressionism focussed on the misery of man's lot (prostitutes, clowns and circus scenes). To Péladan, these works rooted in reality would seem nightmares unworthy of Rouault's master, Gustave Moreau.

Two close disciples of Moreau—not among his Beaux-Arts students—would probably have considered it an insult to be included in this chapter devoted to the Rose + Croix Salons, to which they never contributed any of their works. One would agree, however, that their paintings at this time were eminently eligible for inclusion in Péladan's shows.

George Desvallières (1861-1950) came from a very cultivated family. He took private lessons with Moreau and was strongly marked by the latter's influence between 1890 and 1900, when he painted pictures of a recherché Symbolism, for instance *Narcissus* (1893, Private Collection, Paris) and *The Annunciation* (1897, Private Collection, France). One of Moreau's friends (he and Rouault were among the first curators of the collection Moreau bequeathed to the State), Desvallières developed a more realistic manner after 1900, and painted in a fiery, colorful style the rundown demi-mondaines of London and Paris. He was one of the founders of the Salon d'Automne which saw the birth of Fauvism in 1905. Desvallières later became a devout believer and gave himself to religious paintings and church decorations. In 1919, he and Maurice Denis founded the Ateliers d'Art Sacré with the goal of reviving authentic religious art freed from sentimental stereotypes.

Grandson of the Romantic painter Henry Scheffer, son of the famous religious historian Ernest Renan, Ary Renan (1857-1900) was disfigured by Pott's disease, but seemed to have received more than his fair share of intellectual gifts. Poet, historian, and art critic, he traveled widely in Asia, illustrated his own books, and was a refined painter stamped by the twofold influence of Puvis de Chavannes (a family friend) and Gustave Moreau, whose life Renan was the first to chronicle. His father's native Brittany was the younger Renan's greatest source of inspiration, its seascapes and rocky coasts providing the setting for many of his mythological compositions. *Sappho* (1893, Maison natale d'Ernest Renan, Tréquier) and *Scylla* (1894, Musée Renan-Scheffer, Paris) are evocations of man's fate and death. Geneviève Lacambre, whose work has vastly improved our knowledge of this painter, compares him to the Pre-Raphaelite, John Everett Millais.

Georges Desvallières
Annunciation
1897, oil on canvas, 87 × 134
Private Collection, France
Desvallières charged this very Pre-Raphaelite religious scene with a multiplicity of meanings and motifs: for example, the angels draping a mantle over the Virgin's shoulders and presenting her with the emblems of celestial sovereignty, and the solemn angel brandishing the cross, that symbol of the moral sufferings the mother of Christ will undergo during the Passion. In later years, the artist turned away from this type of composition and developed a more Expressionist manner.

117

Lucien Lévy-Dhurmer
Portrait of
Georges Rodenbach
c. 1895, pastel on blue-gray paper, 36 × 55
Musée d'Orsay, Paris
Few portraits match the sitter's personality as exquisitely as this. The poet Georges Rodenbach got his inspiration from the heart of the old Flemish towns: "In the listless solitude of
[cities
Drowzing on the banks of
[vacuous rivers."
The artist painted the background view of Bruges—which he had never visited—from a photograph.

The musical correspondences of Lévy-Dhurmer

Lucien Lévy-Dhurmer (1865-1953), who began his career as a ceramist, first came to public notice as a painter in 1896 with a one-man show at the Galerie Georges Petit. He was invited to send works to the Salon de la Rose + Croix but declined. He owed his fame to the Belgian Symbolist writer Georges Rodenbach, well known at the time in Paris for his poetry and, mainly, his tale *Bruges-la-Morte* (1892), a book which contributed to the rediscovery of that forgotten town. Lévy-Dhurmer's masterpiece is, in fact, his pastel portrait of Rodenbach (around 1895, Musée d'Orsay, Paris), whose delicate, dreamy features are depicted against the background of the celebrated Flemish town with its Gothic spires, bridges, and somber canals. It is a remarkable portrait and an exquisite evocation of the poet's character and his work, which obsessively revolves around silence and melancholy.

A virtuoso with pastels, able to draw the best from the velvety textures and singular tones of that medium, Lévy-Dhurmer centered many of

Lucien Lévy-Dhurmer
Medusa (The Furious Wave)
1897, pastel and charcoal on beige paper, 59 × 40
Musée d'Orsay, Paris
Like many of the artist's paintings, this face grimacing with terror, crowned with seaweed and twisting snakelike branches of coral, defies interpretation. Does it picture a nightmare, the metamorphosis of a natural force into a human being, the passage from life to death?

his often mysterious compositions around a human face: *Silence* (1895, Zagorowsky Collection, Paris), *The Woman With a Medal* (or *Mystery*, 1896, Musée d'Orsay, Paris), *Medusa* (or *The Furious Wave*, 1897, *ibidem*), *The Witch* (1897, *ibidem*), *Circe* (1897, Musée des Beaux-Arts, Brest).

After the year 1900, Lévy-Dhurmer increasingly depicted nudes, very much in the turn of the century vein, modeled with a dreamy vaporousness, in an endeavor to make the female anatomy render an equivalent of the auditory impressions of Beethoven, Fauré, and Debussy's music (*The Moonlight Sonata*, Musée d'Orsay, Paris; *La Marche Funèbre*, Musée des Beaux-Arts, Brest; *The Appassionata*, around 1906, Petit Palais, Paris). Although based on the characteristically Symbolist notion of "correspondances," these somewhat artificial and flaccid works are not as convincing as the earlier portraits, but they bear witness to the fashion for artistic haziness which pervaded even the photographic portraits of the early twentieth century.

From Symbolism to parody: Gustav-Adolf Mossa and Marcel Duchamp

Trained by his father, himself a painter and the originator of the Nice carnaval's floral parade, Gustav-Adolf Mossa (1883-1971) was eighteen when he painted his first canvas, *Salome Dancing Before Herod*. It soon became clear that he was thoroughly familiar with both the repertory of abnormal sexuality and every art style, from Gustave Moreau to Beardsley, the Florentine Quattrocento to Art Nouveau. He juggled myths and symbols with a disconcerting ease, slyly combining them with turn of the century decors, clothes, and jewelry, and evidently expected painting to liberate him from his private obsessions, a fact which sometimes makes it difficult to draw the line between satire and confession in his work.

Until the First World War, Mossa's reputation rested on his oils and above all his watercolors, with their brilliant coloring and carefully cal-

Gustave Adolf Mossa
She
1905, oil and gold on canvas, 80 × 63
Musée des Beaux-Arts Jules Chéret, Nice
This young female giant is not the one Baudelaire dreamt of spending his life with, "like a voluptuous cat at a Queen's feet." A baby-faced sphinx bearing the emblems of death, she towers above a heap of bloody corpses. Possibly influenced by a painting in the Musée Gustave Moreau, which opened its doors to the public in 1903, this canvas is a good example of the profound misogyny of this artist (aged twenty when he painted it) who seems to have been incapable of viewing love except in terms of death.

Marcel Duchamp
Spring
(Youth and Young Girl
in Spring)
1911, oil on canvas, 65.7 × 50.2
Vera and Arturo Schwarz
Collection, Milan

Duchamp in his youth was deeply impressed by the Symbolist poets he read (Mallarmé and Laforgue) as well as artists like Redon, from whom he borrowed the idea of the embryo and the halo encircling the two figures floating in space. This painting, a wedding gift from the artist to his sister, expresses the fertility of the male-female couple through allusions like the Tree of Life and the homunculus inside an alchemical sphere.

culated linear excesses intended to show that man, as a rule, is but the plaything of grasping females, with the artist's native Nice apparently offering plenty of material to draw from. He gradually gave up painting after 1918 and, as curator of the Nice museum, devoted the rest of his life to preserving other painters' works. He was rediscovered after his death thanks to J.-R. Soubiron, who calls him, "a Symbolist who pokes fun at Symbolism," an example "of the turn-of-the-century counter-culture spawned by a sophisticated superculture," an artist who "put an expiring movement into question and opened the door to a new mode of perception."

Was there a similar dose of humor in the first paintings of the artist who was to devote most of his life to tilting at the very idea of the work of art—Marcel Duchamp (1887-1968)? Duchamp's earliest works, in any case, reveal a strong Symbolist bias, which some critics have interpreted as evidence of an esoteric mysticism underlying all the later output of the artist who created *The Bride Stripped Bare*. Around 1910 the young Duchamp was painting canvases like *Spring* (1911, Vera and Arturo Schwarz Collection, Milan) which draw heavily on Redon's compositions ("my starting point," as Duchamp once admitted). It has even been suggested that his famous *Nude Descending a Staircase* (1911, Philadelphia Museum of Art) is in some ways an illustration of Mallarmé's poetry, which Duchamp is known to have admired.

Not the least paradox in Duchamp's oeuvre, which has inspired volumes of exegesis, is that one is only able to grasp the meaning of his most important composition, *The Bride Stripped Bare by Her Bachelors, Even* (1915-1923, Philadelphia Museum of Art) with the help of clues gleaned from a thorough knowledge of the Symbolist atmosphere of his youth.[5]

Notes

[1] F. Fénéon, an article published in *Le Chat noir*, 19 March 1892; reprinted in *Œuvres plus que complètes*, Paris and Geneva, 1970, p. 211.

[2] O. Mirbeau, "Botticelli proteste!" in *Le Journal*, October 4-11, 1896; reprinted in *Des artistes*, Paris, 1922-1924, 2 vols., and Paris, 1986, p. 248.

[3] P. Signac, *D'Eugène Delacroix au néo-impressionnisme*, op. cit., pp. 154-155.

[4] I. Millman, *Georges de Feure*, unpublished thesis, University of Paris-Nanterre, 1986; and "Georges de Feure. The Forgotten Dutch Master of Symbolism and Art Nouveau," in *Tableau*, Amsterdam, September-October, 1983, pp. 41-47.

[5] See J. Clair, *Marcel Duchamp. Catalogue raisonné*, Centre Georges Pompidou, Paris, 1977.

Léon Spilliaert
Vertigo,
the magic stairs
1908, ink wash, watercolor,
and color pencils, 64×48
Museum voor Schone Kunsten,
Ostend

Spilliaert excelled at both re-
ducing the perception of a particular place or vista to a few
essential lines and using perspective to create an oppressive
atmosphere. Thanks to the disproportionate treatment of the
steps, these stairs suggest a sort
of dream tower soaring into thin
air. The female figure with her
blowing hair increases the
nightmare effect.

122

THE SPREAD OF SYMBOLISM IN EUROPE

1

Belgium, the Netherlands, and Switzerland under the spell of the Rose+Croix

In the end, Péladan's aesthetic theories aroused more curiosity than serious interest in France, and were generally regarded with ironic amusement by critics. But in neighboring countries, especially Belgium, Holland, and Switzerland, they were received with deep respect. Péladan even delivered a series of lectures in the principle towns of Flanders and the Netherlands and made numerous converts there among writers and artists. True, the ground had already been prepared. In Brussels, the Groupe des XX (Group of the Twenty, 1883-1893)—consisting of twenty of the most innovative artists in Belgium, whose annual art shows, moreover, included international avant-garde artists chosen with a rare degree of discernment—was steeped in literary Symbolism[1]. The leading Belgian writers of the era, Emile Verhaeren, Maurice Maeterlinck, Grégoire Le Roy, Georges Rodenbach, all wrote influential art criticism. As early as 1889 the periodical *L'Art Moderne*, which transmitted the principles of the new artistic movement in Belgium, stated that there existed "a need for the otherworldly, for remote and mystical ideas evoking dreams, extending reality—hard, substantial, precise reality with its solid contours—prolonging it in hazy chimera, haloing it, surrounding and covering it with an incense of thought." These literary Symbolists regularly visited Paris—sometimes for long stays—and were thoroughly acquainted with the latest artistic developments in the French capital, where some of them were better known than in their own country. The moving spirit of the Groupe des XX, the art critic Octave Maus, was an indefatigable scout for new talent—the most knowledgeable in this fin de siècle—and even after the group broke up in 1893 he continued his activities, founding a new movement, "La libre esthétique," which lasted until the outbreak of the First World War.

Félicien Rops
Sentimental Initiation
(Frontispiece for a novel
by Joséphin Péladan)
1887, black pencil and
watercolor with gouache and
pastel highlights, 29.2 × 18.2
Graphic Arts Department,
Musée du Louvre, Paris

This watercolor is a characteristic example of the artist's erotic-macabre fantasies. The symbolic attributes of death are associated here with a generous female anatomy. The Latin inscription, drawn from St Augustine, lends a sarcastic irony to this work: "The Devil's power lies in the loins."

The satanic Félicien Rops

Older than any other member of the Groupe des XX, Félicien Rops (1833-1898) enjoyed the remarkable honor in the eyes of his turn-of-the-century countrymen of having been noticed before 1870 by Baudelaire himself, who had written after a trip to Belgium,

The frolicsome Monsieur Rops
Is no great Prix de Rome,
But his talent is as grand
As the pyramid of Cheops.

The poet regarded Rops as the only artist alive in Belgium worthy of that name, and it was in his company that, in 1866, while visiting a church, he suffered a paralyzing attack from which he would never recover.

During Baudelaire's lifetime, Rops had begun to gain notoriety with his licentious and anticlerical drawings. Like him, the poet had been keenly interested in licentious subjects, even going as far as to claim that "an obscene book sweeps us toward the mystical oceans of blueness." Huysmans in turn had stated that Rops "celebrated that spiritualism of Luxury that is Satanism, and painted, in pages that cannot be perfected, the supernaturalism of perversity, the otherworld of Evil." Péladan, too, adulated Rops, seeing in his album of lithographs *Les Sataniques* (1882) the "poem of the devil's possession of woman, wherein Rops elevates himself to the level of Dürer while remaining more Rops-like than ever."

Our eyes are less blinkered by sexual taboos than were those of Rops's contemporaries, and this is perhaps why we see in the drawings and engravings of that artist more prurient eroticism than moral significance. But in his time, Rops was regarded as the artist who revealed Satan's hold on mankind (it was an era of belief in the Devil) and exposed the sexual and religious hypocrisies of the late nineteenth century with a pencil dipped in acid. He was in fact a rake and, unlike his admirers Baudelaire, Huysmans, and Péladan, does not appear to have been burdened with metaphysical preoccupations.

He drew the frontispiece for Baudelaire's *Epaves* (1866), the poems that had earlier been banned in criminal court. During the Symbolist era, a number of writers, Verlaine, Mallarmé, Barbey d'Aurevilly, and of course Péladan, asked him to illustrate their works. Rops designed frontispieces for several of Péladan's books and correspondend with him fairly often, though nothing indicates that the painter ever shared the magus' theories.

Rops found his type of *femme fatale* in the streets and brothels of Paris, the girl who inflames the desire of man—or saint—to the limit of exhaustion. A vitriolic draftsman and remarkable connoisseur of the female body and its arsenal of provocative finery, Rops knew how to manipulate the Symbolist motifs of his time with superb irony. An atheist, he was thoroughly versed in the vocabularies of religion and mythology. Sphinxes, serpents, crosses, masks, severed heads, angels, and skeletons surround his buxom women, who exhibit themselves immodestly to men while frolicking with symbols. Sigmund Freud himself, in "Delirium and Dreams in Jensen's *Gradiva*" (1907), an essay treating the problem of death and immortality, cites one of Rops's engravings to illustrate the process of repression. Basically, Rops expressed with remarkable force the situation of the fin de siècle male, convinced of his superiority over the "weaker sex," but filled with anxieties about woman and struggling to repress the libido that drove him toward venal sex and exposed him to the frightening diseases that were often its consequence.

Félicien Rops
Death at the Ball
1865-1875, oil on canvas, 151 × 85
Rijksmuseum Kröller-Müller, Otterlo
Rops has given us a perfect illustration of the following lines from *Danse macabre* by his friend Baudelaire:
Elle a la nonchalance et la désinvolture
D'une coquette maigre aux airs extravagants.
Vit-on jamais au bal une taille plus mince?
Sa robe exagérée, en sa royale ampleur,
S'écroule abondamment sur un pied sec que pince
Un soulier pomponné, joli comme une fleur.

125

From Baudelaire to Gauguin, there is a long list of victims of the *Mors syphilitica*, which Rops depicts as a disease-wasted woman brandishing a scythe. "Rops," observed Octave Mirbeau, "constantly strips man down to the skeleton, and upon this macabre frame he knots his tortured muscles, twists his flesh gouged by the claws of chimaera and whipped by furious passions."

There was a whiff of sulphur in Rops's talent, which is one of the reasons why he was so popular in his day. A prolific illustrator and inventive engraver, he painted few pictures. It seems a pity that there are not more paintings like *Death at the Ball* (1865-1875, Rijksmuseum Kröller-Müller, Otterlo) in his oeuvre. The raw sensitivity of his technique, the richness of the colored impasto are qualities that would have made this brilliant draftsman a great painter as well, like Honoré Daumier.

James Ensor, the disguised Symbolist

There is plenty of vindictive irony, too, not to mention skeletons and devils, though more spiritual anguish, in the oeuvre of the greatest Flemish painter of the nineteenth century, James Ensor (1860-1949). Although the painting of this rebel displays a chromatic brilliance rarely encountered among those of his fellow-artists who were influenced by the Rose + Croix movement (which was not his case), his biographers have found it easy to link his inspiration to Symbolism[2].

A founding member of the Groupe des XX, yet always fiercely jealous of his independence, Ensor had trouble at first getting his contemporaries to accept his "monstrous fantasies." The virulence of his social criticism shocked them. They were

James Ensor
Christ Calming the Tempest
1891, oil on canvas, 80 × 100
Museum voor Schone Kunsten, Ostend
The anarchist James Ensor was also a mystic obsessed by Christ, with whom he sometimes identified. Stylistically indebted to Turner's luminous effects, this surrealistic vision of nature's raging elements is given meaning by the tiny figure of Christ standing at the prow of the boat.

James Ensor
Death and the Masks
1897, oil on canvas, 79 × 100
Musée d'Art Moderne, Liège
Beneath the grotesque spectacle
of the grimacing carnaval masks
of his native Ostend, Ensor depicted the human comedy dominated by the pale specter of
death—a ubiquitous theme in
his work.

outraged by his *Christ's Entry into Brussels* (1888, The J. Paul Getty Museum, Malibu), both be- cause of its satire of bourgeois mores and because of its stylistic daringness. A profound mysticism underlies Ensor's approach, concealed by the artist's anarchism, as one can deduce from the six superb drawings inspired by the life of Christ, dating from the years 1885-1887. *Christ's Haloes or the Sensitivities of Light* (Taevernier Collection, Ghent) is a suite of "visions," as the artist himself puts it, in which the mysteries of Christ's life (in the theological sense of the word mystery) are suggested by successively "gay," "bright," "sad and crippled," and "intense" qualities of light that translate the mystical feelings they produced in the artist. Like Gauguin, Ensor was inclined to identify with figures of Christ persecuted because he too had been misunderstood. The painter, who viewed himself as a martyr to art, also de- picted himself as a new St. Luke kneeling at the

feet of the Virgin, who has appeared to him while he paints (*The Virgin of Consolation*, 1892, Private Collection, Ghent). As F.-C. Legrand observes, the great themes that inspired this modern Bosch were an "obsession with death represented by skeletons, fear of the devil, paradise lost, tempta- tion, the disguises and masks that personify the Human Comedy, all derived from the funda- mental repertory of Symbolism, the Symbolism rooted in the heart of the Romantic nineteenth century[3]".

Ensor's period of creativity was short. He produced his first significant works at the age of twenty, but his art stopped renewing itself before the end of the century, which led one critic to write that, like Christ, he died at the age of thirty-three. Actually, Ensor lived to a ripe old age and witnessed the flowering of pictorial movements he had anticipated by many years, Expressionism and Surrealism. Unlike Gauguin,

Xavier Mellery
Autumn
1893, watercolor and chalk on silver background, 90.5 × 57
Musées Royaux des Beaux-Arts, Brussels
This highly personal interpretation of falling Autumn leaves could be set beside this line by Homer, which probably inspired it: "The generations of man fall like leaves from the trees."

CHUTE DES DERNIERES FEUILLES D'AUTOMNE

he was able to enjoy at least some rewards in this life; in his final years, he was even knighted.

"A powerful conjurer of tragic dreams," is what Georges-Albert Aurier called Henry de Groux (1867-1930). De Groux was an isolated artist. His eccentricities and sectarian views got him voted out of the Groupe des XX—he had refused to allow his paintings to be hung on the same wall as pictures by Van Gogh, Toulouse-Lautrec, or Seurat at the group's annual show. Yet he had begun his career brilliantly enough, with a *Christ Insulted* (1890, Foundation Flandreysi-Espérandieu, Palais du Roure, Avignon), a violent, highly colorful great machine of a painting that scandalized some and was admired by others (notably the writer Léon Bloy). "My fate is to compromise everything," he once acknowledged. Appropriately enough, the part of his oeuvre that remains of any worth is a series of pastels and lithographs illustrating the operas of Wagner, the artist who embodied what de Groux would have liked to have been.

Fernand Khnopff, or the retreat into oneself

Fernand Khnopff (1858-1921) was the most international of the Belgian Symbolist painters, equally at home in the artistic circles of Paris, London and Vienna. He was, in that respect, a link between these major art centers in the late nineteenth century.

His first master had been the self-effacing and likeable Xavier Mellery (1845-1921) who dreamt of becoming the Belgian Puvis de Chavannes and devoted many years of his life to sketching vast allegorical compositions with which he hoped in vain to obtain commissions for decorating public buildings in Brussels. All that remains of his ambitious projects is a series of lush, harmonious watercolors, mostly with gold or silver backgrounds, which appear at first glance to be conventional allegories, though in fact their dreamlike, mysterious atmosphere goes far beyond the limits of the strictly allegorical—*The Awakening, Terpsichore, Immortality, Autumn* (Musées Royaux des Beaux-Arts, Brussels). In the words of F.-C. Legrand, Mellery "viewed the universe with a feeling of love, of human communion... In his eyes, everything in it partook of a hidden order, of occult harmonies. He saw it as being

engendered, organized, pervaded by intelligence."[4] His quest for interiority also unfolded on another level, that of his often very somber drawings of silent domestic or monastic interiors, collected under the title *The Soul of Things*. "Everything is alive," Mellery was fond of repeating, "even things that do not move."

It was from this artist, then, that Khnopff probably got his taste for a secret and hieratic art. At the age of twenty he discovered contemporary French art at the 1878 Universal Exposition in Paris, and was particularly struck by the paintings of Delacroix, Gustave Moreau, and Burne-Jones. His earliest compositions were mainly influenced by Moreau, especially the latter's sphinx theme, and it was not long before he was noticed by Péladan, who would later call him "the Gustave Moreau of Flanders." A sojourn in London in 1891 gave him an opportunity to familiarize himself more thoroughly with the painting of Burne-Jones and Rossetti—Khnopff's dreamy-eyed auburn beauties are clearly derived from the latter. A refined man of the world and great connoisseur of poetry and music—Mallarmé, Schumann, Wagner—he made woman his one

and only subject, or nearly. His favorite model was his younger sister Marguerite, to whom he was deeply, narcissistically attached, as if she were the female half of an androgynous creature, brother and sister formed together. Indeed, Khnopff shared his friend Péladan's fascination with the Platonic theme of the androgyne.

Khnopff regularly exhibited at the Groupe des XX shows and the Salons de la Rose + Croix, and illustrated Péladan's books as well. His art is an art of introversion; his paintings seem to have no place in time, no action, no story, more often than not no explanation. His titles themselves are usually vague and uninformative: *Memories, Of Silence, Solitude, The Offering, A Blue Wing, Incense, The Secret*, and so on. Even when his pictures draw inspiration from literary sources, like his masterpiece, *I Lock My Door Upon Myself*, based on a poem by Christina Georgina Rossetti (the painter's sister), their message is obscure, for Khnopff's interpretations of literature are highly personal. The objects that surround his women with their transfixed looks only seem to increase their mysteriousness and inscrutability: flowers, masks, ancient statues, precious objects and

Fernand Khnopff
I Lock My Door Upon Myself
1891, oil on canvas, 72 × 140
Neue Pinakothek, Munich

A mystical poem by Dante Gabriel Rossetti's sister, Christina Rossetti, inspired this painting which expresses a withdrawal from the outer world to the inner world of dreams, symbolized by the bust of Morpheus, the god of sleep. The three lilies—budding, blossoming, and withered—in the foreground are an allusion to life's passage.

129

Fernand Khnopff
The Secret and the Reflection
1902, pastel medallion: diameter 49.5; below: color pencil drawing: 27.8 × 49
Groningenmuseum, Bruges
This mysterious work would appear to be an evocation of the artist's childhood in Bruges (the drawing at the bottom represents the lateral facade of the Hospice of St John), while the priestess (a portrait of Khnopff's sister!), pressing her finger against a mask's lips seems to be silencing some unspeakable memory.

jewelry, backgrounds consisting of views of dead cities, like Bruges, or deserted landscapes. Khnopff had a villa built for himself in Brussels —it is now destroyed unfortunately—the walls of which were covered with white enamel paint, as in a hospital; the rooms were graced with a few choice collector's objects, and in the center of his studio was a large golden circle into which the artist would step and concentrate before starting a painting.

Emile Verhaeren wrote that "tormented and tormenting," Khnopff strove "to translate the anxieties, sorrows, perversities, dramas that never cross the limit of dreams to fade away in deeds."[5] Closer to us, the work of a painter like Paul Delvaux produces similar impressions of repressed actions and strange associations.

Khnopff was certainly the most famous of the turn-of-the-century Belgian painters. His pictures were shown in Vienna and Munich as well as London and Paris. At the inaugural show of the 1898 Vienna Secession exhibit, Khnopff had twenty pictures on display in a separate room and was enormously successful, even more so than other illustrious Symbolists such as Puvis de Chavannes, Rodin, Böcklin, Klinger, Segantini. In December of that same year, the Secession periodical *Ver Sacrum* devoted an entire, lavishly illustrated issue to him. Nor did his popularity decline at later Viennese art shows. It is for this reason that we will return to him in a later chapter when we seek to gauge his influence on the development of Gustav Klimt's painting.

Jean Delville, the quintessential Rose+Croix artist

Enamored with swirling arabesques, which held for him a spiritual significance, Jean Delville (1867-1953) was first noticed for his charcoal drawings inspired by Wagner's operas, especially *Tristan and Isolde* (1887, Musées Royaux des Beaux-Arts, Brussels). Very early on he became interested in spiritualism and the Cabala, and naturally gravitated around Joséphin Péladan. After showing his works several years running at the Salon de la Rose+Croix (Péladan inscribed one of his books to him with the words, "To the Chevalier Jean Delville, the dearest to my heart of the artists of the Order because he has never exhibited elsewhere than at the Rose+Croix"),

Delville organized a Salon of Idealist Art in Brussels in 1896. The Belgian Idealist school, he declared, was "analogous if not identical to the one in Paris and the Pre-Raphaelite movement in London." The French artists Point and Séon sent in works, as did the Belgian artists Albert Ciamberlani, Emile Fabry, Léon Frédéric, Constant Montald, all of whom we will encounter below. A theorist as well as a painter, Delville wrote a book called *La mission de l'art*, published in 1900 with a preface by Edouard Schuré, in which he defined form and line as "the symbolic expression of the mysterious affinities linking mind to matter." He wanted to create a plastic equivalent of Péladan's theory of androgyny. The result was a series of ambiguous works that arouse or amuse, depending on one's inclinations. *Plato's School* (1900, Musée d'Orsay, Paris) groups twelve naked youths around the famous philosopher; their arms lovingly entwined, they seem to be drinking in the master's words of wisdom.

At the entrance of the Salon of Idealist Art Delville hung reproductions of paintings by Puvis de Chavannes, Moreau, Rossetti, Burne-Jones, and Böcklin. His own work reveals traces of all these artists, especially Moreau (*Orpheus*, 1893, Private Collection, Brussels; *The End of a Reign*, 1893, Private Collection). Like Puvis de Chavannes, he liked to work with large surfaces and elaborated vast theatrical compositions which, after having been locked away in the store rooms of Belgian museums for half a century, are once again on display. *L'Homme-Dieu* (1901-1903, Groeningemuseum, Bruges), a rather macabre variation on the theme of the Last Judgment, or *The Treasures of Satan* (1895, Musées Royaux des Beaux-Arts, Brussels) are of less interest today than a more modest canvas such as *Soul Love* (1900, Musée d'Ixelles, Brussels), in which the musical arabesques of two chastely entwined bodies express sublimated physical love.

Delville's disciple Constant Montald (1862-1944) was more influenced by Puvis de Chavannes. His figures stroll through bucolic landscapes or drink from sacred springs (*The Font of Inspiration*, 1907, Sarub Collection, on permanent loan to the Musées Royaux des Beaux-Arts, Brussels). A close friend of Emile Verhaeren, Montald, whose Symbolism was far less ethereal than Delville's, taught decorative painting for years at the Brussels Academy, where René Magritte and Paul Delvaux were his students.

Jean Delville
Soul Love
1900, egg-base paint on canvas, 238 × 150
Musée d'Ixelles, Brussels
Apart from its subject—the Platonic fusion of two beings recreating the primordial androgyny through love—this painting is remarkable mainly for the harmonious decorative effect of the arabesque constituted by the two bodies drifting upward through ideal blue clouds.

Two portrayers of human suffering: George Minne and Emile Fabry

George Minne
The Fountain of Kneeling Youths
c. 1898, plaster, height 168, diameter 240
Museum voor Schone Kunsten, Ghent

The kneeling naked youth hugging himself or bearing awesome relics is a recurrent theme in Minne's oeuvre. This group is sometimes called the *Narcissus Fountain*, a better name for these introverted, self-absorbed figures kneeling with their backs to the viewer, searching their own reflection for the solution to their anguish.

The Ghent draftsman and sculptor George Minne (1866-1941) depicted the woes of motherhood, much as his counterpart in France, Eugène Carrière, had specialized in painting the joys and griefs of the maternal lot. Virtually self-taught, Minne became a close friend of Maurice Maeterlinck and illustrated a volume of his poetry, *Serres chaudes* (1889), a book which brought a measure of fame to both men. Rarely has the collaboration between a poet and a painter been as harmonious as it was between these two artists who portrayed, one in verse, the other in drawing and sculpture, tormented, silently suffering souls.

Minne's oeuvre is indeed a lengthy meditation on grief and anguish, both in his charcoals (*Mother Grieving Over Her Dead Child*, 1886; *Grief*, 1888) and in his sculptured, or rather modeled,

figures for he never actually carved stone or wood. His best-known sculpture is *The Fountain of the Kneeling Youths* (1898, Museum voor Schone Kunsten, Ghent), which shows five lanky naked adolescents kneeling around a pool, hugging themselves and staring at their reflections. This group was particularly popular in northern Europe and influenced artists such as Kokoschka, Schiele, Lehmbruck, and Kollwitz. Minne continued to work on the same themes as he grew older, but from a Christian perspective, producing a series of Virgins with Child, Christs, and relic bearers after 1900. His is a very ascetic sculpture, marked by the striving after the archaic that often characterizes Symbolism and devoid of any expressionistic effects, yet nevertheless possessing an inner tension that reflects the anguished temperament of a uniquely talented artist who in his works expressed unconscious childhood recollections of war and disease brought to light by his regular association with Symbolist poets.

Like George Minne, Emile Fabry (1865-1966) exhibited at the Rose + Croix Salons. He depicted beings in the grips of existential anguish. All the titles of his paintings evoke the inexorability of fate and the ubiquitous presence of death (though the artist himself lived to be 101): *Salome, Delilah, The Fates, Autumnal, The Ages of Man, The Gestures, The Path*. F.-C. Legrand, in her essential book, *Le symbolisme en Belgique*, gives a good description of Fabry's women. They are all "strangely alike," she says, with their "sallow anguished faces, crazed eyes, deformed profiles, flattened noses, pinched lips and sucked-in mouths, prominent chins and foreheads; enigmatic as sphinxes, bowed down toward death, clutching funereal flowers between their over-long fingers."[6]

Léon Frédéric (1856-1940) began his career painting in the Naturalist style. His early work, after the manner of Bastien-Lepage, had a social message and depicted in detail the landscapes of his native Ardennes, the harsh lives of the indigent Ardennais peasants or the jobless in the

Léon Frédéric
The Lake.
Dormant Waters
1897-1898, right panel of the triptych, *The Stream*, oil on canvas, 205.5 × 127.5
Musées Royaux des Beaux-Arts, Brussels
The oneiric, unwittingly Surrealist quality of this painting is unmistakable. The dormant water suggests sleep, as does the swan, a bird associated with still waters. Yet one wonders what all those babies floating among aquatic flowers rendered with the precision of a Millais are meant to signify.

Emile Fabry
The Offering
c. 1884-1886, oil on canvas, 45 × 100
Musées Royaux des Beaux-Arts, Brussels
Deeply influenced by the poetry of Verhaeren and Maeterlinck, Fabry frequently painted mute anxious female faces—the faces of future victims baffled by the dolorous mysteries of life and death, with nothing to offer save their own resignation.

133

**William Degouve
de Nuncques**
Nocturnal Effect
1896, pastel, 47×68
Musée d'Ixelles, Brussels
The artist often depicts isolated
houses in the night and the fog,
with only a few weakly lit windows to suggest that they are
inhabited.

proletarian suburbs of Brussels. His sources of
inspiration changed when, under Delville's influence, he converted to Idealist art, while his
meticulous technique remained the same. The
result appears very odd to us, a painting that
teeters between the mystical and the bizarre, its
almost finicky brushwork recalling some of the
English Pre-Raphaelites. The most memorable
examples of his art are the triptychs (a supremely
Flemish form), like *The Golden Age* (1901, Musée
d'Orsay, Paris), obviously inspired by Puvis de
Chavannes's *Sleep* (Musée des Beaux-Arts, Lille),
and *The Stream* (1897-1898, Musées Royaux des
Beaux-Arts, Brussels). Although Beethoven's
famous *Pastoral Symphony* contains a movement
called *The Stream*, suggesting birds singing over a
murmuring brook, it is difficult to imagine how
on earth that piece of music ever prompted this
vision of hundreds of rosy little children snuggling
against each other, sleeping, playing, or running
as they are swept along by the stream. Granted
that the turn-of-the-century public may have
been more innocent of Freudian associations than
we are, one cannot help but wonder at the unconscious eroticism of their poses. Be that as it
may, far from being scandalous, Frédéric was

highly regarded as an official artist, a painter of
touching scenes from the lives of the poor. The
King of Belgium even gave him a title of nobility.

The nocturnes of
William Degouve de Nuncques

The very sensitive and cultivated artist William Degouve de Nuncques (1867-1935) expressed himself on a modest scale compared with
the ambitious compositions of Delville and
Frédéric; pastels were his favorite medium and
the landscape his chosen genre. Though he was
well acquainted with the Symbolist circles,
having shared a studio first with Jan Toorop
and later Henry de Groux, and married Emile
Verhaeren's sister-in-law, he did not exhibit at
any of the Rose+Croix shows. Widely read, passionately fond of music and the natural sciences,
he was practically a self-taught artist. His non-
academic training left an imprint on his work, a
certain naïveté in his manner, particularly in his
treatment of figures. He is most convincing when
he paints landscapes. His characteristic pictures
are gardens and woods at night, weakly illumi-

134

nated by the lingering glow of twilight or the luminous haloes of streetlamps, nocturnal scenes from which every human trace is banished but where each tree, plant, and flower is described with an amateur botanist's loving precision. The only living creatures in these havens of silence, with their dormant pools, are swans or peacocks, sometimes an angel or two. From his travels through Europe, Degouve brought back nocturnal views—he was plainly familiar with Whistler's *nocturnes*—of the public gardens of Milan, Schönbrunn, Paris, Brussels, Venice, transfigured and hallowed by the blue-green tones of their shadowy foreignness.

Some of Degouve's pictures, for instance *The House of Mystery* (1892), Rijksmuseum Kröller-Müller, Otterlo, where most of his works are preserved), are said to prefigure Magritte's famous paintings (his *Empire of the Lights*, for example), but, aside from the fact that Surrealism owes a great deal to Symbolism, it seems more relevant to compare these dreamy canvases to the poems of Degouve's contemporaries and friends, Rodenbach, Verhaeren, and Maeterlinck. *The Reign of Silence*, to borrow the title of one of Rodenbach's volumes, was a theme that all of them were drawn to. After 1899, Degouve began to spend long periods in southern Europe, in luminous Mediterranean landscapes, and his palette became brighter, his landscapes sunlit, and the mysterious atmosphere that makes for the charm of his earlier work dissolved like mist.

William Degouve de Nuncques
The Black Swan
1896, pastel, 38 × 47
Rijksmuseum Kröller-Müller, Otterlo
This pastel is characteristic of the artist's Symbolist period, when he often strove to create an atmosphere of mystery by eliminating any trace of a human presence from his delicately shaded blue and green twilight scenes.

Jan Toorop
O Grave, Where Is
Thy Victory?
1892, grease-paint stick on
yellow cardboard, 62 × 76
Rijksmuseum, Amsterdam
A pair of wiry angels (inspired by Indonesian puppets) are removing thorns from a corpse coveted by the forces of Evil, on the right. The curved lines express good, the broken lines, evil.

The macabre probings of Jan Toorop

The Dutch painter Jan Theodor Toorop (1858-1928) spent his first thirteen years on the island of Java, where his father was a settler. His Indonesian origin explains the more original aspects of his style, the figures with unnaturally long arms that recall the *wayang* shadow puppet theater, the tendency to cover every inch of the picture plane with a profusion of details, reminiscent of Javanese art. He did not receive his artistic training in Holland, where the teaching was dominated by the landscape painting of The Hague school, but in Brussels, where he was admitted to the Groupe des XX as early as 1885. Toorop, a receptive, musical youth who spoke several languages and was drawn to literary circles, was influenced by two artists who exhibited with the Groupe des XX as early as 1887, Ensor and Seurat. He frequently sojourned in Paris and London, where he married. He was forever on the look-out for the latest innovations in art, which he would promptly absorb into his own style. Thus, by turns he was a Realist after the manner of Courbet, an Impressionist *à la* Manet, a Pointillist in the vein of Seurat, with Socialistically tinted scenes depicting the lives of ordinary fishermen.

He was among the artists who welcomed Verlaine and Péladan to Holland in November 1892, and promptly fell under the magus' spell, contributing to the first Salon de la Rose + Croix a canvas called *The Young Generation* (1892, Museum Boymans-van Beuningen, Rotterdam) that portrayed his own child in a cradle in the middle of a hostile forest. Until 1900 he combined the thematic repertory of Symbolism with a pessimistic vision of human existence: sphinxes and angels, crosses and skulls, lilies and thorns, swans, skeletal women with an abundance of wavy hair. He was particularly fond of macabre subjects fraught with complicated, if not somewhat confused, significance set, more often than not, in cemeteries. Equally skilled at drawing with pencil and chalks, at pastels, watercolors, and oils, he had a remarkable gift for creating striking, sometimes even strident, color combinations, and a taste for arabesques that led him to cover surfaces with a mesh of curves that intertwine and unfurl inextricably toward the edges of the frame, producing decorative effects that are pure Art Nouveau.

The reflection on man's ultimate destiny that underlies his inspiration was doubtlessly rooted in something far deeper than the Symbolist vogue: in 1905, Toorop converted to Catholicism. He subsequently reverted to the Divisionist manner of his painting prior to 1890 and concentrated on religious subjects which now seem of little interest.

Toorop, like Khnopff, was well known outside of Belgium, notably in Vienna where he participated in the Secession exhibition two years running, in 1900 and 1901. His influence is clearly discernible in Klimt's work after the turn of the century, particularly in the parade of figures flying past the great sphinx representing the riddle of mankind at the center of the famous Beethoven Frieze (1903).

Some ten years younger than Toorop, Johan Thorn Prikker (1868-1932) was introduced by the older painter to the Groupe des XX. Trained as a landscape painter at The Hague Academy, he was more drawn to the mysticism of the Flemish primitives than to the rustic scenes dear to the Dutch school. "The Symbolist artist," he stated, "rebels against those who paint a tree simply because it is a tree and are lacking in that sense that precisely distinguishes the artist from the painter."

His inspiration was tied even more closely than Toorop's to the Christian doctrine of redemption through suffering, which was widespread in Catholic circles in the late nineteenth century. *Holy Women Beneath the Cross*, *Christ Upon the Cross*, *The Descent From the Cross*, *The Madonna of the Tulips at the Foot of the Cross*, *The Entombment*, these are the titles of his most well-known works, all at Rijksmuseum Kröller-Müller in Otterlo. Even his masterpiece, *The Betrothed* (1892-1893, *ibidem*) depicts a young bride beneath a crucifix. Like Toorop, Thorn Prikker adopted Seurat's Pointillist technique, but employed it to a strictly decorative end, though attributing a precise symbolic meaning to lines: curves stood for charity or mercy, thick lines suggested a strong emotion, thin lines expressed nuances, like the musical signs for crescendo and decrescendo.

Johan Thorn Prikker
The Betrothed
1892-1893, oil on canvas, 146 × 88
Rijksmuseum Kröller-Müller, Otterlo
This scene represents a mystical marriage: one distinguishes the bride's veil and her crown of flowers intertwining with Christ's crown of thorns. The phallic tulips and skull-shaped snapdragons symbolize carnal love. The artist was familiar with Seurat's Pointillist technique (whose works hung beside Thorn Prikker's at the Groupe des XX shows in Brussels), but he uses it here to express the essence of a vision rather than to decompose light scientifically.

Jan Toorop
The Sphinx
**1892-1897, grease-paint stick
and watercolor on canvas,
126 × 135
Gemeentemuseum, The Hague**
Also called *Sphinx Surrounded by
Dead Souls*, this intricate drawing expresses (according to the
artist), "The eternal dualism
within man who in spite of
everything struggles to attain
the Ideal on earth." The figure
laid out on a sphere—obviously
a poet—symbolizes man's quest
for truth through the ages and
through different religions (the
Gothic portal, sphinx, and
statue of Buddha in the background).

Unlike Toorop, however, Thorn Prikker was
not a successful painter, and in 1895 he turned
toward the applied arts, influenced notably by
Henry Van de Velde; like many of his fellow
Symbolists, he wanted art to serve human needs.
He devoted himself thereafter to creating mural
decorations, designing stained glass windows and
coloring cloth using the Indonesian technique of
batik. From 1904 on, he taught at the Krefeld
Kunstgewerbeschule in the German province of
North Rhine-Westphalia.

Other, less well known Dutch painters followed briefly in Toorop's footsteps. His companion in Brussels, Antoon Derkinderen (1859-
1925), realized his ambition of becoming an
artist-craftsman in the manner of the medieval
masters by painting vast Giottoesque mural decorations for the town hall of Bois-le-Duc. Essentially a lithographer, Roland Holst (1868-
1938), a Rosicrucian, was strongly influenced by
Rossetti. Léonard Sarluis (1874-1949) came from
a family of rich antique dealers; an angelic-look-
ing youth, he was fond of reading the Bible and
Petronius' *Satiricon*. At the age of twenty he went
to Paris, spent his time there with Oscar Wilde
and Jean Lorrain (which tells us something about
his inclinations), and practiced a painting inspired, or so he claimed, by da Vinci, but sexually

even more ambiguous. Péladan inducted him in the Order of the Rose+Croix, and Armand Point gave him art lessons. It was Sarluis who designed, at least in part, the poster for the fifth Rose+Croix Salon, namely Perseus (drawn by Point) brandishing the head of Emile Zola. Péladan's theory about androgyny gave Sarluis a wonderful excuse for painting variations of hermaphroditic anatomies which had nothing to do with spiritualism.

There was more authenticity in the work of Christoph Karel de Nerée tot Babberich (1880-1909) who, after contracting tuberculosis and giving up his career as a diplomat, devoted the final years of his life to drawing and poetry, which he composed indifferently in French and Dutch. He identified mainly with Aubrey Beardsley whose destiny foreshadowed his own. The subjects and manner of the British artist are easily recognizable in the 300 ink and pastel drawings de Nerée tot Babberich is known to have produced (Gemeentemuseum, Arnhem and The Hague), with perhaps a deeper expressivity, though a more mannered graphic style; yet at the same time he was able to combine, with a rare degree of refinement, the twin influences of Toorop and Thorn Prikker.

Karel de Nerée tot Babberich
Black Swans
1901, chalk and pastel on canvas, 97.5×54.5
Gemeentemuseum, The Hague
In a graphic oeuvre steeped in Aubrey Beardsley's influence, de Nerée chiefly painted turn-of-the-century women, frail *femmes fatales*. The black swan, a presage of ill fortune, and the woman's wavy hair are stock items in the Symbolist iconography of Maurice Maeterlinck, whose poems often inspired the artist.

Jan Toorop
Assuagement
1893, pastel on beige paper, 76×90
Musée d'Orsay, Paris
This sketch for a stained glass window (hence its simplified forms) represents desire, shown full-face, her eyes wide open, waiting for a dew drop (or drop of blood) to fall from the cross —for it will bring inner peace. The personification of assuagement, seen in profile, has already collected one of these drops in a lily. More than its obscure symbolism inspired by Christian mysticism, what makes this work interesting is its composition and teeming arabesques which show that Toorop was well acquainted with Japanese prints.

139

The lingering twilight of Symbolism: Léon Spilliaert and Piet Mondrian

Two landscape artists, the first Belgian, the second Dutch, perpetuated the influence of Symbolism into the early twentieth century, although one difference distinguishes them, for the latter was to become a master of abstract art.

Léon Spilliaert (1881-1946) was born and lived in Ostend, like his senior, James Ensor. Restless by nature, he would spend part of the night roaming alone through that resort town in the off-season, sketching the dark, deserted beaches, breakwaters, and public squares. His pictures create a powerful impression of loneliness and melancholy which is further heightened by their geometric construction, as if the artist wanted to bore deep down beneath the picture plane toward elusive vanishing points. There are few human figures in these paintings, and those few only seem to accentuate the solitude and mysteriousness of the setting. Influenced by Munch, Spilliaert seems in turn to announce Giorgio de Chirico's metaphysical art, though the latter was surely not acquainted with this artist's little-known and only recently discovered work. Deeply influenced too by the Symbolist atmosphere and the dead cities that Khnopff and Degouve de Nuncques evoked, Spilliaert produced a pictorial oeuvre closely allied to the melancholy poetry of Maurice Maeterlinck, whose books he illustrated as well.

Piet Mondriaan (1872-1944)—the artist dropped the second "a" of his last name only after his arrival in Paris in 1912—was at the beginning of the century a meticulous landscape artist in the luminous vein of The Hague school. He does not appear to have been much interested in the Rosicrucian doctrine at the time Toorop and Thorn Prikker were, but after 1908, specifically after encountering Toorop (who taught him the rudiments of the Pointillist technique), he too became fascinated with spiritualism. He may have read some of the theosophical classics around this time; it is known that he owned a copy of the Symbolists's bible, Schuré's *Les grands initiés*, as well as Madame Blavatsky's *Isis Unveiled*, which he annotated carefully. In 1909, he joined the Theosophical Society in Amsterdam[7]. He might have passed for a belated Symbolist were it not for the fact that already at that time

Léon Spilliaert
White Robes, White Sheets
1912, gouache and pastel, 90 × 70
Museum voor Schone Kunsten, Ostend
This pair of white silhouettes seen from the rear, walking through a flat landscape delimited by a row of poplars bending in the wind, might be medieval monks—or figures in fancy dress returning from a carnaval ball. Most of Spilliaert's pictures have this feeling of mystery and strangeness.

his works had begun to reflect the formal innovations of Cubism: for instance, *Evolution* (1910-1911, Gemeentemuseum, The Hague), a triptych that depicts in each panel a woman at different stages of her ascent toward supreme knowledge, or *The Passion Flower* (1908-1909, *ibidem*), an inspired portrait that Delville would not have disowned. Like Péladan, Mondrian the theosophist believed it was the mission of the artist to guide mankind spiritually. After his years of Symbolist apprenticeship while evolving along similar lines as Franz Kupka, he elaborated the theory that was to lead him, during his stay in Paris, toward total abstraction.

Piet Mondrian
Evolution
1910-1911, oil on canvas, in three panels forming a triptych; (central panel: 183×87.5; side panels: 178×85)
Gemeentemuseum, The Hague
The artist has used the medieval triptych to express his symbolic message. Before attaining the perception of divine light, that is to say complete knowledge (central panel), man must withdraw from the material world (left panel) and focus on his inner self (right panel). Blue is the astral color *par excellence*; the six-pointed star (Solomon's seal) symbolizes the sum of hermetic wisdom; the triangle stands for divine mystery.

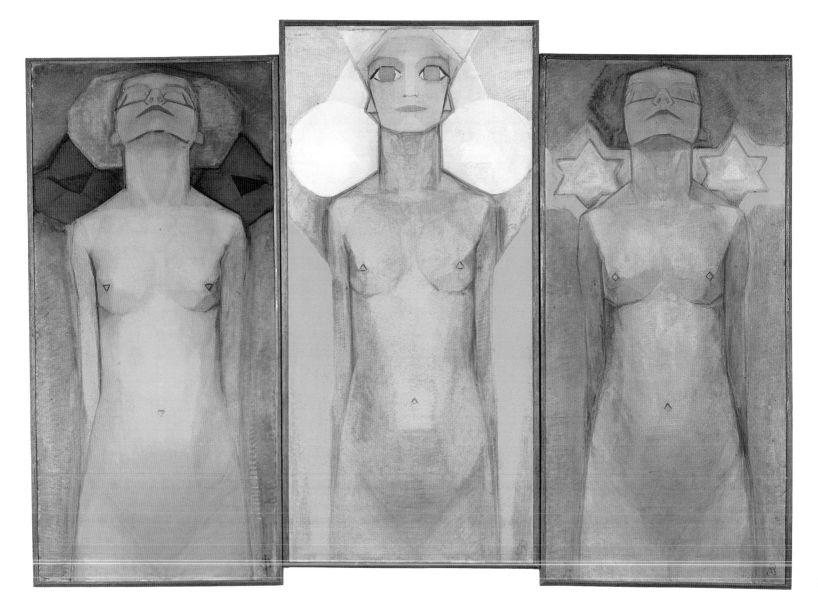

Ferdinand Hodler's pantheism

Ferdinand Hodler
Night
**1889-1890, oil on canvas,
116 × 299
Kunstmuseum, Bern**

This painting, according to the artist, does not represent a particular night, but "the totality of diverse nocturnal impressions." The key idea is that sleep prefigures death. The central figure is a sleeper in the throes of a nightmare; his wracked body and twisted features also seem to express fear at the coming of death. Thus the inscription on the frame: "More than one man has gone to sleep calmly in the evening not to wake up again in the morning."

The Bernese painter Ferdinand Hodler (1853-1918) had an often difficult life, overshadowed by unhappiness and death, complicated by stormy love affairs; his work was deeply affected by the alternating periods of hardship and hope he lived through.

Trained as a landscape artist in the school of Barthélemy Menn, he also studied Dürer, Holbein, and Courbet, who spent his last years in Switzerland. Throughout his life, he created compositions that were, whatever their subjects, robust and down to earth, and he never stopped painting landscapes; few painters have rendered the majesty of the Alps as powerfully as he did.

However, as early as 1880, Hodler began to frequent Symbolist circles, under the aegis of the Geneva poet Louis Duchosel, who ran a review promoting Symbolist writing and the taste for Wagner in Switzerland. Inevitably, Hodler was drawn to Paris, where he discovered Puvis de Chavannes's murals: they were to be a lasting influence on his art.

His conversion to Idealist art came early. In 1884, he painted *Private Dialogue* (Kunstmuseum, Bern) which depicts a nude youth gesturing ecstatically as he climbs a path slanting through a steep landscape. In the following years, he tackled the ambitious theme of mankind confronting the mysteries of life and death in compositions that combine realism (more than once his nudes and embracing couples fell afoul of the censorship in Geneva and even Paris) with complex allegorical messages. He conceived his first masterpiece, *Night* (1889-1890, Kunstmuseum, Bern), as "the great symbol of Death."

Hodler was soon noticed by Péladan, who considered him the "foremost contemporary Germanic painter," and was invited to show his work at the Salon de la Rose + Croix. During the 1890s Hodler mainly painted pessimistic paintings, such as *The Disappointed Souls* (1891-1892, Kunstmuseum, Bern), *The World-Weary* (Foundation for Art, Küsnacht), *Eurhythmy* (1894-1895, Kunstmuseum, Bern), with their rows of dejected old men or women composed according to the artist's "principle of parallels." In the last years of the decade, Hodler began to turn toward less lugubrious subjects, and evoked the mysteries of life and love in gentle, luminous landscapes centered around gaunt female figures. *Day* (1899-1900, Kunstmuseum, Bern) and *Spring* (1901, Museum Folkwang, Essen) are good examples of

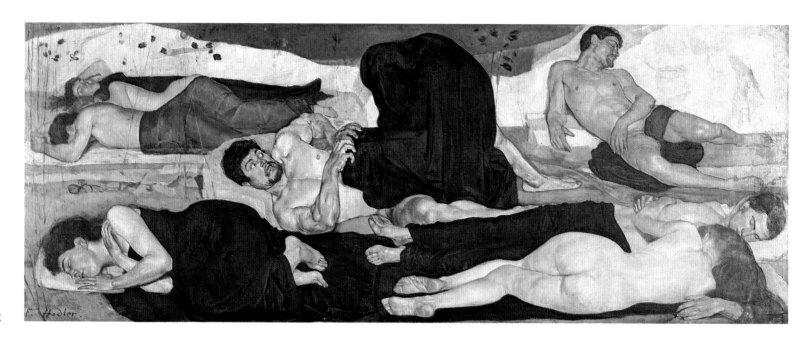

this new phase in his art reflecting a more relaxed period in his life, when Hodler was beginning to attain fame.

Much of Hodler's time and energy, like Puvis de Chavannes's, went into large-scale commemorative paintings for public buildings, such as *The Retreat From Marignan* (1899-1900, Schweizerisches Landesmuseum, Zurich), the decorations for the town hall of Hanover and the University of Iena, which bear witness to his popularity in German-speaking countries (whereas in Paris he counted relatively few admirers).

Hodler has given us his theory of art in *The Mission of the Artist* (1897), which shows clearly that, even around the time he came under the influence of the Rose+Croix, he retained his pantheistic sense of connection to nature. "When the artist makes a picture," he wrote, "he borrows elements from the pre-existing world he lives in. The more imaginative artist is guided by nature; she is the greatest source of facts; it is she who stimulates the imagination. The deeper one probes into the mind of nature, the more complete is the notion of it one renders." Hodler attached a great deal of importance to the emotional weight of tones and colors (somber tones expressed sadness, light ones were joyful, in a symbolic system derived from Goethe), but his most original contribution is the "principle of parallels." This consists of arranging comparable figures or motifs in a symmetrical or frieze-like composition, in order to give the painting a greater unity through repetition and thus to capture the spectactor's attention more effectively by creating a more powerful and durable impression.

This approach to composition owes more than a little to Puvis de Chavannes and has much in common with Maurice Denis's ideas as well; nevertheless, Hodler produced a strong, highly individual oeuvre in which, to cite one of his contemporary critics, "man is always, even in his most abstract appearances, a son of the earth, wholly in the grips of earthly passions and an earthly fate."

We might associate Hodler and his robust personality with his more retiring friend Albert Trachsel (1863-1929), who studied architecture at the Zurich Polytechnicum and the Ecole des Beaux-Arts in Paris. Well acquainted with the literary world of the French capital—he himself wrote Symbolist verse—Trachsel showed a large

Ferdinand Hodler
The Dream
1897-1903, watercolor, 95 × 65
Private Collection, Zurich
Hodler often links the episodes in human life to the seasons' cycle. Here love is associated with spring. The artist has unwittingly illustrated the theory of sexual sublimation (notice the phallic shape of the rose in the young girl's fingers), and it is tempting to speculate that Sigmund Freud saw this watercolor in 1904 at the Twentieth Vienna Secession exhibit where Hodler was guest of honor.

Albert Trachsel
Dream Landscape
After 1905, oil on canvas,
102 × 127
Private Collection, Switzerland
Trachsel, in his dream landscapes, transforms his country's
natural phenomena into symbolic worlds that border on abstraction.

number of drawings highlighted with watercolors, in the style of the late eighteenth century
architectural fantasies, at the first Rose + Croix
Salon. "The artist's aim was to create an architectural poem, to erect a dream in stone," he
wrote in the presentation of his series of *Real
Celebrations*. Each plate depicts a temple or palace
celebrating Infinity, Eternity, Mystery, the
Mountain, the Ocean, Heroism, Liberty, Purity,
Justice, Joy, the Will, Dreams, and so on, ending
with Silence, Rest, Grief, and Death. The series
was published in an album in 1897, and was
followed by a new series, *Dream Landscapes*, more
abstract in manner, based on the annual cycle of
the seasons in the artist's native Switzerland (*Sunrise*, *The Cascade*, *The Island of Blossoming Trees*,
etc., preserved in the Solothurn, Bern, and Geneva art museums).

Carlos Schwabe, a mystic of death

Of German extraction and raised in Geneva,
Carlos Schwabe (1866-1926) first arrived in Paris
at the age of ten and rarely left France after that.
In 1891, Péladan noticed one of his first paintings, *The Evening Bells* (Museo Nacional de Belas
Artes, Rio de Janeiro), and entrusted him with
the task of designing the poster for the first Salon
de la Rose + Croix. This poster, which shows two
gauzily-clad women climbing the stairs that lead
to the ideal, while a third figure, mired in materialism, looks on helplessly, contributed significantly to the success of the show. Although
Schwabe exhibited at only one of Péladan's
salons, he placed his considerable gifts as a draftsman (which, thanks to the work of J.-D. Jumeau-
Lafond, have at last been recognized) in the

Carlos Schwabe
Grief
1893, oil on canvas, 155 × 104
Musée d'art et d'histoire,
Geneva
Schwabe's imagination fed on
the haunting themes of death
and grief. Here the artist gives
us an arresting plastic translation of grief: a slender silhouette
veiled in black pacing between
graves.

145

service of Symbolist literature and composed remarkable drawings, many of them enhanced with watercolors, for volumes of poetry by Baudelaire, Catulle Mendès, Albert Samain, Maurice Maeterlinck, Stéphane Mallarmé, and above all Emile Zola's *Le rêve*, the only novel in the Rougon-Macquart cycle devoted to the transcendent.

Combining the influences of Dürer, Hokusai, and the Pre-Raphaelites, Schwabe's meticulous, analytic draftsmanship lends a definite meaning to each detail. Thus the flowers and plants he drew from nature at different stages of their life —their budding, blossoming, and withering— appear as so many symbolic correlatives of human existence. Haunted by the notions of virginal purity and death, Schwabe painted watercolors and oils whose cold tones and themes are strange indeed. His masterpiece is unquestion-

ably *The Death of the Grave-Digger* (1895, Musée du Louvre, Paris), depicting an angel of death with long green scythe-like wings come to fetch an old man who is digging a grave. Nor is this the only picture in which Schwabe gave death a woman's features (those of his own wife, in fact); there is *The Day of the Dead, Grief* (1893, Musée d'art et d'histoire, Geneva), and *The Wave* (1907, *ibidem*) which, with hindsight, seems a premonition of the chaos of World War One, with its unfurling wave of screaming women's faces. The preliminary charcoal sketches for that disturbing work bear witness to the exceptional graphic gifts of this secretive painter who unhappily was unable to renew his art and wound up becoming a rather caricatural figure of the Symbolist artist trapped in an imagery—lilies and spiritlike figures—that was quickly outmoded after the turn of the century.

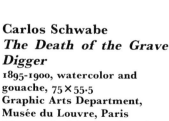

Carlos Schwabe
The Death of the Grave Digger
1895-1900, watercolor and gouache, 75 × 55.5
Graphic Arts Department, Musée du Louvre, Paris
The angel of death, whose long green wings are shaped like scythes, has just alighted like a great bird on the edge of a grave being dug by an old man in a snowy cemetery. The artist has used the entire Symbolist repertory of signs and plants.

Augusto Giacometti
Night
**1903, tempera on canvas,
251.5 × 110
Kunsthaus, Zurich**
This large canvas combines the
typically Symbolist themes of
woman, night, dreams, and
death, with decorative floral
motifs inspired by the plates of
his master Eugène Grasset's famous book, *La plante et ses ap-
plications ornementales*, published
just before the turn of the century.

Other Swiss artists influenced by Symbolism

Eugène Grasset (1845-1917), one of the
pioneers of Art Nouveau in France, was briefly
a Symbolist. Fascinated, like the English Pre-
Raphaelites, by all that was medieval, he exhibited at the first Salon de la Rose + Croix. In
the 1890s he painted a series of watercolors on the
theme of women's feelings—*Apprehension, Anxiety,
Jealousy, Meditation,* and *Women and Wolves* (1892,
Musée des arts décoratifs, Paris), the last showing
several women (witches?) flying through a wood,
panicking at the gleaming eyes of black wolves
lurking among tree trunks.

Grasset exerted a decisive influence on his
young countryman, Augusto Giacometti (1877-
1947), who came to Paris in 1897 to study the
decorative arts and frequent the literary scene. A
fervent admirer of Puvis de Chavannes and the
stained glass windows and mosaics of the Middle
Ages, Giacometti (a cousin of the sculptor, many
of whose works, like his own paintings, can be
seen at the Zurich Kunsthaus) painted a number
of canvases in the Symbolist vein in the early
years of the twentieth century. They are, by their
tones and forms, highly original pictures (*Night*,

147

1903, and *Adam and Eve*, 1907, both at the Kunsthaus, Zurich). Keenly interested in the experiments with color in the decorative arts around this time, Giacometti evolved after 1910 toward an abstraction of sorts, which consisted in placing extremely tactile spots of color in juxtaposition. "I began to paint a picture of flowers," he once said, "and ended up keeping only the colors."

The Zurich artist Albert Welti (1862-1912) went to Munich for his training and studied under Böcklin. Influenced by the Wagnerian cult, he produced a series of etchings to illustrate the composer's works and painted pictures in a voluntarily archaic manner, many of them inspired by Nordic legends. *The Horsemen of the Fog* (1896, Kunstmuseum, Basle) and *Walpurgis Night* (1896-1897, Kunsthaus, Zurich) depict savage nightmares, in contrast to *The House of Dreams* (1897, *ibidem*) which expresses the isolation of individuals locked in their own reverie.

Albert Welti
The House of Dreams
1897, tempera on cardboard,
32 × 44.5
Kunsthaus, Zurich
Practicing a deliberately archaic kind of art, not unlike that of his master, Arnold Böcklin, Welti has set this scene in a Swiss-style summerhouse overlooking the Lake of Zurich. Each member of the family shown here seems absorbed in some private dream or fantasy, oblivious of his or her surroundings.

Notes

[1] See the exhibition catalogue, *Le groupe des XX et son temps*, Musées Royaux des Beaux-Arts, Brussels, and Rijksmuseum Kröller-Müller, Otterlo, 1962.

[2] Francine-Claire Legrand, *Ensor cet inconnu*, Brussels, 1971.

[3] Francine-Claire Legrand, *Le symbolisme en Belgique*, Brussels, 1971, p. 114.

[4] *Ibidem*, pp. 36 and 45.

[5] Emile Verhaeren, "Le Salon des XX," in *La Revue indépendante*, March 1887.

[6] Francine-Claire Legrand, *Le symbolisme en Belgique*, op. cit., p. 96.

[7] See Herbert Henkels, "Portrait de l'artiste par lui-même: éléments pour une biographie intellectuelle," in *L'atelier de Mondrian*, Paris, 1982, pp. 104-123.

2

The Scandinavian countries

The young Scandinavian painters of the late nineteenth century, after studying the rudiments of art in their own country, often spent years in Italy, Germany, and, increasingly after 1880, France. Paris, for example, boasted nearly fifty Swedish artists toward 1885. They usually enrolled in the ateliers of recognized masters (members of the Academy, teachers at the Ecole des Beaux-Arts), but this did not prevent them from keeping abreast of the latest literary and artistic movements. Not too surprisingly, Gauguin's circle included several Danes, notably Francesco Mogens Ballin (1871-1914) and Jens Ferdinand Willumsen (1863-1958)—after all, the artist's wife Mette came from Copenhagen and, following their separation, returned there with her children to make a living of sorts selling her husband's paintings. A number of Swedish and Finnish painters also lived and worked in Brittany. Toward the end of the century, northern Europe was swept by a Christian revival, and this undoubtedly contributed to the spread of Symbolism and the ideas of Joséphin Péladan in that part of the world. Upon their return, these Scandinavian artists, many of whom harbored deeply nationalistic feelings, tended to reinterpret their own peculiarly luminous landscapes, their myths and legends and folk traditions, in much the same way that Gauguin and his friends had approached the landscapes and peasants of Brittany. This produced a true renaissance of Scandinavian painting which is known as National Romanticism[1].

149

Sweden

Ernst Josephson (1851-1906) arrived in Paris in 1879 and lived for almost a decade in France. Drawn at first to painting out of doors yet fascinated too by Scandinavian mythology, he devoted painting after painting to the folktale figure Näcken, who had the gift of bewitching humans with his music (*Näcken or the Water Spirit*, 1882, Nationalmuseum, Stockholm). Seeking solitude, he fled to Brittany where he engaged in spiritualist séances, summoning the spirit of his famous eighteenth-century countryman, Emanuel Swedenborg, the founder of a religious sect

△ **Richard Bergh**
Death of the Day
1895, charcoal and oil
on canvas, 37 × 83
Nationalmuseum, Stockholm

▷ **Ernst Josephson**
Näcken
(The Water Spirit)
c. 1890, oil on canvas, 144 × 114
Nationalmuseum, Stockholm
A tormented artist who immersed himself in a dreamworld of spirits, to the extent of losing his sanity, Josephson was fascinated by this divinity in Scandinavian mythology, a sort of evil Orpheus who, with his music, cast spells on human beings.

that the Symbolists, beginning with Baudelaire, thought very highly of. The quest for mystical "correspondences" between nature and the other world, however, eventually unhinged Josephson's mind, though it did not diminish his creativity. Identifying with Christ, he produced highly original canvases in which he endeavored to render his mystical visions with an energy that recalls Expressionism. For example, *The Holy Sacrament* (around 1890, Nationalmuseum, Stockholm) depicts a radiant Christ surrounded by El Greco-like figures in ecstatic poses.

Son of a landscape artist, Richard Bergh (1858-1919) followed in his father's footsteps yet was deeply influenced, during his stay in France, by Puvis de Chavannes and Gauguin. In his canvas *Death of the Day* (1895, Nationalmuseum, Stockholm), with its two figures sleeping by the seaside at sunset, the imprint of the master of Pont-Aven is clearly discernible. Bergh had, moreover, bought one of Gauguin's paintings in 1892. After he returned to Sweden, the artist had a major role in the National Romantic movement as president of the Swedish Artists's Association and leader of a group of painters who rebelled against the conservatism of the Stockholm Academy and the Nationalmuseum, which he was eventually named director of. A great believer in national art, he strove in his landscapes to render the symbiosis that unites the artist and his native soil. The couple gazing religiously at the forest from their balcony in *Summer Evening in the North* (1899-1900), Göteborgs Konstmuseum, Göteborg) is the expression of an almost pantheistic fervor for nature.

It is impossible not to mention August Strindberg (1849-1912) in any discussion of Symbolism in Sweden[2]. That literary giant, who escapes easy classification for his genius drew on Zola's Naturalism as much as the esoteric, was a powerful influence over turn-of-the-century Scandinavian artists, many of whom were friends of his, in particular Richard Bergh, Ernst Josephson, and above all Edvard Munch. As an art critic he himself was influenced by Péladan's ideas. Of the latter he wrote: "...he brought the Germanic civilization to his country and, for all of Europe, opened hitherto closed doors." Strindberg admired Puvis de Chavannes and was well acquainted with Gauguin; he himself painted on occasion, more or less as a therapy when depressed. It is his seascapes that are the most widely known, painted in a tormented vein between 1892 and 1900, almost abstract visions of storms which are clearly pretexts for expressing the primal chaos, reflecting the artist-writer's principle that an art work has "an exoteric side that every one can see, even if it is difficult, and an esoteric side, reserved for the artist and the happy few." In an article written in French ("Des arts nouveaux! ou le hasard dans la production artistique," 1894), Strindberg describes the creative process as an unconscious operation that the artist himself cannot control, leading him to paint Tännhäuser's cave, for example, instead of the forest he set out to render. "The art to come," he concludes, will "imitate nature more or less, mainly nature's way of creating."

Denmark

The Danish artist Jens Ferdinand Willumsen (1863-1958) became acquainted with Gauguin and his circle at Pont-Aven and was especially receptive to their spiritual and pictorial message. He was drawn to the same books as Gauguin—notably Carlyle's *Sartor Resartus*—who wrote to him in 1890, "You are right to say that we are somehow related. If we learn to recognize each other and to band together, and if we certify our faith through mutual affection, we will in time acquire the strength to accomplish our work."[3]

His paintings and bas-reliefs, on display for the most part at the Willumsens Museum in Frederikssund near Copenhagen, often depict Breton scenes and landscapes in a style akin to Sérusier's. Willumsen later lived in Norway where he applied the Synthetic principles he had learned at Pont-Aven to mountain views. His masterpiece, *Jotunheim* (1892-1893, Willumsens Museum, Frederikssund) seeks to render man's harsh relationship with nature in that "bleak and austere" locality of the Far North, "covered year-round with snow and ice, in a world uninhabitable to man." The artist has given the painting a frame cut from a copper sheet and decorated with the "symbolic, carved figures shaped by this sinister environment." Some of them stand for learning and the quest for knowledge, others represent life without aim; altogether, the artist's intention was to "produce effects analogous to those created by architecture and music." Still later, Willumsen adopted a more directly Expressionist style, particularly in his violent use of color, but continued to express the anguish and fear of man confronted with hostile elements (*After the Storm*, 1905, Nasjonalgalleriet, Oslo).

Jens Ferdinand Willumsen
Jotunheim
1892-1893, oil on zinc and enamel on copper, 105 × 277
J.F. Willumsens Museum, Frederikssund
"The figures on the left," says the artist, "represent those who, through their knowledge and rational powers, seek obstinately to discover the link between the infinitely great and the infinitely small. The infinitely great is symbolized by a starry nebula, the infinitely small, by microbes... The right panel represents goalless beings: at the bottom, a man repairing a net which another man is undoing; in the middle, a group of unconcerned people; at the top, a figure who stands for chimerical dreams."

Finland

In an era when Finland still rankled at being a grand duchy in the Russian Empire, having previously been under Swedish domination, its more enlightened minds, writers, artists, and musicians (Sibelius), longed for freedom and independence—finally obtained in 1920—and cultivated their national pride by extolling the *Kalevala*, that epic of 23,000 verses celebrating the mythic deeds of the Carelians. Toward 1890, a number of young Finnish artists traveled to France in order to study art there, following the example of Albert Edelfelt (1854-1905) who had settled in Paris and made a career as a portraitist after the manner of Bonnat.

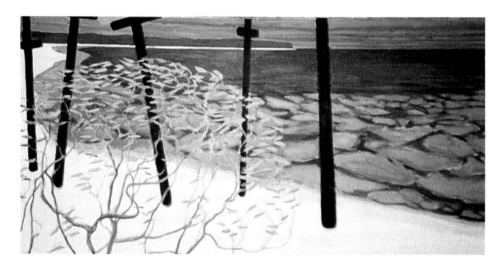

Akseli Gallen-Kallela
Autumn
**1902, tempera on canvas,
77 × 143
Sigrid Juselius Foundation,
Helsinki**
With a remarkable economy of means and in a highly stylized manner, the artist gives this landscape a manifestly symbolic dimension. Autumn presages winter which will soon bury all of nature beneath a thick blanket of ice and snow like a shroud, an image that the four black crosses planted in the middle of the road readily suggest.

Trained in the Impressionist Naturalism of Bastien-Lepage, Akseli Gallen-Kallela (1865-1931) was a familiar figure in Symbolist circles in Paris and Berlin. In themselves the titles of his paintings—*Ad Astra*, *The Road to Death*, *The Symposium*—make it eloquently clear that this was an artist who sought to translate metaphysical preoccupations into pictorial terms. An earnest patriot, he found his vocation in illustrating the *Kalevala*, a task that occupied him until his death. His vast knowledge of symbols allowed him to render the great existential themes of Finnish mythology.

Gallen-Kallela's disciple, Hugo Simberg (1873-1917) explored a very different area. He began by declaring his obsession with death and

his fear of the devil in watercolors that combined a naive gaucherie with a miniature-like precision, as if he hoped to tame his lugubrious preoccupations with irony. "I believe that an art work is something which speaks to me of another world and plunges me into the atmosphere that the artist set out to create," he once explained. "It ought to turn my thoughts toward subjects I do not reflect on every day and which I will continue to ponder over long, long after."[4] This evocative art, in some ways like Redon's conception of painting, is expressed, in a manner at once highly colored and extremely detailed, in small gouaches that inevitably recall Paul Klee. Simberg's elves, devils, and skeletons are of course related to the *danses macabres* of Scandinavian and Germanic medieval frescoes which Simberg, a great admirer of Böcklin, studied closely, along with the engravings of Holbein and the frescoes of the Campo Santo in Pisa. But, as one critic has remarked, "In Simberg's work death is not the grim reaper... His figures of death are generally not cruel. Death does not carry out its labor of destruction amid a reveling crowd seeking to lose themselves in mundane pleasures, as in the writings of Edgar Allan Poe; it picks an impoverished peasant or (as often happened in those times of high infant mortality) an innocent child... Death is as natural as life itself."[5] Seen in this light, the artist's *Garden of Death* (1896, Ateneumin taidemuseo, Helsinki), with its three almost affable skeletons lovingly tending their modest flower patch, has a certain poetry, as does his *Death Listening* (1897, *ibidem*), which depicts a skeleton bringing three little white flowers to a dying woman who is listening for the last time to a tune played by a young village fiddler.

Simberg did not limit himself to painting such fascinating vignettes, however; he also worked in oil and fresco, repeating the same Symbolist themes on a much larger scale, as can be seen in the decorations and stained glass windows he executed after the turn of the century for the Cathedral of St John at Tampere (Finland).

Magnus Enckell (1870-1925) also pursued at length a dialogue with death. He came to Paris in 1891, where his philosophical inclinations (he was already familiar with Plato and Swedenborg) naturally drew him to read Schuré and Péladan and to attend the meetings of the Rose+

Magnus Enckell
*Youth before
a Skull*
1893, watercolor and charcoal
on paper, 70 × 100
**Ateneumin taidemuseo,
Helsinki**
The treatment of space and the
sober tones reveal the influence
of Carrière. Thoroughly steeped
in the mysticism of the Rose +
Croix, this work can nevertheless be compared to the seventeenth century "vanity" paintings whose message reminds
man of his own mortality. The
originality of this work derives
in great part from the figure's
youthfulness.

Croix. He seems to have been particularly impressed with the Platonic myth of androgyny as
interpreted by Péladan. The brooding naked
adolescents that are the subject of many of his
paintings between 1892 and 1895 illustrate this
at once equivocal and idealist theory; the extremely simple plastic means by which they are
rendered reveal the double influence of Puvis de
Chavannes and Eugène Carrière. Paintings like
the *Two Boys* (1892), *Youth before a Skull* (1893),
The Awakening (1894), *Fantasy* (1895)—most of
them hanging in the Ateneumin taidemuseo in
Helsinki—are timeless evocations of adolescents
confronted with the problems of existence; they
also reflect the inner struggle of the artist torn between his longings for purity and the yearnings
of the flesh. Enckell left Paris in 1895 and moved
to Italy, where he came under the influence of
Böcklin (who spent his final years in Tuscany),
and, thence, commissioned to decorate the
Tampare cathedral with Simberg, he returned to
Finland.

Hugo Simberg
The Wounded Angel
1903, oil on canvas, 127 × 154
**Ateneumin taidemuseo,
Helsinki**
Pessimistic by nature if not de-
pressive, the artist expresses
here his tragic view of existence.
The wounded angel symbolizes
love and the impossibility of
ever attaining happiness (one of
his wings is broken). Simberg is
expressing his belief that life is
suffering and grief, and reality
is inherently rotten (reality is
two pigheaded village boys and
a desolate landscape whose
monotony is barely alleviated
by a few timid flowers).

153

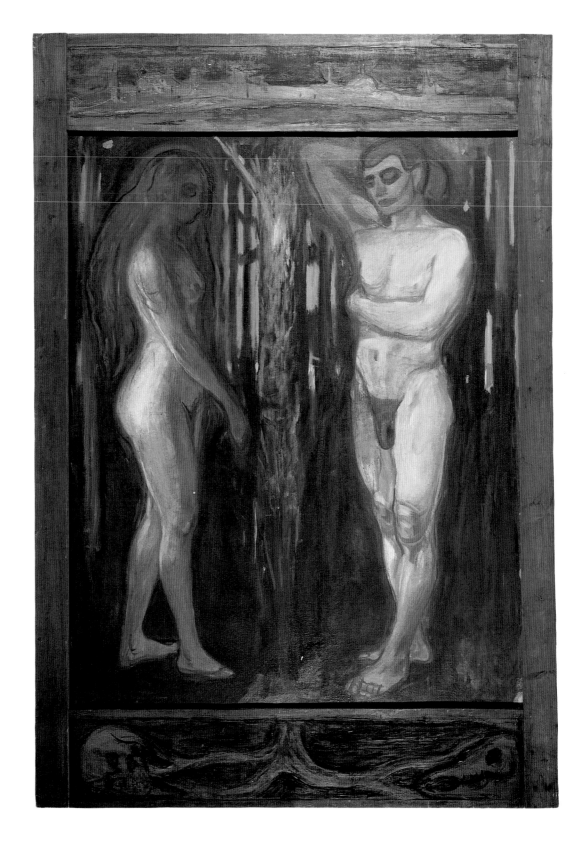

Edvard Munch
Metabolism
1899, oil on canvas, 172.5 × 142
Munch-museet, Oslo

Around 1900, after portraying human suffering in an autobiographical manner, the artist began to approach the great problems of existence from a more philosophical standpoint. Here he shows Adam and Eve standing on either side of the Tree of Life, whose roots find nourishment in the earth where the dead lie buried.

Edvard Munch: the torn self as source for the art work

At first glance, the painting of the Norwegian artist Edvard Munch (1863-1944) seems so free, so full of experimental truth, that one is inclined to describe it as Expressionist rather than Symbolist. Yet Munch belonged wholly to the Symbolist generation. The emotions in his paintings which have human feelings or states of mind as their titles (melancholy, anguish, jealousy, despair, loneliness, consolation, attraction, separation) were felt deeply by the artist himself before they were set down on canvas and made into art works[6].

As a child Munch had witnessed death, and it is hardly surprising that one of his very earliest paintings, *The Sick Child* (1885, Nasjonalgalleriet, Oslo), was conceived not as a simple Naturalist scene but as an expression of genuine grief, a resurrection of a private memory—the death of the artist's sister—which left him with a permanent scar. On his arrival in Paris in 1889, with a grant to study in Léon Bonnat's reputed atelier at the Ecole des Beaux-Arts, Munch mapped out a program for himself, giving art an essentially moral task. In the diary he kept throughout his life, he noted: "We will not paint interiors any longer, no people reading, no women knitting. We must paint living beings who breathe and feel, suffer and love. The public will have to understand the sacredness and power that this reveals, and will have to doff their hats, as in church."

A sedulous reader of Kierkegaard (whose philosophy, in a nutshell, is that subjectivity is Truth) and Maeterlinck, Munch shared the poverty and riotous living of many writers who were, like himself, Bohemians (and were often the first to understand and defend his art). In Paris, he befriended the Danish Symbolist poet Emanuel Goldstein, who compared literary creativity to a "blood flower" rooted in the author's entrails —an image that the artist was to express visually in a number of his paintings as an enormous reddish flower or plant. Later, in Berlin, Munch became closely acquainted with the Polish critic and novelist Stanislaw Przybyszewsky (who, in his more or less autobiographical writings, describes a world dominated by sexual impulses) and above all the Swedish dramatist August Strindberg. Strindberg became more than just a

Edvard Munch
Madonna (Conception)
1895-1902, color lithograph, 60.5 × 44.2
Munch-museet, Oslo
"The tree of the knowledge of good and evil. The pause—the entire world has stopped turning. Your face reflects all the beauty of the earth. Your lips, crimson like the fruit to come, are dolefully ajar. A corpse's smile. Behold life reaching out to death. The chain linking the thousand departed generations to the thousand generations yet to be born is once again made whole." (From the artist's notebooks.)

Edvard Munch
Woman (The Sphinx)
1894, oil on canvas, 164 × 250
Rasmus Meyer und Bergen
Billedgalleri, Bergen
This large canvas sums up the whole Symbolist generation's attitude toward woman. On the right, man like a new Oedipus is trying to fathom the enigma of woman, who is "at once a saint, a courtesan, and a heart-sick lover," as the artist puts it. Between the man and the woman on the right blooms a blood-flower, a motif that, found throughout Munch's work, symbolizes artistic creation, "An art conceived with the heart's blood."

drinking companion: he was one of the first to champion Munch's painting, and he even absorbed its intensity into his own universe. It was Strindberg who gave the lasting title _Vampire_ to a canvas Munch had originally named _Love and Suffering_ (1893-1894, Göteborgs Konstmuseum). Around this time too, Munch discovered the art of Gauguin, Rops, and more importantly Böcklin, whose _Island of the Dead_ he ranked above every other painting.

Even though his canvases seem reactions to situations that the artist endured in the course of his alcohol-sodden existence (he was eventually interned in a psychiatric clinic because of his drinking), his work nevertheless reflects a deeply pessimistic, and at the same time resolutely coherent, outlook on life. Nearly all of the pictures he painted between 1893 and 1902—his most productive years—are parts of a grand project he called _The Frieze of Life_ which was exhibited in its entirety in Berlin in 1902. Munch

had organized all his work until then around four fundamental themes: "Birth and Love," "The Flowering and Waning of Love," "The Anxiety of Living," and "Death." He wanted to house these works in a "Temple of Art" which he designed himself in the hope that the Norwegian government would build it to house the _Frieze_ permanently. This it may have been in order to fulfil a lifelong ambition that he bequeathed his studio—containing thousands of paintings, drawings, and engravings—to the City of Oslo, where the museum that bears his name opened its doors in 1963.

Munch's pessimism, contrary to that of many other artists of his generation, was unrelieved by any otherwordly considerations. Life is one long trial, without a glimmer of hope or redemption, at least in his work prior to 1910. He endlessly repeats the same leitmotif of the struggle between the sexes or, even more darkly, of woman's possession of man. Strindberg hardly exaggerated the artist's underlying message when he commented à propos of *The Kiss* (1896-1897, Munch Museet, Oslo): "The fusion of two beings, of which the smaller, shaped like a carp, seems about to devour the larger, as do microbes, vermin, vampires, and women." Munch's attitude toward the female gender—the sphinx woman, the she-spider—is fundamentally no different than that of the artists of Gustave Moreau's generation.

Munch, who began to elaborate his oeuvre as early as 1890, an oeuvre of strikingly original forms and colors, created a new plastic language that has much in common with that of the Fauves (who were the scandal of the 1905 Salon d'Automne) but does not appear to have influenced them, even though Munch had exhibited works earlier at the Salon des Indépendants. He uses color to create emotions, whereas they tend to employ it to construct space. On the other hand, the link between Munch's art, which was very well known in Germany, and Expressionism and the *Brücke* movement hardly needs to be demonstrated.

During the early years of the twentieth century, Munch's paintings were at once intensely admired and violently attacked—a state of affairs which the artist took some satisfaction in. Munch wrote, "Like Leonardo, who studied the interior of human anatomy and dissected cadavers, I seek to dissect the soul. He was obliged to write in ciphers, for in his time it was a crime to cut open bodies. Today, it is the dissection of psychic phenomena that people consider immoral and inconsiderate." After 1909 (the year he underwent psychiatric treatment) he dominated the art scene, even in his native land where, being elevated to the rank of a Puvis de Chavannes, he was commissioned to decorate the main lecture hall at the University of Oslo. Settling with a degree of permanence in that city, he reiterated the themes of his youth right up to the end of his life, but less convincingly and less authentically as an established master than he had as a struggling young artist, as if the fact of having gained a certain mental equilibrium and leading a more orderly existence had deprived him of the ability to plumb the depths of the self with his former acuity.

The other great Norwegian artist of the era, the sculptor Gustav Vigeland (1869-1943), never acquired the universal recognition that Munch enjoyed. One has to travel to Oslo to see his works: he has his museum there and even his park graced by 200 of his sculptures[7]. In a style that betrays the influence of Rodin, whose studio he frequented during his sojourn in Paris, Vigeland evoked, in a production that spans almost four decades, the themes of life and death in creations of monumental proportions, the most successful of which is a fountain surrounded by twenty sculptured groups portraying figures of all ages enacting, in the branches of a tree of life, the different stages of human existence.

Notes

[1] For this chapter the author has relied extensively on the well-documented catalog of two recent exhibits: *Northern Light. Realism and Symbolism in Scandinavian Art. 1880-1910*, by K. Varnedoc, Washington, New York, Minneapolis, Göteborg, 1982-1983; and *Lumières du Nord. La peinture scandinave. 1885-1905*, Musée du Petit Palais, Paris, 1987.

[2] See the catalog of the *August Strindberg* exhibit by G. Söderström, Rijksmuseum Vincent Van Gogh, Amsterdam, 1987.

[3] Letter quoted in W. Jaworska, *Gauguin et l'Ecole de Pont-Aven, op. cit.*, p. 216.

[4] Letter cited in S. Sarajas-Korte, *Lumières du Nord, op. cit.*, pp. 294-298.

[5] *Ibidem*, p. 294.

[6] See A. Eggum, *Edvard Munch. Peintures. Esquisses. Etudes*, Paris, 1983; and U.M. Schneede, *Edvard Munch. Les chefs-d'œuvre de jeunesse*, Munich-Paris, 1988.

[7] See the catalog of the *Gustav Vigeland* exhibit by T. Wikborg, Musée Rodin, Paris, 1981.

Mikhail Vrubel
Demon's Head
1890-1891, illustration for Lermontov's poem,
The Demon
Obsessed by the idea of the devil, whom he did not consider an evil being at all but a
rejected, woebegone angel, Vrubel depicted him ceaselessly over fifteen years as a
desperate-looking and beautiful androgynous being.

3

Central and Eastern Europe

The Russian artist Mikhail Vrubel and the devil's mystique

Mikhail Alexandrovitch Vrubel (1856-1910), a tormented and mystical artist, from his childhood was keenly interested in philosophical literature; Goethe's *Faust* was one of his favorite books. His reading of Mikhail Lermontov's long Romantic poem, *The Demon* (1840), molded his world view and took hold of his imagination so powerfully that, from 1885 on, it became a kind of psychotic obsession which eventually drove him insane[1].

Always on the edge of Russia's main artistic currents—particularly the somewhat Messianic realism of the "Wandering Artists"—Vrubel was drawn, on completing his art studies at the St Petersburg Academy of Fine Arts, to medieval religious painting. He made several trips to Italy, to Venice and Ravenna specifically, to complete his training as a decorator and fresco restorer, and there he acquired his characteristic manner of juxtaposing brightly colored touches in mosaic fashion.

Though he traveled widely in Europe, Vrubel does not seem to have been directly in touch with Symbolist circles. Yet his notion of the devil—a proud, wretched spirit, not originally evil, who struggles desperately to fathom the meaning of life and the universe—has much in common with Péladan's. His fallen angels are lonely, extra-ordinarily handsome youths whose tragic features inspire pity rather than hatred. He depicts them in different poses, seated, flying, sprawling brokenly on the earth, defeated in their struggle which is also the Faustian struggle of the human mind. In 1902, after completing his great canvas, *The Vanquished Devil* (Tretyakov Gallery, Moscow), Vrubel had to be committed to an insane asylum.

Thus Vrubel's career ended at the very moment he was gaining prominence. He was not only a brilliant painter but an interesting decorative artist as well, for he also devoted his talents to creating fine pieces of pottery, founding the "Modern" style, akin to Art Nouveau, in ceramics. Yet his approach, which has more to do with the Romantic world than the world of Symbolism, remains an isolated example in Russian art. Two other Russian artists, Victor Borissov-Mussatov (1870-1905) and Kosma Petrov-Vodkin (1878-1939), lived for some time in Paris and were both influenced by Puvis de Chavannes and Maurice Denis. However their commitment to idealist art remained rather superficial; at the most one notices a touch of gravity present in their harmonious landscapes where pretty young girls are shown dreaming on the banks of reflecting pools.

Polish Symbolists

A kingdom in name only under the rule of the Russian empire beginning in 1815, Poland was shaken repeatedly in the course of the nineteenth century (not to mention other periods of its history) by heroic uprisings. The most desperate of these rebellions occurred in 1863 and brought in response a merciless program of Russification. This, however, failed to eradicate the Polish people's deep-seated nationalism bolstered by the clergy, artists, and writers who, either within the country or in Polish communities throughout Europe, continued to nurture the national identity. The Polish elite banded together in movements like *Modla Polska* (Young Poland) that enjoyed ties with the rest of Europe, notably France, Germany, and Austria. Under the rule of the two latter countries, moreover, several Polish provinces, in particular Cracow, retained a measure of self-determination. The indissoluble attachment the Poles felt for their native soil may be why Polish artists rarely omitted landscapes of their homeland in their paintings[2].

Gauguin's circle at Pont-Aven included a Polish artist, Wladyslaw Slewinsky (1854-1918). Slewinsky seems, however, to have been impervious to the master's spiritual message and was influenced only superficially by the Synthetist technique which he used exclusively for landscapes and still lifes, even after his temporary return to Poland where, incidentally, he never succeeded in adapting.

Jacek Malczewsky (1854-1929) studied art in Cracow under Jan Matejko, the great artist famous for celebrating heroic moments in Polish history. Malczewsky completed his training in Paris and Munich. He seems to have wanted to make a career of illustrating Polish history, but around 1890 began to evolve toward a tormented visionary Symbolism, influenced on the one hand by literary sources and on the other by artists like Segantini, whose work could be seen in Munich, where Malczewsky exhibited his own paintings. His canvas, *The Swirl of Dust* (1893-1894, Muzeum Narodowe, Poznan), depicting a female figure in chains trailing a straggling band of children (a symbolic projection of the motherland abandoning her sons) was clearly inspired by the Italian artist's *Shameless Mothers*.

One of Malczewsky's favorite subjects was the Polish peasant on a country road encountering Death in the guise of a strapping young woman whose wings seem as sharp as the scythe she is honing. Often portraying himself as the central figure in paintings which he occasionally grouped in triptychs, he depicted life around a family mansion, not as a dream but as a long circular journey at the end of which man returns to his birthplace for a fated encounter with Death.

The author and art critic Stanislaw Przybyszewsky (1868-1927), an admirer of Edvard Munch, whose work was made known to the public thanks in part to Przybyszewsky, was also an important source of inspiration for a number of other painters. Fascinated with the cult of Satan (as were Huysmans and Péladan) and inclined to flaunt his scandalous behavior, he began one of his books with the following blasphemous paraphrase of Genesis: "In the beginning was lust." In his writings, woman was of course

▷ **Jacek Malczewsky**
Thanatos (1)
1898, oil on canvas, 124.5 × 74
Muzeum Narodowe, Poznan
Death in the guise of a statuesque young woman appears frequently in the paintings of this artist who usually depicts her honing a scythe or luring a resigned-looking victim (here, the artist's own father standing in front of the family mansion). The metallic tones accentuate the uncanny feeling of this nocturnal scene.

▷▷ **Wladyslaw Podkowinsky**
Madness
1894, oil on canvas, 310 × 275
Muzeum Narodowe, Cracow
In this monumental composition representing a shapely, somewhat Pre-Raphaelite bacchante straddling a raging stallion, the artist undoubtedly sublimated his own erotic drives for he later slashed the canvas when it was exhibited.

an agent of Evil. The artist Wojciech Weiss
(1875-1950) was particularly receptive to Przybyszewsky's message as well as that of his favorite
artists, Goya, Rops, and Munch. In compositions
like *The Dance* (1899, Private Collection, Poland)
and, above all, *Obsession* (1899-1900, Muzeum
Adama Mickiewicza, Warsaw), he recreated the
decadent atmosphere of Przybyszewky's novels,
rendering in orgiastic rhythms crowds in hot pursuit of carnal pleasures.

The same frenzied pitch is seen in the work of
Wladyslaw Podkowinsky (1866-1895) who died
of tuberculosis while still very young. He discovered Impressionism in Paris in 1889 and began to paint out-of-doors in a style that recalls
Monet's. This new technique met with little success in Poland and, sensing perhaps that he would
not live long, he soon discarded it to begin painting macabre visions dominated by madness, unattainable love, and death. The titles of these
canvases—*The Skeletons' Dance, The Resurrection,
The Funeral Procession*—indicate from what sort of
themes the artist drew his inspiration. His most
famous work, *Madness* (1894, Muzeum Narodowe, Cracow), which he mutilated even as the
public was praising it, reiterates the theme of
Gustave Moreau's *Chimaera* by depicting an amorous woman embracing a wild horse plunging
into an abyss.

161

Jozef Mehoffer
The Strange Garden
**1903, oil on canvas,
222.5 × 208.5
Muzeum Narodowe, Warsaw**
In the midst of a dream garden where a toddler is taking his first steps watched fondly by his mother, the artist has introduced a giant Gallé-like dragonfly—a dramatic touch straight out of an Alfred Hitchcock script, which serves to underscore the painting's message that happiness and indeed life itself are precarious things.

Boleslas Biegas
The Sphinx
**1902, plaster, 46 × 39 × 11
Musée d'Orsay, Paris**
Biegas was obsessed with images of the sphinx, not as expressions of the war between the sexes, but as representations of the eternal riddle of life. Through his severely geometrical treatment of form and his way of emphasizing the forehead's height and the figure's deep-set eyes, the artist creates an original plastic work which owes almost nothing to the direct observation of nature and verges on abstract art.

Like Malczewsky, Jozef Mehoffer (1869-1946), before moving on to Paris, was a pupil of Jan Matejko in Cracow, whom he even assisted in decorating churches, an experience that determined the course of his career (in particular the stained glass windows decorating the Cathedral of St Nicholas in Fribourg, Switzerland are the work of Mehoffer). Keenly interested in landscapes, he was fond of introducing extraneous elements into otherwise sunny scenes, shifting them to a completely different plane. For example, in his picture *The Ravine* (1897, Muzeum Narodowe, Poznan), he turns a young woman's excursion in the Alps into a meditation on the fleetingness of happy moments. And in *The Strange Garden* (1903, Muzeum Narodowe, Warsaw), he injects a bizarre and disquieting note in an otherwise peaceful domestic scene by depicting a giant dragonfly hovering threateningly above a toddler taking his first steps as his mother watches fondly, apparently unaware of the outsized insect.

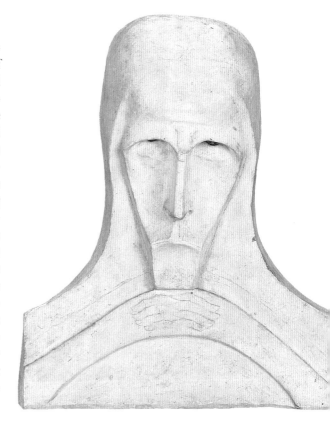

Boleslas Biegas (1877-1954) is surely the most personal and original Polish artist of this period[3]. A shepherd until the age of sixteen (which made critics compare him to Giotto), he studied the rudiments of art in Cracow and completed his training first among the Viennese Secession artists and then, beginning in 1901, in Paris. Strongly drawn to literary coteries, having written himself several plays, he expressed his ideas on often rather abstract metaphysical issues—the universe, thought, the future, infinity—in compositions filled with spirals and wavy lines and very much marked by Viennese art. It was as a sculptor, however, that he translated his ideas into plastic forms most effectively; he modeled flat, almost two-dimensional statues, and, by means of the interplay of minimal geometric forms, created figures with elongated faces, domed and disproportionately high foreheads, embodying man's fundamental questions about life's mysteries.

The retrograde career of Alphonse Mucha

In an era when the former kingdom of Bohemia was merely a province of the Austro-Hungarian empire, Alphonse Mucha (1860-1939) and František Kupka (1871-1957), two artists who settled in Paris relatively early, were both steeped in the spirit of this Symbolist age and both drawn to spiritualism—a fact that explains their subsequent careers.

Remarkably gifted for drawing and designing theater sets, Mucha studied first at the Academy of Fine Arts in Munich; then, aged twenty-eight, he enrolled at the Académie Julian in Paris, where his illustrations of history books soon earned him a certain renown. In 1894, almost overnight, thanks to a poster he designed for a play starring Sarah Bernhardt, he became a leading poster artist, a genre that he regarded more as a way of making a living than as a true vocation. Over the next six years, he was commissioned to design the posters for every play that the famous actress had a role in; and this brought a multitude of advertising jobs. Without taking anything away from the profound originality of the "Mucha style," one can nevertheless perceive, as Jana Brabcova has pointed out[4], that the composition of his posters was influenced by Rossetti,

Schwabe and the "atmosphere surrounding the Salons de la Rose + Croix," as well as by Byzantine and Japanese art. In his 1897 design for the poster announcing his own one-man show, Mucha represented a young Moravian girl (a tribute to his native land) holding a page on which she appears to have painted three crowns over a heart, an esoteric motif only an initiate could understand.

Shortly before the turn of the century, Mucha began to grow weary of his success with posters and gradually moved away from the genre that had made him one of the most prominent Art Nouveau artists. Increasingly, he devoted his attention to what he considered more important tasks: elaborating a spiritual message by means of the language of symbols and painting grandiose murals celebrating the heroic deeds of the freedom-loving Czechs. The ten years during which he designed posters seem the more significant period insofar as his contribution to art history is concerned, but Mucha himself set more store by the forty years he devoted to his other

Alphonse Mucha
Poster for the Mucha Exhibit at the Salon des Cent
1897, color lithograph, 68.5 × 45.5
Cabinet des Estampes, Bibliothèque nationale, Paris
A contemporary commentator explained this composition as follows: "A young girl resting pensively on a cardboard sheet decorated with a flaming heart which foolishness crowns with thistles; genius, with thorns; and love, with flowers."

Alphonse Mucha
The Abyss
**c. 1898-1899, pastel on paper mounted on canvas,
129 × 100**
Musée d'Orsay, Paris
After 1898 Mucha gradually abandoned his famous
poster style and began to paint mystically inspired
works whose message is often obscure. Here two
corpses, which seem to be emerging from a pit, stand
out against the horizon glowing with orange light. A
resurrection?

undertakings. In 1898-1899, he did a series of illustrations for the *Lord's Prayer*, adding personal comments which clearly owe more to Joséphin Péladan than to the canonical interpretation of the paternoster. This too was the period of his obscure pastels, *The Abyss* (Musée d'Orsay, Paris) and *The Seven Deadly Sins*, both exemplifying a fairly radical change of style, with something in common with the pictures of Redon and Lévy-Dhurmer.

After he returned to settle in his native Moravia in 1910, Mucha concentrated on painting twenty huge canvases illustrating *The Slavic Epic*, an ambitious yet retrograde project that marked a return to the historical painting he had learned in his youth and was inspired simultaneously by his patriotic fervor and his mystical vision of his nation's destiny.

František Kupka
The Way of Silence
c. 1900, pastel on paper, 58.1 × 65.1
Narodni Galerie, Prague
Always fascinated by the enigmatic, the artist depicts himself here as a tiny human figure walking down a sphinx-lined road. The Latin inscription on the pedestal of one of the sphinxes translates thus, "Wherefore are we," a query that recalls Gauguin's well-known question, but which Kupka to answer dabbling in spiritualism.

František Kupka
The Lotus Soul
1898, watercolor, 38.5 × 57.5
Narodni Galerie, Prague
In the Hindu myths the lotus floating on water is a symbol for the primordial indetermi-
nateness blossoming on the surface, like the egg of the world (both macrocosm and
microcosm) which the artist pictures here as a kind of homunculus emerging from a flower.

František Kupka,
from Symbolism to abstraction

At the age of thirteen, František Kupka[5], then apprenticed to a village saddler in Bohemia, was introduced to spiritualism. He exhibited such an extraordinary aptitude for communicating with the dead that he became famous locally as a medium. This helped to pay for art studies in Prague and, later, Vienna where he discovered and was deeply impressed by the Nazarenes (the early nineteenth-century German painters who preached that painting must above all have a spiritual mission). Kupka joined a Viennese theosophical sect founded by a fellow artist, who introduced him to the religions of the Far East and even got him to take up a severely ascetic life style based on nudism. One of Kupka's first works is a charcoal entitled *Meditation*, in which the artist depicts himself nude, on his knees, worshipping a sunny mountain. Other drawings and aquatints followed, with evocative titles such as *The Black Idol*, *The Road of Silence*, *The Beginning of Life*, *Quam ad Causam Sumus* (Why Are We?), *The Witches*, and so forth.

Kupka settled in Paris in 1896. He admired Redon and plunged headlong (and with no prior training) into philosophical and scientific studies, becoming particularly interested in the analysis of movement and light, in astronomy and human genetics, subjects that he integrated in his esoteric view of the universe. "The work of art being in itself an abstract reality," he stated, "it demands to be assembled from invented components." From 1906 on, he gradually began to move toward abstract art, which Kandinsky and he were to invent around 1910-1912. *The Dream* (1906-1909, Bochum Museum, Bochum), a typical example of Kupka's visionary art, shows a wraith-like human figure levitating amid fluid volumes. *The First Step* (1909-1913, The Museum of Modern Art, New York) is less a depiction of a planetary system than a vision of a luminous, colorful universe that exists somewhere beyond the limits of the visible world; such a work by Kupka exemplifies the transition from Symbolism to abstraction.

Notes

1 See M. Guerman, *Mikhail Vrubel*, Leningrad, 1986.

2 The best survey of Symbolist painting in Poland is: A. Morawinska's *Symbolism in Polish Painting* (catalog), The Detroit Institute of Art, Detroit, 1984.

3 Totally forgotten until recently, Biegas's work, most of it preserved at the Société Historique et Littéraire Polonaise de Paris, has at last been rediscovered thanks to several studies by Xavier Deryng: "Un arrêt d'Apollinaire: Boleslas Biegas," in *Cahiers du Musée National d'Art Moderne de Paris*, No. 6, Paris, 1981, pp. 41-47; "Le Sphinx de 1902 de Boleslas Biegas au Musée d'Orsay," in *La Revue du Louvre*, 1, Paris, 1988, pp. 53-56.

4 See his contribution to the catalog for the Mucha exhibit at the Grand Palais, Paris.

5 See M. Mladek and M. Rowell, *František Kupka. A Retrospective* (catalog), The Solomon R. Guggenheim Museum, New York, 1975.

Hans von Marées
The Golden Age II
1880-1883, oil on wood,
185.5 × 149.5
Neue Pinakothek, Munich

4

German-speaking countries

A German Puvis de Chavannes:
Hans von Marées

The last chapter of the Marquis de La Maze-lière's well-documented survey of nineteenth-century German painting, *La peinture allemande au XIXe siècle*[1], published in 1900, is devoted to Symbolist artists, whom the author places under the joint tutelage of Wagner and Nietzsche. De La Mazelière begins with a discussion of the Basel artist Böcklin, "the greatest of the German Symbolists," then proceeds to examine the works of Klinger, von Stuck, and Thoma.

To this list he might have added Hans von Marées (1837-1887), another *Deutsch-Römer* painter who, though, far less influential than Böcklin, had surely more in common with Puvis de Chavannes than any other German artist of the period; his gift for decoration is comparable to Puvis de Chavannes's and so is his commitment to expressing the Ideal by pictorial means[2]. Like many of his countrymen, he became enamored with Italy and, dreaming of finding a new Arcadia isolated from the modern world, eventually settled there. In 1873, he painted a fresco depicting the Garden of the Hesperides, with figures modeled on local fishermen, in the library of the Stazione Zoologica in Naples. He elaborated his idyllic visions in vast compositions, many of them grouped in triptychs, with titles like *The Ages of Man* (1873-1878, Nationalgalerie,

Berlin), *The Golden Age* (1879-1885, Neue Pinakothek, Munich), *The Hesperides* (1884-1885, *ibidem*). Unfortunately, his habit of thickening the coat of pigment on his canvases, in order to produce a glassy or lacquer-like iridescent surface and give his figures the illusion of some sort of organic existence, was not altogether successful and has resulted in irreversible damage to his paintings.

Both Böcklin and von Marées had a number of followers whom we might mention here rapidly in passing. Ferdinand Keller (1842-1922) started out his career as a historical painter but then, relatively late in his life, began to draw inspiration from more or less the same sources that Böcklin made use of. His *Tomb of Böcklin* (1901-1902, Staatliche Kunsthalle, Karlsruhe) manifestly owes its fame to the Basel painter's *The Island of the Dead*. Ludwig von Hofmann (1861-1945), an artist influenced by Keller, von Marées, and Puvis de Chavannes whom he had discovered during one stay at the Académie Julian, painted dream landscapes and nymphs haunting sacred springs; his colors are remarkably fresh and he possessed a fine and pleasing sense of ornamentation, a trait that often led him to carve himself the frames of his paintings.

eschatology. His *Judgement of Paris* (1887, Kunst-historisches Museum, Vienna), his *Christ on Olympus* (1889-1897, Museum der Bildenden Künste, Leipzig), and above all his *Crucifixion* (1890, *ibidem*), all gave rise to heated discussions, due more to their philosophical content than to their technique. Today we find it difficult to take their theatricality seriously, but they are characteristic of a certain fin de siècle taste for florid paintings in elaborately carved and colored frames which seem to grow out from the picture and lend it a sort of reality. Klinger's aspiration to give more life to his works drove him to try sculpture. His style of sculpturing owes a good deal to Rodin, whom he admired, yet there is originality in his use of colors and rich materials, inspired by the example of Phidias. His *New Salome* (1893, Museum der Bildenden Künste, Leipzig) clearly reflects Parisian influence. However, it was mainly music that inspired Klinger, a close friend of Brahms. If his masterpiece, the *Monument to Beethoven* (1901-1902, *ibidem*), was the crowning exhibit at the Fourteenth Secession Show in Vienna, it is the mural decoration against which it was placed that we now remember: Klimt's *Beethoven Frieze*.

It was not, however, in the paintings and sculptures that brought him fame that Klinger's genius manifested itself most clearly; it was in his engravings. He himself, in his theoretical statement *Malerei und Zeichnung* (Painting and Drawing), written in 1891, contrasted painting, the goal of which is to express "the physical world in a harmonious way," to drawing and creative engraving, the true instruments of the "strong subjectivity of the artist" who translates his "feeling for the world" and for "life's dark side" into lines. A master at etching. Klinger has left us some 400 engravings grouped in fourteen "opus." These series often have bizarre subjects and are filled with autobiographical references and, rather unexpectedly for this period, humor. The suite called *Ovid's Sacrifices Rescued* (1879) offers alter-

Max Klinger, the engraver of life's dark side

In the words of Giorgio De Chirico, who wrote a long article in praise of the artist shortly after his death, Max Klinger (1857-1920) was "a painter, sculptor, etcher, philosopher, writer, musician, and poet."[3] Klinger aspired to a *Gesamtkunstwerk*, a "total" art work that would express his metaphysical ideas steeped in the writings of Schopenhauer. As a student and young artist he had lived in most of Europe's capitals and was strongly influenced by Böcklin and Puvis de Chavannes. This led him to paint enormous pictures, using the ancient Greek and Roman canons of beauty to elaborate a syncretic vision combining pagan mythology and the Christian

native and entirely unexpected denouements to some of the tales the Latin poet recounts in *The Metamorphoses*. *The Paraphrase on the Finding of a Glove* (1881) shows that Freud was not the first to discern the unconscious riches or sexual undertones of what he would later term "the psychopathology of everyday life." However, it was mainly in his subsequent series such as *A Life* (1887), *Brahmsphantasie* (1894), and the two opera on *Death* (1882-1889 and 1889-1910) that Klinger, in his unique way, confronted the great questions of life, suffering, and death, with a power to evoke such themes that at times rivals Goya and Redon.

Max Klinger
Twilight
1890, oil on canvas, 191.5 × 176
Museum der Bildenden
Künste, Leipzig

The Symbolist generation's favorite time of day was what the French call *l'heure bleue*, that twilight hour when night's approach fills the mind with melancholy daydreams. In Klinger's words, "It was the clean light of Paris and the color studies I did several years earlier that drove me to paint this canvas. Since one naturally introduces an idea, I tried to characterize as clearly as possible three different kinds of silent contemplation: the amorphous dream that bathes in the darkness of twilight, the contemplative shiver one experiences looking into flames, and the liberating dream."

Max Klinger
The Philosopher
1910, aquatint etching,
49.5 × 33.4
Cabinet des Estampes,
Musée d'art et d'histoire,
Geneva

This etching belongs to a series of twelve entitled *Of Death, Part II*, in which the artist, deeply influenced by Schopenhauer's thought, opposes the frailness of the individual to nature's inexhaustible capacity for renewal. The thinker's meditations debouch on an insubstantial reflection of his own existence, whereas the superhuman female earth encompasses all of mankind's future in her sleep.

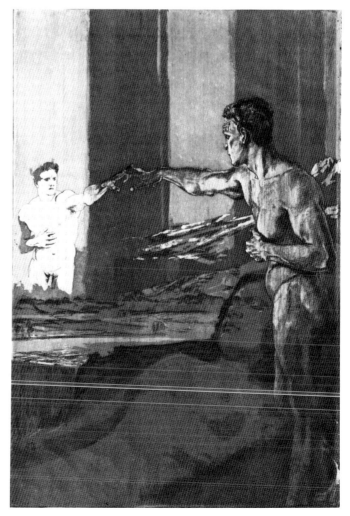

Franz von Stucl
Sin
1893, oil on canvas, 124.5×95.5
Neue Pinakothek, Munich

Franz von Stuck's poisonous Symbolism

In an era when Munich was still the art capital of Germany, Franz von Stuck (1863-1928) was regarded as the "Empire's foremost draftsman." In 1892, he played a leading role in the birth of the Munich Secession (the inspiration for the subsequent Berlin and Vienna Secession movements) and as a result was regarded as an avant-garde artist. Painters from all over northern Europe —notably Klee and Kandinsky—flocked to his class at the Munich Academy of Fine Arts[4].

Von Stuck had mastered the thematic repertory of allegory and symbolism by closely examining the work of Böcklin and Klinger while keeping an eye on what Rossetti and Khnopff were doing. He produced an album entitled *Allegories and Emblems* and very quickly built up a reputation as the "best painter of ideas" in his country. His painting was at first strongly influenced by the Pre-Raphaelites, notably his *Guardian of Paradise* (1889, Villa Stuck Museum, Munich), awarded a gold medal at one of the annual exhibitions at the Munich Glaspalast. He imitated Böcklin's scenes of centaurs and satyrs fighting or playing, but his imagination never had the originality or depth possessed by the other artist. Soon spoiled by his success, he began to repeat images that produced facile effects: seductive but deadly sphinxes which had none of

Gustave Moreau's restraint; endless depictions of *Sin* and *Vice* represented as nude women, shown from the waist up or sprawling full length, perversely entwining with disproportionately large reptiles that have nothing to do with Biblical symbolism but are simply bizarre sexual objects. The ultimate expression of this fascination with vice, which must have shocked many spectators at the time, is the *Altar of Sin* (Villa Stuck Museum, Munich), a construction enshrining one of von Stuck's many versions of *Sin*, which the artist erected in his studio around 1898, next to two other altars, one consecrated to Orpheus, the other to Athena.

The "prince of artists," as he was called, colored his themes by bathing them in the lurid red glow of hellfire. Under the moral pretext of admonishing his contemporaries, he offered them the spectacle of their own fantasies. And he made a fortune, judging from his villa in Munich, an extravagant and narcissistic "folly" he himself designed: it is now a museum housing his oeuvre as well as Jugendstil art, lavish examples of which adorn the reception rooms.

Franz von Stuck
The Sphinx
1904, oil on canvas, 83 × 157
Hessisches Landesmuseum,
Darmstadt

Gustav Klimt
and the consecration of Eros

Gustav Klimt
The Aspiration Toward
Happiness Is Appeased
in Poetry
(Beethoven Frieze,
last panel)
1902, casein on stucco,
220 × 506
Osterreichische Galerie,
Vienna

A pictorial translation of the *Ninth Symphony*, the Beethoven Frieze expresses the lenitive influence of the arts on mankind which, in an earlier panel, confronts and triumphs over the forces of evil. The airborne figures, whose silhouettes owe something to Toorop, represent the hopes and ardent desires of a humanity aspiring toward peace through music, symbolized by the woman playing a lyre.

International Symbolism produced a late but brilliant flowering in the work of Gustav Klimt (1862-1918) and the Viennese Secession. By the time he was thirty-five, Klimt had already reached prominence by decorating large cultural edifices (the Burgtheater, the Kunsthistorisches Museum, the University) erected toward the end of the nineteenth century in the capital of the Austro-Hungarian empire. Thoroughly familiar with the repertory of allegorical painting, he was considered the most promising heir of the previous generation's foremost painter of historical scenes, Hans Makart (1840-1884). In 1897, Klimt, along with a group of young artists, founded and became the first president of the Vienna Secession, patterned after the Munich and Berlin Secession movements. The title of the new movement's magazine, the luxurious *Ver Sacrum* (Sacred Spring), eloquently expresses the group's longing for renewal and its idealistic aspirations. "Art is moving away from Naturalism," wrote one of its members; "it is seeking something new [...]. What we want is to escape, whatever the cost, from visible reality; to take refuge in the shadowy, the unknown, the secret."

The first exhibit organized by the Secession was held in 1898 and brought together, among others, the great names of European Symbolism: Khnopff (who was lionized), Puvis de Chavannes, Rodin, Böcklin, von Stuck, Klinger, Segantini, and Mucha. Subsequent Secession exhibits included works by these artists, as well as Toorop, Minne, Hodler. Klimt's plastic language began to change under the impact of their art, and his thematic iconography expanded and came to embrace the favorite subjects of his fellow European Symbolists. Obsessed with woman and female sexuality, Klimt began to paint his own versions of those lethal heroines, Salome and Judith, and to place the erotic and the libidinous on a sacred plane. The desiring woman, the pleasure-giving and pleasure-receiving woman decked in gold, the procreating woman (he was among the first to depict women in the last stage of pregnancy) and, inevitably, Woman-and-Thanatos: these are his characteristic themes. *Hope* (1903, National Gallery, Ottawa) associates an expecting mother with skulls and corpse-like faces; *Life and Death* (before 1911, R. Leopold Collection, Vienna) juxtaposes a blissfully slumbering family group with the hideous specter of Death wielding a bludgeon[5].

Profoundly influenced by the ideas of Schopenhauer and Nietzsche, Klimt's pessimistic view of man's fate was expressed so uncompromisingly in the ceiling decorations he executed for the main auditorium at the University of Vienna (1898-1907) that they raised a storm of protest. Klimt had been commissioned to paint traditional allegories of Philosophy, Medicine, and Jurisprudence; instead, with an abundance of symbols and images that seemed scandalous to his contemporaries, he chose to express his own subversive ideological values—values which so enraged the university professors that they signed a petition to have his decoration removed.

The long frieze Klimt devoted to Beethoven (1902, Secession Pavilion, Vienna) exemplifies even more clearly his ideal of an art expressing mankind's collective aspiration toward happiness, an aspiration that can never be fully satisfied except by destroying the forces of evil[6]. On close examination this masterpiece of forms and colors, which is one of the pinnacles of mural painting, reveals itself to be an extraordinarily convincing example of the kind of plastic "correspondences" between thought, music, and painting that the artists of this generation aspired to. In fact, it was Wagner's commentary on the *Ninth Symphony* that inspired Klimt's composition; and the frieze must be read thus, as a mapping out of coded images, the key to which, as Klimt himself hinted in the lines he wrote to present this work to the visitors at the Secession exhibition, is the sublimation of the sexual drive.

As Carl Schorske has written, "Klimt was a questioner and a prober of the questionable, the problematical, in personal experience and culture. Like Freud, he sought answers to his riddles by exploring his own depths, and often made the

Gustav Klimt
Judith II
1909, oil on canvas, 178×46
Museo d'Arte Moderna, Cà Pesaro, Venice

This Judith, who seems indistinguishable from Salome, represents (like her counterpart in the New Testament) the castrating *femme fatale*. She is depicted here as a *demi-mondaine* attired for a formal soirée. Judith was in fact a "positive" figure: her act of heroism was a response to Holofernes's lust; a sort of self-punishment for profligacy. Perhaps an allusion to the artist's libertine existence given over to sexual pleasure?

175

it has been called; *The Kiss* (1908, Öster-
reichische Galerie, Vienna) and the elegant
mosaics at the Palais Stoclet in Brussels are its
most attractive expressions. However, even in
these works, when one delves beneath the glitter-
ing gold and gemstones, one discovers mystical
and erotic meanings that the artist has tucked
away in the depths of his paintings, where they
go unnoticed by the hasty viewer whose eye is
caught solely by their dazzling surface.

Following in Klimt's wake, the painter Wilhelm List (1864-1918) produced an oeuvre that
deserves to be rescued from the relative neglect
into which it has fallen. List was one of the founding members of the Vienna Secession and devoted much of his time and energy to editing
Ver Sacrum (for which he designed numerous
chromolithographs, such as *Daphne*, 1899, and
Salome, 1900). One of his finest canvases, *The
Offering* (around 1900, Musée des Beaux-Arts,
Quimper), shows that, like Klimt, he was particularly receptive to the style of Puvis de
Chavannes, whose painting he had studied in
Paris.

Alfred Kubin
and the lure of death

In the epilogue to *The Other Side*, a fantasy
novel he wrote and illustrated in 1909, Alfred
Kubin (1877-1959) wrote, using the first-person
"I" to emphasize the personal nature of the experience he was describing: "I loved that death,
loved her ecstatically, as if she were a woman; I
was transported with rapture. In the ensuing
nights, all of them brimming with a lunar bright-
ness, I surrendered completely to her, I gazed at
her, drank her in with my senses, and thrilled to
supernatural delights. I was the lover of that
glamorous mistress, that glorious princess of the
world who is indescribably beautiful in the eyes
of all those she touches."[8]

In other writings, Kubin stressed the importance of dreams as the main source of his inspiration. In many respects he resembled Redon,
whom he had in fact visited while in Paris. Like
Redon, he gained a reputation as a masterly
graphic artist; with pen and India ink, gripped
by "unspeakable psychic tremors," he produced
his innumerable macabre visions, although, un-

Alfred Kubin
The Graveyard Wall
**c. 1900, pen and India ink
wash on paper, 24.8 × 18.2
Oberösterreichisches
Landesmuseum, Linz**
Kubin devoted his career almost exclusively to the art of
pen and ink drawing, bringing
to it remarkable technical refinements like the device of spat-
tering ink to suggest three-
dimensionality. Kubin's entire
artistic production is dominated
by obsessive images of death
and destruction, as is Schopenhauer's philosophy which had a
decisive influence on the artist's
world view.

answers plain to others by exhibiting himself.
What he began as a cheerful quest for sensual
liberation very nearly ended in professional—
perhaps even personal psychological—disaster.
But in the process Klimt became a kind of meta-
psychologist in the world of vision."[7]

Following the scandals caused by those paintings permeated with a symbolism drawn from the
depths of his unconscious, Klimt fell back for a
time on the security of less provocative works—
landscapes and society portraits—which concealed his private obsessions behind purely ornamental research. This was his "golden style," as

like the French artist, he stuck to black and white techniques throughout his life and only rarely resorted to color.

His discovery of Schopenhauer's philosophy at the age of nineteen permanently shaped his outlook on life; similarly, his first viewing of Klinger's engravings for *The Paraphrase on the Finding of a Glove* determined his calling. "What I saw" in those engravings, he writes in his *Autobiography*, "was an absolutely new art giving sufficient scope to the allusive expression of all the worlds of sensation, the only possible ones."

The 6,000 to 7,000 drawings produced by this "artistic gravedigger of the Austrian Empire" (as Kubin called himself) offer a sort of recapitulation of the graphic oeuvres of Goya, de Groux, Rops, Munch, Ensor, Redon, Beardsley—artists whom he had studied carefully, retaining only their most morbid aspects. For Kubin transformed everything he saw into a nightmare vision, even women and love, as if the death urge were the only tangible reality. Not even Freud himself gave it such pride of place.

The Kingdom of Hungary

An independent kingdom in the heart of the Hapsburg empire, Hungary closely followed the example set by Vienna in art, even if the millenium celebration, in 1898, of the foundation of the kingdom led many to cultivate still more so their Magyar heritage. Yet Hungarian artists regularly worked and studied in the studios of Munich, Paris and London.

János Vaszary (1867-1939), who studied art in Munich and Paris, produced during one period of his career a body of Symbolist works. The finest example of these, *The Golden Age* (1898, Hungarian National Gallery, Budapest), depicts two contemplative lovers embracing in a mysterious park. The greenish monochrome hues of the canvas, the painting's sculptured and gilded frame show that the artist had perfectly absorbed the art that was then fashionable in Munich as well as Paris. In 1902 Aladár Körösföi Kriesch (1863-1920) created a small artists' colony in Gödöllö under the influence of the ideas promoted by Ruskin and William Morris. A painting like *Ego sum via, veritas et vita* (1903, Hungarian National Gallery, Budapest) typifies the religious nature of his inspiration and abounds in emphatic references to the art of the Middle Ages. Kriesch's friend Sandor Nagy (1868-1950) drew inspiration from similar sources. As for Tivadar Csontváry Kosztka (1853-1919), this mystical visionary and quite original colorist worked as a pharmacist for twenty years before devoting himself completely to art. Following stays in Munich and Paris, he traveled throughout the Middle East executing strange naive landscapes peopled with various enraptured figures, as in *The Savior in Prayer* (1903, Janus Pannonius Museum, Pécs) and *Pilgrimage to the Cedar of Lebanon* (1907, *ibidem*).

Notes

[1] Marquis de La Mazelière, *La peinture allemande au XIXᵉ siècle*, Paris, 1900. (Part 6 of this book is entitled "The Symbolists.")

[2] The most recent survey is: C. Lenz, *Hans von Marées* (catalog), Neue Pinakothek, Munich, 1987-1988. See also J.P. Marandel, "Arcadia Germanica," in *FMR*, Milan (French edition), No. 12, January-February, 1988, pp. 47-64.

[3] See the following exhibit catalogs: *Max Klinger. Gravures*, Musée d'art et d'Histoire, Geneva, 1982; *Max Klinger. Wege zum Gesamtkunstwerke*, Roemer- und -Pelizacus-Museum, Hildesheim, 1984.

[4] See *Franz von Stuck. 1863-1928. Maler. Graphiker. Bildhauer. Architekt* (catalog), Villa Stuck Museum, Munich, 1982.

[5] See: S. Sabarsky, *Gustav Klimt* (catalog), Musées Royaux des Beaux-Arts, Brussels, 1987.

[6] J.-P. Bouillon, *Klimt: Beethoven*, Geneva, 1986.

[7] Carl E. Schorske, *Fin-de-Siècle Vienna. Politics and Culture*, New York, 1981; reprinted Cambridge, 1985, p. 226.

[8] A. Kubin, *L'autre côté*, French translation, Paris, 1986, pp. 251-252.

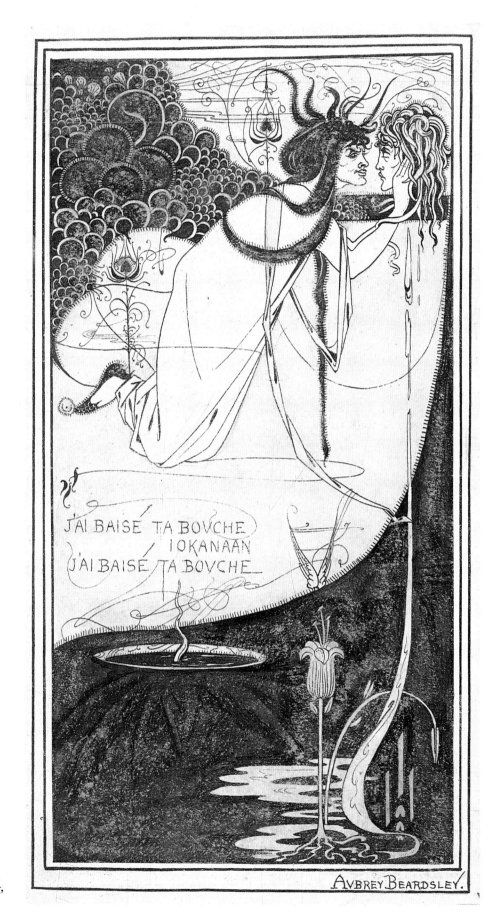

Aubrey Beardsley
J'ai baisé ta bouche
Iokanaan
1893, pen and India ink and
green watercolor
Galatin Beardsley Collection,
Princeton University Library,
Princeton

5

English-speaking countries

A perverted Pre-Raphaelite: Aubrey Beardsley

In Great Britain in the last decade of the nineteenth century, Edward Burne-Jones, still as prolific as ever, embodied Pre-Raphaelitism almost by himself. He spurred the growth of the Arts and Crafts Movement led by his friend William Morris (1834-1896). Morris dreamt of making art available to the masses by founding crafts studios devoted particularly to printing illustrated books and wallpaper for which Burne-Jones created numerous designs. This socio-medieval utopia hardly outlived its founder. The most innovative painter of the period was undoubtedly the American artist James McNeil Whistler (1834-1903), who is beginning to be recognized throughout Europe as an artist of genius after having long been regarded as a provocative dauber, a reputation for which he himself was partly to blame. A portraitist and landscape artist, Whistler introduced an intangible element into his paintings that places him beyond Realism and bears witness above all to his indomitable individualism. Of all his creative output, he was especially admired by young artists of the day for his blue and gold *Peacock Room* (1876-1877, Freer Gallery of Art, Washington) which he had decorated in the "Japanese manner" for the London residence of a wealthy shipping magnate.

The virtually self-taught Aubrey Vincent Beardsley (1872-1898) picked up his remarkable gift for drawing from illustrated books[1]. His earliest works were influenced by Burne-Jones who, with Puvis de Chavannes, was the first to encourage him to follow his chosen calling. He drew inspiration as well from Whistler (whose *Peacock Room* he was familiar with), Mantegna, and Japanese printmakers, combining elements from all three to create a highly personal style whose beauty rests at once on pleasing arabesques and artful arrangements of black and white areas. At the age of twenty, Beardsley defined his main source of inspiration, which quickly earned him a scandalous reputation: "The subjects are rather unsettling and daring. Strange hermaphroditic creatures saunter about in Pierrot costumes or modern robes. In short, a universe that springs entirely from my own imagination."

Beardsley's imagination was in fact not unlike that of many young people of his generation. He went into raptures over Wagner's operas (and illustrated scenes from *Siegfried*, *Tristan and Isolde*, and *Das Rheingold*), waxed enthusiastic over medieval legends (*Le Morte d'Arthur*), and was obsessed by the idea of the *femme fatale* whom he soon associated with Salome. Indeed Oscar

Wilde's drama *Salome* (1893) provided him with an opportunity to execute a series of twenty outstanding drawings remarkable for their linear purity and original layouts. Beardsley's treatment of the by then somewhat hackneyed theme of Salome is perverse and cynical, even grotesque, with its provocative allusions to crude sexual acts, as if the artist had wanted to exorcise all the fantasies and forbidden impulses repressed by the prevailing morality of Victorian society and by his own illness (tuberculosis which, contracted when Beardsley was a child, would carry the artist off at the age of twenty-six).

There is a good deal less overt salaciousness in the work of Charles Ricketts (1866-1931), a very

refined artist who was, after Beardsley, the best English illustrator in the 1890s. During a sojourn in Paris, Ricketts discovered the paintings of Puvis de Chavannes and, in particular, Gustave Moreau. Moreau's influence combined with that of Rossetti is manifest in the drawing that brought him fame, *Oedipus and the Sphinx* (1891). A great admirer of Wilde, who wisely chose, however, not to provoke the public by stressing the latter's homosexuality, Ricketts devoted the better part of his considerable gifts to illustrating the Irish writer's works, notably "The Sphinx" (1894), translating that poem's timeless esoteric atmosphere into elegantly hieratic and artfully archaic engravings.

Mackintosh and the mystique of plants

Echoes of European Symbolism reached as far as Scotland, where students at the Glasgow School of Art were acquainted not only with the

work of Rossetti and Burne-Jones but also with that of Beardsley, Toorop, and Schwabe, widely reproduced as prints or illustrations in art journals like *The Studio*, launched in London early in 1893. It was in this manner that the future architect and decorator Charles Rennie Mackintosh (1868-1928), unsure whether to become a painter or an architect, began in 1894 to exhibit in the classrooms of the School of Art strange watercolors painted in a very fluid technique, depicting long winged angels alighting amid trees and flowers[2]. The attention to stylized forms and symmetrical motifs that characterize these youthful experiments reemerged a few years later in Mackintosh's decorations for several Glasgow tearooms. The very titles of some of his almost abstract watercolors (*The Tree of Personal Effort*, 1895, Glasgow School of Art, Glasgow; *The Tree of Influence*, 1895, *ibidem*) speak eloquently of recondite metaphysical reflections that revolve around the feeling that the elementary organisms of plant life (especially flowers, which Mackintosh studied and drew repeatedly throughout his life, as if he wanted to dissect their inmost structures) are clues that will help us understand the elementary forces governing nature's order.

The same restless fascination with the riddles of nature and human existence can be discerned in the colored drawings and decorative designs of the Macdonald sisters, Margaret (1865-1933) whom Mackintosh married, and Frances (1874-1921), an artist influenced by Burne-Jones's graphic style.

American analogies

Young American artists in the late nineteenth century were eager to complete their training in Europe, but as a rule attended the ateliers of official masters, especially in France and Italy, avoiding avant-garde movements. However, there were brilliant exceptions, such as the unclassifiable Whistler (whom art historians have endeavored to connect alternately with Impressionism and Symbolism) and Mary Cassatt who was, for her part, close to Degas and exhibited with the Impressionists.

Certain American artists of this period shared the attitude of their European counterparts respecting the philosophical problems of existence. Colored by an introspective pessimism that ran counter to the realism of their fellow citizens, their disposition of mind led them to execute works that can be easily identified with the main currents of European Symbolism and are obviously inspired by that movement's favorite themes.

The New York artist Elihu Vedder (1836-1923) became fascinated with Rome at a very early age and spent most of his life in Italy[3]. In the course of his travels through Europe he discovered the English Pre-Raphaelites and, as early as 1865, began to tackle subjects that have a good deal in common with Moreau's themes. *The Riddle of the Sphinx* (1866, whereabouts unknown) was painted precisely after one of the artist's visits to Paris. In his memoirs, *Digressions*, Vedder states: "I am not mystical, nor well-versed in the occult sciences... and yet I like to immerse myself in the unknowable and refresh myself there, and I have a strong tendency to see in things more than meets the eye."

This bent for metaphysical speculation, which led Vedder to take a deep interest in Oriental mystics, manifests itself in his fifty-six remarkable drawings inspired by *The Rubáiyát of Omar Khayyám* (1883-1884, National Museum of American Art, Washington). They are not mere illustrations, as the artist himself pointed out, but "companion-pieces" that depict in a rather unexpected fashion the riddles of life and death rather than the Epicurean celebration of earthly pleasures that one usually associates with the Persian philosopher-poet's verses. Vedder's best-known picture, *The Cup of Death* (1885, Virginia Museum of Fine Arts, Richmond) is incidentally

Elihu Vedder
The Cup of Death
1885, oil on canvas, 112.7 × 52.7
Virginia Museum of Fine Arts, Richmond
The hypnotic quality of this painting, which depicts a journey down the dark river of death, is striking. The theme was suggested by a quatrain from *The Rubáiyát* of Omar Khayyám:
So when that Angel of the darker
[drink
At last shall find you by the river
[brink
And offering his Cup, invite your Soul
Forth to your Lips to quaff—you shall
[not shrink.

based on a quatrain of the *Rubáiyát*, or rather one image which the artist interprets as a symbol for the inexorable character of death and which he renders in a manner reminiscent of George Frederic Watts.

Albert Pinkham Ryder (1847-1917), like Vedder, rejected illusionist reproduction of natural scenes. He chose to remain on the edge of the art world (though this did not prevent him from making several short trips to Europe), and built up a reputation as a hermit living in reclusion in his New York studio and emerging only to attend performances of Wagner's operas. A keen reader of the Bible, Edgar Allan Poe, and Walt

181

Albert Pinkham Ryder
The Flying Dutchman
c. 1887, oil on canvas,
36.1 × 43.8
**National Museum of American
Art, Washington**
His imagination fired by Wagner's operas, Ryder does not seek to paint an accurate visual translation here but to set down a pictorial equivalent of the sea's awesome power, making use of brushtrokes that seem about to crush the foundering boat whose three passengers are gesticulating with terror at the ghost ship's approach, the latter's sails blending in with the clouds.

Whitman, he coined aphorisms that might have been written by Odilon Redon: "The artist should be wary of becoming a slave to details. He must endeavor to express his thought and not just the surface of his thought [...]. The artist must only remain true to his dream and not see anything other than his vision."

Whether they draw their inspiration from Wagner (*The Flying Dutchman*, 1887, National Museum of American Art, Washington) or Poe (*The Temple of the Spirit*, 1885, Albright-Knox Gallery, Buffalo). Ryder's paintings, left for long periods on the easel and constantly reworked (a practice that has greatly contributed to the poor state of these canvases) are not attempts to depict scenes from musical or fictional sources but visual translations of the artist's exalted feelings expressed through contrasting light and dark masses or through the movements of the pictorial material to which he sought to give musical rhythms.

Although Ryder's quest for an art conceived independently of the facts of reality drew criticism from his contemporaries (who objected to what they regarded as obscurity and careless draftsmanship), he has since come to be viewed as one of the forerunners of abstract art in the United States. Jackson Pollock, who as a young painter was strongly influenced by Ryder, even went so far as to declare: "He is the only American master who interests me."

During the 1890s several younger American artists made long sojourns in Paris. An enthusiastic admirer of Puvis de Chavannes (who, it is worth recalling, executed a mural for the Boston Public Library), Arthur Bowen Davies (1862-1928) painted idyllic landscapes in pale tones as a setting for groups of dancing girls whose features recall those of Maurice Denis's female figures. Pinckney Marcius-Simons (1865-1909) spent part of his youth in France and was a regular exhibitor at the Salons de la Rose + Croix, he made a name for himself with religious themes. An ardent admirer of Wagner, he illustrated the composer's works and ended up settling in Bayreuth and devoting himself almost exclusively to designing the sets for performances of Wagner's operas.

Notes

[1] See S. Weintraub, *Beardsley*, London, 1976; K. Clark, *The Best of Aubrey Beardsley*, London, 1978; J.-J. Mayoux, "Aubrey Beardsley, satanique et pervers," in *Sous de vastes portiques... Etudes de littérature et d'art anglais*, Paris, 1981, pp. 177-187.

[2] See R. Billcliffe, *Mackintosh Watercolours* (catalog), London, 1978.

[3] See R. Soria, *Perceptions and Evocations: The Art of Elihu Vedder*, Washington, 1979.

6

Southern Europe

In Italy, unlike France, Symbolism was closely associated with the Divisionist technique, which does not seem to have stemmed directly from Seurat and Signac's Neo-Impressionism. Though the latter preceded the former by several years, it was virtually unknown among Italian artists during this period. Moreover, while French painters practiced Pointillism, their counterparts in Italy, basing their own researches on Ruskin's writings and Rood's theories, endeavored to reconstruct the optical synthesis by juxtaposing thick or thin touches of different colors[1].

In May 1891 two canvases were displayed at the First Triennial Exhibition of the Brera Academy in Milan: Previati's *Maternity* and Segantini's *The Two Mothers*. The subject matter of these pictures and their unusual execution aroused a considerable amount of interest. It is hard to distinguish the foreign influences in them, so alien are they to most Italian painting of the day, but it has often been stressed that the art critic and dealer Vittore Grubicy de Dragon (1851-1920) played a vital role in the development of both artists. Grubicy, who was also a painter, was acquainted with the writings of the Groupe des XX in Belgium and had seen their exhibits. He was in fact the champion of anti-Realist art in Italy. "When the artist directs his efforts to expressing ideas," he wrote, "the objects which contribute to their expression must not have any value in themselves, but only as signs, after the fashion of letters in an alphabet; and these signs, indispensable as they are, represent nothing in themselves: the Idea is everything." As a painter, Grubicy was himself strongly influenced by The Hague school and painted a series of idealized landscapes, many of which he combined in polyptichs. One fine example of such compositions is *Winter in the Mountains. A Pantheistic Poem*, 1894-1911, Galleria d'Arte Moderna, Venice, and Civica Galleria d'Arte Moderna, Milan.

Death in the Engadine:
Giovanni Segantini

Giovanni Segantini
The Punishment for Lasciviousness
1891, oil on canvas, 99 × 173
Walker Art Gallery, Liverpool
The artist devoted several canvases to this theme inspired by an Indian poem, the *Pangiavahli*: "Up yonder, in the sky's boundless space, shines Nirvana [...]. Thus the evil mother wanders ceaselessly in a circle, in the livid valley, amid eternal glaciers where no flower ever blooms, no branch ever greens [...]. Behold her, drifting restlessly like a leaf, her woefulness surrounded by silence."

The painter Giovanni Segantini (1858-1899) could have been the protagonist of a nineteenth-century romance of wretchedness. Orphaned at a very early age and almost illiterate, he none the less managed to attend art classes at the Brera Academy and was noticed at the outset of his career by Vittore Grubicy de Dragon, who took him under contract and became his mentor. An anxiety-ridden figure who craved solitude, Segantini gradually drifted away from the city and ended up settling in the high mountain country of the Engadine in Switzerland. In 1898, driven toward purer skies and ever more pristine natural scenery, he moved to a mountain hut 9,000 feet above sea-level and began painting his *Triptych of Nature*, intending to send the work to the Universal Exposition in Paris. He died, however, at forty-one before completing it. The un-

finished triptych and a number of his other paintings are now housed in the Segantini Museum in the resort of St Moritz.

Already something of a legend in his own lifetime, Segantini and his work became the subject of one of the very first psychoanalytic studies devoted to an artist. Karl Abraham, one of Freud's closest disciples, saw Segantini's premature death as the fulfillment of a suicidal urge in an artist deeply obsessed with the idea of death[2].

Segantini had begun his career in the footsteps of Millet, close to the latter in both his choice of subjects (shepherds surrounded by flocks of sheep, scenes of peasant life rendered with sentimental Realism), and style. After withdrawing to the mountains, he began to educate himself and, some time after 1890, discovered the writings of Nietzsche (he even illustrated an Italian edition

of *Thus Spake Zarathustra*) and Schopenhauer, whose deep pessimism suited his own essentially gloomy nature. His reading of Schopenhauer fostered a belief in metempsychosis and led him to search for inspiration in the literature of India. "Yes," he wrote in 1893, "true life is but a single dream, the dream of gradually approaching an ideal at once as remote as possible and elevated, elevated to the point that matter vanishes."

These meditations gave rise to a series of works between 1891 and 1897 that evoke the fate of wayward mothers (first version of *The Punishment for Lasciviousness*, 1891, Walker Art Gallery, Liverpool) in which the artist illustrates passages from the *Pangiavahli*. Somewhat like Dante's *Inferno*, this Indian poem details the torment in store for promiscuous women who do not live up to their responsibilities as mothers; they are condemned to wandering forever in a frozen wasteland. Aside from the strangeness of the theme, Segantini displays a great technical originality in these paintings, which derives partly from his use of the Divisionist technique and partly from the fundamental naturalism that drove him to paint landscapes out-of-doors amid glaciers and year-round snow. As for the underlying meaning of these works, Karl Abraham has shown that it

expresses the artist's repressed feelings about his own mother.

Segantini hoped to reach the ideal, the azure so dear to Mallarmé's heart, by isolating himself high in the mountains, far above the rest of mankind. Thus, as we have seen, he spent the last three years of his life in an alpine hut, working on *The Triptych of Nature*. Like Gauguin, who painted *Whence Come We? What are we? Whither go we?* in 1897, Segantini conceived this last, monumental painting as a pantheistic testament in three panels—*Life (Childhood)*, *Nature (Maturity)*, and *Death*, also called *Becoming, Being,* and *Dying* —against a background of snowy peaks shining in the sun.

Kandinsky, who regarded Segantini as one of the three "seekers of immaterial spheres" who, together with Böcklin and Rossetti, wished to illustrate art's progress toward the spiritual, described his work in the following terms: "He took nature's most accomplished forms, mountain ranges, stones and animals, and reproduced them down to their smallest details. Nevertheless, he was able to create images that are abstract despite their strictly realist appearance and thus was probably the least materialist of the three."[3]

185

Two painters of virginity:
Gaetano Previati and
Giuseppe Pellizza da Volpedo

Gaetano Previati
Maternity
1890-1891, oil on canvas,
174×411
Banco Popolare, Novara
Exhibited at Milan in 1891, where it met with a storm of criticism, and at the Salon de la Rose + Croix in Paris a year earlier, this large canvas can be read on several levels. The Christian message of divine virginity is manifest in the halo-shaped lighting and the frieze of angels; while the fruit-laden tree (a tree of life) suggests a more pagan interpretation centering on woman's fertility and the cycles of nature. The technique of juxtaposing filaments of different colored pigment is characteristic of Italian Divisionism, for which this painting was a manifesto.

186

Before long, another artist trained at the Brera Academy, Gaetano Previati (1852-1920), began to broach non-realist themes too, illustrating Poe's tales (1887-1890) and painting scenes like *The Opium Smokers* (1887, Private Collection, Turin). *Maternity* (Banca Popolare, Novara) was his first Symbolist canvas. Its bizarre mystical atmosphere caused a scandal at the Milan Triennial in 1891, for instead of depicting a traditional Nativity, it showed a woman nursing her child under the Tree of Life. Exhibited at the Salon de la Rose + Croix the following year, it went unnoticed, even though its technique derived from Divisionism was highly original—but then the public that visited these shows was more interested in the subjects of the works on display than in matters of style. In Italy, Previati's only supporter was Grubicy, who was endeavoring to interest a largely hostile public in the new "Ideaist" art. Unlike Segantini, whose works were internationally successful, Previati was never popular. Despite their original technique, his *Madonna With*

Lilies (1894, Civica Galleria d'Arte Moderna, Milan) and his *Funeral of the Virgin* (Galleria Nazionale d'Arte Moderna, Rome) were too narrowly Pre-Raphaelite in inspiration to have much of an impact in a country where memories of the Renaissance are ubiquitous.

Though Previati remained loyal to the themes of Symbolism (for instance, presenting a "dream room" at the 1907 Venice Biennial), he was the theorist of Divisionism in Italy, as Signac had been the theorist of Neo-Impressionism in France, but in an altogether different spirit: Previati undertook his experiments with light and color in order to give spiritual energy to the pictorial material by drawing on the laws of optics. His books, *La tecnica della pittura* (1905) and *I principi scientifici del divisionismo* (1906) had a decisive influence on the Futurist artists Balla, Carrà, and Boccioni. "Previati is the only great Italian artist in our time," wrote Boccioni, "to have conceived art as a representation in which visual reality is merely a point of departure. In

Italy he was the forerunner of the idealist revolution which is crushing Naturalism and the documentary treatment of reality."

Influenced by Segantini, Giuseppe Pellizza da Volpedo (1868-1907) employed the Divisionist technique in works of a somewhat maudlin Symbolism with social overtones. This led him at times to tackle rather unusual themes; *The Fourth Estate* (1901, Civica Galleria d'Arte Moderna, Milan) depicts, for example, a trade union demonstration. But his real preoccupations emerged in other works: *The Procession* (1892-1895, Museo Nazionale della Scienza e Tecnica, Milan), *The Crushed Flower* (1896-1902, Musée d'Orsay, Paris), *The Round* (1890-1900, Civica Galleria d'Arte Moderna, Milan). These paintings represent life's joyful or painful mysteries in a manner that was based on an accurate observation of nature and the interplay of light and shade rendered with originality. The artist's refined technique often compensates for his affected subject matter.

Previati's growing interest in the symbolic significance of light combined with his discovery of Monet's painting led him, after 1900, to celebrate the poetry and landscapes by breaking down the solar spectrum into its rainbow of colors. A canvas like *The Rising Sun* (1903-1904, Galleria Nazionale d'Arte Moderna, Rome) is more than just a foreshadowing of the light effects that were to occupy Balla, Boccioni, and Severini several years later. The artist's suicide at the age of thirty-nine—he could not bear his wife's premature death—brought to a close any further pursuit of his "glorifications" of nature which, as he himself put it, had allowed him to "sacrifice to Idealism, not the mystical Idealism, but the Idealism that rests on scientific and philosophical positivism. The ancient Greeks and Romans glorified their gods, the Middle Ages glorified its saints, and as for us, we glorify Nature in her most grandiose spectacles, her most typical forms, her most vital organisms."[4]

Giuseppe Pellizza da Volpedo
The Crushed Flower
c. 1896-1902, oil on canvas,
79.5 × 107
Musée d'Orsay, Paris
Pellizza was fond of depicting scenes from the village life of his native Volpedo and giving them a symbolic dimension. Despite its rather *passé* sentimentalism, this painting of a funeral procession is worth attention for its composition (the figures turn their back to us to signify that they are paying their respects to someone departing toward another world) and the interplay of light and shadow (the sun illuminating the coffin), which is typical of Italian Divisionism.

Luigi Bonazza
The Legend of Orpheus
1905, oil on canvas, 154×369
S.O.S.A.T. Collection,
Museo d'Arte Moderna et
Contemporanea di Trento
e Roverto

The Roman artist Giulio Aristide Sartorio (1860-1932) expressed a form of Symbolism akin to that of Moreau, Böcklin, and the Pre-Raphaelites. On close terms with D'Annunzio, who had brought to Italian literary and artistic circles a taste for the decadent and had made the perverse, castrating female the heroine of many of his poems, Sartorio was fond of evoking ancient Greek and Roman rites in gigantic theatrical canvases with such titles as *The Ephesian Diana and Her Slaves* (around 1890, Galleria Nazionale d'Arte Moderna, Rome) and *The Gorgon and the Heroes* (1895-1899, *ibidem*), whose setting recalls that of Gustave Moreau's *Hercules and the Hydra* and *The Suitors* (Musée Gustave Moreau, Paris).

A native of Trenta, a city that remained under Austrian rule until 1918, Luigi Bonazza (1877-1965) studied at the Kunstgewerbeschule of Vienna, where he was very much influenced by the art of the Secession movement; it was, moreover, at the 29th Secession Exposition that he successfully exhibited *The Legend of Orpheus* (1905, Trenta, Society S.O.S.A.T.), a sumptuous tryptich very clearly inspired by the flying figures Klimt created for the Vienna University. For the same work Bonazza also adopted a Pointillist technique similar to what Segantini and Toorop practiced, both of whom exhibited as well in the Hapsburg capital.

Until the end of the 1920s Bonazza would continue to interpret themes drawn from classical mythology in a style that recalls Klimt's technique, as well as the manner of von Stuck and Hodler.

An avatar of Symbolism: the metaphysical art of Giorgio De Chirico

Giorgio De Chirico (1888-1978), an Italian citizen born in Greece, studied art at the Munich Academy of Fine Arts from 1906 to 1908. He reserved his enthusiasm for Böcklin (his first paintings were virtually pastiches of that artist) and Klinger, two artists whom he admired and studied. He also immersed himself in the writings of Schopenhauer, Nietzsche and Otto Weininger. Weininger's books, in particular *Sex and Character*, revealed to him the existence of sexual symbolism and convinced him of the reality of close correlations between the human microcosm and the universe as a whole. It was in fact from Weininger that he borrowed the term "metaphysical art," the earliest examples of which he painted in Paris around 1912. The first to notice the birth of this new painting was the poet Guillaume Apolli-

naire, who wrote: "The art of this young painter is an interior, cerebral art that has no connection with the art of the painters who have become known these last few years... Here are several singular titles for these strangely metaphysical paintings: *The Riddle of the Oracle*, *The Melancholy of Departure*, *The Riddle of Time*, *Solitude*, *The Locomotive's Whistle*[5].

Obviously, the vast squares surrounded with arcades, the towers and clocks and bunches of bananas that De Chirico painted are no part of the Symbolist iconography of the 1890s and early 1900s, but the titles of his pictures have a resonance that is undeniably that of the fin de siècle generation. It is therefore hardly surprising that André Breton should have felt indebted to De Chirico for "the revelation of the symbols that

Giorgio De Chirico *The Transformed Dream*
1913, oil on canvas, 63 × 152 Saint Louis Art Museum
Drawing inspiration from books he read, notably the works of Nietzsche and Otto Weininger, De Chirico sought to express a universal symbolism and update ancient myths by setting them in the modern urban and industrial world. His paintings between 1910 and 1916 all convey images of impotence and the incompleteness of being. The ancient head, the bananas, and the two pineapples are covert symbols for vacuity and proscribed virility.

189

preside over our instinctual life and which, as we suspected, are distinguishable from those of savage periods. It is now and then salutary to give terror its due, and I cannot prevent myself from seeing, in the canvases that De Chirico painted from 1912 to 1914, so many rigid images of, for example, the outbreak of war. Putting aside all our qualms, there is plenty in the machinery of prophecy to keep us long entranced. And De Chirico has allowed us to hear, for the first time in centuries, the irresistible, unjust voice of the soothsayer."[6] It was once again Breton, a few years later, who rejected the post-1919 De Chirico, when the latter, trying to renew his style, turned toward a Neo-Classicism stamped with Greek mythology and became in the eyes of most critics a sort of "living corpse" consumed with a thirst for lucre, at best plagiarizing his own work.

Picasso's blue period

Even though Spanish art seems to have gone into a slumber following Goya's death until the early 1900s, Barcelona, Spain's most active city, kept in touch with developments elsewhere in European art. The last decade of the nineteenth century in fact witnessed the flowering of *modernismo*, a term that was symptomatic of the Barcelonians' openness, particularly to neighboring France, where most of the Catalonian artists sojourned.

Typical of the more cosmopolitan Catalonian artists, Joan Brull i Vinoles (1863-1912) went to Paris to finish his art studies and, between 1890 and 1900, exhibited his paintings in most of the European capitals. His most famous picture, *Reverie* (1898, Museu d'Art Modern, Barcelona), depicts a young girl seated on the shore of a moon-lit lake and is saturated with reminiscences of the Pre-Raphaelites, though stylistically it has more in common with the work of the French artists Henri Martin and Aman-Jean. The same type of inspiration is found again in *The Dew* (1897, Museu d'Art Modern, Barcelona) by Adria Guall i Queralt (1872-1944) who as a young artist, before he became mainly a stage designer, expressed the Catalonian variety of Pre-Raphaelitism, with its long-haired auburn daughters of the night weeping at the approach of dawn and (as the artist spells out in a poem engraved on the frame) reviving the flowers and trees with their tears.

This atmosphere of Symbolism influenced Pablo Picasso (1881-1973) during his blue period (blue being of course the color of melancholy)[7].

In Barcelona, the young artist frequented *Els Quatre Gats*, the favorite café of the Catalonian modernists. In Paris, where he visited the Universal Exposition in 1900, he discovered the new trends in European art, including the painting of Puvis de Chavannes and Eugène Carrière. After returning to Barcelona he wrote to his friend the poet Max Jacob: "I show what I am doing to my artist friends here, but they find it has too much soul and no form." One discerns traces of French artists' influence, combined with memories of El Greco, in *The Evocation* (1901, Musée d'Art Moderne de la Ville de Paris, Paris), an allegorical canvas Picasso executed as a tribute to his friend Casagemas, who had killed himself in a fit of lover's despair. This painting marks the beginning of the then twenty-year-old artist's series of pictorial broodings on love and death, two themes that were to dominate his work for several years to come.

In 1902, Picasso discovered Gauguin's painting. Its impact nudged his own work further toward the existential themes of his first masterpiece, *Life* (1903, Museum of Art, Cleveland), which could just as well have been called *Whence Come We?...* Here Casagemas's features provide a final opportunity for the young Picasso to ponder over man's fate (with certain autobiographical undertones which have never been fully elucidated). Soon after, Picasso settled in Paris for good, began to paint in a new vein—his pink period—and the metaphysical and affective values in his early work gradually gave way to purely plastic values.

Pablo Picasso
Life
1903, oil on canvas, 196.5 × 123.2
Museum of Art, Cleveland

A masterpiece of Picasso's Blue Period, this carefully meditated canvas is one of the most mysterious works by the artist, who was just twenty-two years old when he painted it. Its central theme is the self-inflicted death of the painter's friend, the artist Casagemas (who lends his features to the male figure). Picasso was deeply upset by this suicide. In addition to the questions "What is love?", "What is life?" posed by the couple on the left and the mother and child on the right, this painting brings into the artist's studio, through the two canvases inspired by Gauguin and Van Gogh, two accursed artists whose destiny furnishes Picasso, at a particularly difficult time in his life, with a third topic to ponder: Where do I belong as an artist?

Notes

1 See A.-P. Quinsac, *La peinture divisionniste italienne. Origines et premiers développements. 1880-1895*, Paris, 1972; A.-M. Damigella, *La pittura simbolista in Italia. 1885-1900*, Turin, 1981.

2 K. Abraham, *Œuvres complètes*, vol. I, *Rêves et mythe* (french translation), Paris, 1965, pp. 217-266.

3 V. Kandinsky, *Concerning the Spiritual in Art, op. cit.*

4 From a letter by Pellizza dated 28 October 1904, cited in A.-M. Damigella, *La pittura simbolista in Italia, op. cit.*, p. 200.

5 See W. Rubin, W. Schmied, and J. Clair, *Giorgio De Chirico* (catalog), Centre Georges Pompidou, Paris, 1983.

6 A. Breton, *Les pas perdus*, Paris, 1924; reprinted 1970, pp. 160-161.

7 Picasso's blue period is analyzed and illustrated in detail in J. Glaesemer and M. Mac Cully, *Der junge Picasso. Frühwerke und Blaue Periode* (catalog), Kunstmuseum, Bern, 1984.

BIO-BIBLIOGRAPHY OF THE SYMBOLIST ARTISTS

GENERAL BIBLIOGRAPHY

INDEX

LIST OF ILLUSTRATIONS

BIO-BIBLIOGRAPHY OF THE SYMBOLIST ARTISTS

We have intentionally limited the bibliography for each artist to the most recent studies, mainly books and exhibit catalogs, containing substantial bibliographies.

AMAN-JEAN, Edmond
Chevry-Cossigny 1859 – Paris 1936

Aman-Jean, a pupil and assistant of Puvis de Chavannes, had close ties with literary Symbolist circles and exhibited works at the Salon de la Rose + Croix. A friend of Verlaine, he was fond of depicting, in pastel shades, dreamy young girls in parks. He was also a fashionable society portraitist around the turn of the century.

Bibl.: *Souvenir d'Aman-Jean*, **exhibit catalog, Musée des Arts décoratifs, Paris, 1970.**

BEARDSLEY, Aubrey Vincent
Brighton 1872 – Menton 1898

Beardsley, a precocious and prodigiously gifted draftsman stricken with tuberculosis at a very early age, was influenced stylistically by Burne-Jones and Puvis de Chavannes. His first success came in 1894 with his drawings for Oscar Wilde's *Salome*. He also illustrated Wagner, Aristophanes, Pope, and Mallory's *Morte d'Arthur*. He was keenly illustrated in the art of printing and book design (*The Yellow Books*).

Bibl.: S. Weintraub, *Beardsley, Imp of the Perverse,* **London, 1976.**

BERGH, Richard
Stockholm 1858 – Stockholm 1919

The son of a famous landscape painter, Bergh made numerous sojourns in France, where he discovered Gauguin's art. He played a significant role in the artistic life of his era. He opened the Scandinavian art scene to modern influences and directed the Nationalmuseum in Stockholm.

Bibl.: *Lumières du Nord. La peinture scandinave 1885-1900,* **exhibit catalog, Paris, Petit Palais, 1987.**

BERNARD, Emile
Lille 1868 – Paris 1941

Precocious and interested in all innovations, Bernard dropped out of the official ateliers before he was eighteen and associated with Van Gogh and Toulouse-Lautrec. He invented "Cloisonnism" (with Anquetin) very early on and became friendly with Gauguin at Pont-Aven in 1888. He later asserted that he was the father of "pictorial Symbolism" and accused Gauguin of having imitated him. He spent part of his life trying to substantiate this claim in writing. He exhibited at the Salon de la Rose + Croix in 1892, then went to Egypt where he spent ten years. His later style was influenced by the Italian Baroque.

Bibl.: *Emile Bernard*, **exhibit catalog, Lille, Palais des Beaux-Arts, 1967; J.-J. Luthi,** *Emile Bernard. Catalogue raisonné de l'œuvre peint*, **Paris, 1982.**

BIEGAS, Boleslas
Koziczyn 1877 – Paris 1954

A shepherd until the age of sixteen, Biegas studied painting and sculpture at the Cracow Academy, then settled in Paris in 1901. He gravitated toward the Symbolists, studied the works of Redon, Moreau, Klimt, and Böcklin, and cultivated with equal ardor painting, sculpture, and playwriting. He was haunted by the theme of the sphinx, which to him represented the riddle of life and the world.

Bibl.: X. Deryng, *"Le Sphinx de 1902 de B. Biegas au Musée d'Orsay,"* **in** *Revue du Louvre*, **Paris, 1/1988.**

BÖCKLIN, Arnold
Basel 1827 – Fiesole 1901

Regarded at the end of the nineteenth century as the leading Germanic painter of his time, Böcklin was deeply influenced by ancient Italian art (Pompeii) and painted mainly mythological compositions whose predominant themes are the cycles of nature and life, war, and death. His loud color hamronies, his deliberately unsophisticated drawing, and his foundness for sometimes overemphatic effects have long been held against him by twentieth-century art lovers. At the beginning of the century critics unfavorably compared his philosophical painting, which they deemed retrograde, to the Impressionist values of an art painted in the open air.

Bibl.: R. Andree, *Arnold Böcklin, Die Gemälde,* **Basel, 1977.**

BRULL I VINOLES, Joan
Barcelona 1863 – Barcelona 1912

Art studies in Barcelona and Paris, where he exhibited from 1897 on. He was influenced both by the Pre-Raphaelites (Millais, Rossetti) and the French Symbolists. His favorite subject was young girls in generally nocturnal landscapes (*Reverie*, 1898, Museu d'Art Modern, Barcelona).

BURNE-JONES, Edward Coley
Birmingham 1833 – Fulham 1898

While studying theology at Oxford, Burne-Jones read Ruskin's works and, with his friend William Morris, decided to devote himself to art. He was deeply influenced by Rossetti and Italian Renaissance art (Botticelli, Michelangelo, Mantegna). His paintings evoke the legends of antiquity and the Middle Ages. A late Pre-Raphaelite, Burne-Jones was also drawn toward the decorative arts and was, with Morris, one of the leading figures of the Arts and Crafts Movement.

Bibl.: John Christian, *Burne-Jones*, **exhibit catalog, The Arts Council of Great Britain, London, 1975.**

CARRIÈRE, Eugène
Gournay 1849 – Paris 1906

Carrière spent his youth in Strasbourg and, later, Saint-Quentin where he studied de La Tour's famous pastel portraits. His early work was in the Naturalist vein, but after 1879 the subjects that inspired him were *intimiste* scenes depicting maternal love—his favorite models were his wife and children. A close friend of Rodin (who collected his pictures) and a militant socialist, he sought to paint reality tinged with the magic of dreams. He frequented literary circles and left a number of oil and lithograph portraits of Symbolist artists and writers.

Bibl.: *Eugène Carrière*, exhibit catalog, Château des Rohan, 1964; R.-J. Bantens, *Eugène Carrière. His Work and his Influence*, Ann Arbour, 1983.

CLAUDEL, Camille
La Fère-en-Tardenois 1864 – Montdevergues 1943

Camille Claudel, the older sister of poet and playwright Paul Claudel, was for ten years Rodin's student, inspiration, and mistress. After her break-up with the sculptor, this passionate woman slowly drifted into madness. In a style close to his, she rendered the joys and sorrows of her liaison with Rodin. She spent the last thirty years of her life in an asylum.

Bibl.: R.-M. Paris, *Camille Claudel*, Paris, 1984; *"L'âge mûr" de Camille Claudel*, exhibit catalog, Musée d'Orsay, Paris, 1988.

DAVIES, Arthur Bowen
Utica 1862 – Florence 1928

After studying art in Chicago, Davies went to Europe in 1893. His paintings depict, in a style reminiscent of Puvis de Chavannes and Maurice Denis, an idealized vision of Nature inhabited by young girls in ancient Greek and Roman attire. He made many sojourns in Italy—which did not prevent him from becoming president of the American Association of Painters and Sculptors in 1912 and organizing the famous Armory Show of 1913.

Bibl.: C.C. Eldredge, *American Imagination and Symbolist Painting*, New York, 1979.

DE CHIRICO, Giorgio
Volo 1888 – Rome 1978

Studied art in Munich, where he discovered the work of Max Klinger and Arnold Böcklin and read Schopenhauer, Nietzsche, and Weininger. His first "metaphysical landscapes" were noticed by Guillaume Apollinaire when they were exhibited in Paris in 1913. De Chirico's metaphysical period ended around 1920. His painting thereafter was mainly influenced by ancient Greek and Roman mythology and the style of the Italian Renaissance.

Bibl.: W. Rubin, W. Schmied, and J. Clair, *Giorgio De Chirico*, exhibit catalog, Centre Georges Pompidou, Paris, 1983.

DEGOUVE DE NUNCQUES, William
Monthermé 1867 – Stavelot 1935

A self-taught artist with close ties to Toorop and de Groux, William Degouve de Nuncques mainly produced pastels depicting landscapes and gardens, often at night, whose atmosphere of mystery, inspired by Poe's tales, derives from the absence of any human figure. After 1900, the artist specialized in Mediterranean landscapes. The main body of his work is housed at Otterlo in the Rijksmuseum Kröller-Müller.

Bibl.: A. de Ridder, *William Degouve de Nuncques*, Brussels, 1957.

DELVILLE, Jean
Louvain 1867 – Brussels 1953

Delville, who was at once a painter, poet, and theorist, was influenced by the esoteric doctrines of the late nineteenth century, notably by those of Joséphin Péladan, whose ideas he propagated in Belgium where he founded a Salon of "Idealist Art." He painted vast mystical compositions.

Bibl.: O. Delville, F.-C. Legrand, *Jean Delville, peintre*, Brussels, 1984.

DENIS, Maurice
Granville 1870 – Paris 1943

One of the founders of the Nabi movement. From the start, Denis's work was dominated by Christian themes. A theorist and historian of the Nabi group, as well as an art critic, his style became more classical in inspiration after 1900. Denis painted large secular and religious decorations. A substantial part of his oeuvre is housed in the artist's home at Saint-Germain-en-Laye, near Paris, now the Musée du Prieuré.

Bibl.: *Maurice Denis*, exhibit catalog, Orangerie des Tuileries, Paris, 1970; M.-A. Anquetil, *Musée du Prieuré, Symbolistes et Nabis, Maurice Denis et son temps*, Paris, 1980.

DERKINDEREN, Antoon Johan
's-Hertogenbosch 1859 – Amsterdam 1925

A companion of Toorop in Brussels and a Wagner enthusiast, Derkinderen was enamored of the medieval arts. In Amsterdam and s'-Hertogenbosch he painted murals in the manner of Giotto. Influenced by Ruskin and William Morris, he was interested too in the art of book design.

DESVALLIÈRES, George
Paris 1861 – Paris 1950

A disciple of Gustave Moreau (and for years curator of the Musée G. Moreau in Paris), Desvallières painted, prior to 1900, elaborate Symbolist pictures heavily influenced by the work of his master. After the turn of the century his work, which had many affinities with Fauvism, was almost exclusively religious in inspiration. In 1919 Desvallières founded the Ateliers d'Art Sacré with Maurice Denis in the hope of fostering a return to a more authentic Christian art. He decorated numerous churches. His art, with its impetuous lines and colors, recalls Expressionism.

Bibl.: **A. Garreau, *George Desvallières*, Angoulême, 1942.**

DUCHAMP, Marcel
Blainville-Crevon 1887 – Neuilly 1968

A student at the Académie Julian, Duchamp began his career under the influence of literary and pictorial Symbolism (particularly Redon's). After 1910 he began to move closer to Italian Futurism, and showed his works in the United States, in an atmosphere of scandal which surrounded the appearance of most of his works thereafter. Notwithstanding the corrosive humor that underlies the "Readymades" he assembled from utilitarian objects, some critics have sought an esoteric meaning in his production.

Bibl.: **A. Schwarz, *The Complete Works of Marcel Duchamp*, London & New York, 1970; *Marcel Duchamp*, exhibit catalog, Centre Georges Pompidou, Paris, 1977, 4 vols.**

ENCKELL, Magnus
Hamina 1870 – Stockholm 1925

Already drawn to the doctrine of Swedenborg when he arrived in Paris from Finland in 1891, Enckell was quickly conquered by the theories of Péladan, and notably by the Magus's ideas about primordial androgyny. He admired Puvis de Chavannes, Carrière, and, later, Böcklin. The works of his Symbolist period depict naked adolescents confronting the mysteries of life and death. He decorated St. John's Cathedral at Tampere, Finland, after the turn of the century.

Bibl.: ***Lumières du Nord. La peinture scandinave 1885-1905*, exhibit catalog, Petit Palais, Paris, 1987.**

ENSOR, James
Ostend 1860 – Ostend 1949

A member of the Groupe des XX, Ensor was influenced by the Flemish primitives, especially Bosch and Breugel. Beneath the masks and carnaval scenes of this tormented artist there lurks a profound mysticism and a horror of death. His themes and pictorial techniques seemed scandalous at first, but he was later recognized as a precursor of Expressionism and was even knighted.

Bibl.: **R.-L. Delevoy, *Ensor*, Antwerp, 1981.**

FABRY, Emile
Verviers 1865 – Brussels 1966

Fabry, who was a painter and lithographer, exhibited works at the Rose + Croix salons and enjoyed close ties with Delville and Mellery. Influenced by the Pre-Raphaelites, his oeuvre depicts figures with anxious, almost uniform features that seem unable to communicate with each other.

Bibl.: ***Rétrospective Emile Fabry*, exhibit catalog, Hôtel communal, Woluwe-Saint-Pierre, 1965-1966.**

FANTIN-LATOUR, Henri
Grenoble 1836 – Buré 1904

At one time close to Manet and the Impressionist group—though he also studied Renaissance Venetian painting—Fantin-Latour first made a name for himself with group portraits of artists, writers, and musicians. He particulary excelled in imaginary scenes inspired by Wagner, Schumann, and Berlioz, only returning to reality with brightly colored paintings of flowers.

Bibl.: ***Fantin-Latour*, exhibit catalog, Grand Palais, Paris/Ottawa/San Francisco, 1982-1983.**

FEURE, Georges van Sluyters, called Georges de
Paris 1868 – Paris 1943

Drawn at first to the art of advertising posters, de Feure painted Symbolist compositions of Baudelairian inspiration on the theme of woman, and showed them at the Rose + Croix salons. Around 1900 he turned to the decorative arts. His contributions to Bing's Art Nouveau pavilion at the Universal Exposition of 1900 were much admired. Gifted with a highly inventive mind, he was as skillful at designing airplanes as theater sets and costumes.

Bibl.: **I. Millman, *"Georges de Feure, the Forgotten Dutch Master of Symbolism and Art Nouveau,"* in *Tableau*, Sept.-Oct., 1983, pp. 41-47.**

FILIGER, Charles
Thann 1863 – Brest 1928

A solitary and retiring person, this companion of Emile Bernard and Gauguin lived the life of a penniless drifter in Brittany. Some of his works were shown at the first Rose + Croix salon. A profoundly mystical artist, he sought to paint in the manner of the Trecento masters. In small gouaches he depicted scenes from the life of Christ, which were set in typically Breton landscapes rendered according to the Synthetist principles evolved at Pont-Aven.

Bibl.: **M.-A. Anquetil, *Filiger*, exhibit catalog, Musée du Prieuré, Saint-Germain-en-Laye, 1980; M. Jacob, *Filiger l'inconnu*, Paris, 1980.**

FRÉDÉRIC, Léon
Brussels 1856 – Brussels 1940

Frédéric's first works were naturalistic scenes from the lives of the peasants and factory workers of his native Belgium. In the 1890s, under the influence of Péladan and Delville, he discovered new sources of inspiration and began to paint polyptichs in the Pre-Raphaelite spirit, all the while bringing to the mystical aspect of his painting a realist, social-minded background. A very popular artist, Frédéric was eventually knighted.

Bibl.: **L. Jottrand, *Léon Frédéric*, Antwerp, 1950.**

GALLEN-KALLELA, Akseli
Pori 1865 – Stockholm 1931

Gallen-Kallela received his training in Paris and began painting in a Naturalist style akin to that of Bastien-Lepage. He first strove to become the pictorial bard of

197

the natural wonders of his native Scandinavia. Then he became fascinated with Finnish mythology and undertook to illustrate the *Kalevala* in a visionary Symbolist manner which reflected his sojourns in Berlin and Paris between 1892 and 1894.

Bibl.: *Lumières du Nord. La peinture scandinave 1885-1905*, exhibit catalog, Petit Palais, Paris, 1987.

GAUGUIN, Paul
Paris 1848 – Atuana 1903

Gauguin, who started out as a Sunday painter, decided at the age of 35 to devote himself to art full time. His earliest work was painted in the Impressionist manner of Pissarro, and he participated in the last Impressionist group shows. He abandoned this style at Pont-Aven in Brittany and evolved a synthetic art midway between realistic representation and rendering psychological states through plastic means. His quest for landscapes unmarred by industrial civilization led him to the South Pacific, where he settled after 1891. The Nabi artists regarded him as their master.

Bibl.: M. Hoog, *Gauguin, Vie et œuvre*, Fribourg, 1987; *Gauguin*, exhibit catalog, Grand Palais, Paris, 1989.

GIACOMETTI, Augusto
Stampa 1877 – Zurich 1947

After studying the applied arts in Zurich, Augusto Giacometti (the uncle of the sculptors Alberto and Diego) attended the classes of his compatriot Eugène Grasset in Paris and discovered Puvis de Chavannes's vast mural decorations. Between 1902 and 1915, he sojourned repeatedly in Italy and studied the Ravenna mosaics. Between 1898 and 1908, while pursuing his career as a decorative artist (mosaics, stained glass windows), he painted canvases in the Symbolist vein and developed an art based on color studies, which verge on abstraction.

Bibl.: *Augusto Giacometti*, Clemens-Sels-Museum, Neuss, 1987.

GRASSET, Eugène
Lausanne 1845 – Sceaux 1917

Influenced by the work of Viollet-le-Duc and the vogue in favor of Japanese art in the 1890s, Grasset was mainly important in the area of the decorative and graphic arts and was one of the pioneers of Art Nouveau. He participated in the first Salon de la Rose + Croix and painted a series of watercolors on the theme of female passions.

Bibl.: *Eugène Grasset*, exhibit catalog, Galerie Plantin-Blondel, Paris, 1980.

GROUX, Henry de
Brussels 1867 – Marseilles 1930

A painter and lithographer, and a member of the Groupe des XX from which he was barred because of his outspoken hostility toward Van Gogh and Seurat, de Groux was chiefly inspired by religious, literary (Dante, Baudelaire), and musical (Wagner) themes. A large part of his oeuvre is preserved at the Fondation de Flandreysy-Espérandieu in the Palais de Roure in Avignon.

Bibl.: E. Baumann, *La vie terrible d'Henry de Groux*, Paris, 1936.

GRUBICY DE DRAGON, Vittore
Milan 1851 – Milan 1920

An art dealer, critic, and painter, Grubicy was a significant influence on Segantini and Previati, both of whom he encouraged. His sojourns in Holland and Belgium brought him into contact with the Groupe des XX and the French Neo-Impressionists. A theorist of pictorial Symbolism in Italy, he painted landscapes which were conceived as pantheistic poems.

Bibl.: A.-P. Quinsac, *La peinture divisionniste italienne. Origines et premiers développements*, Paris, 1972; M. Valsecchi and F. Vercellotti, *Vittore Grubicy de Dragon*, Milan, 1976.

HAWKINS, Louis Welden
Esslingen 1849 – Paris 1910

Of British extraction but trained at the Académie Julian in Paris, Hawkins exhibited at the Rose + Croix salons. His works—some of them close to Rossetti's —often have a gold background, in the manner of the early Siennese masters.

Bibl.: *Le symbolisme et la femme*, exhibit catalog, Paris/Toulon/Pau, 1986.

HODLER, Ferdinand
Bern 1852 – Geneva 1918

Trained as a landscape artist in Barthélemy Menn's studio in Geneva and later turned to other sources of inspiration after making the acquaintance of the Symbolist poet Duchosal. A number of his canvases, clearly influenced by Puvis de Chavannes, were exhibited at the Rose + Croix salons. Around the turn of the century, Hodler undertook several vast decorative paintings for public buildings in Switzerland (Zurich) and Germany (Iena and Hanover). He also had close ties with the Viennese Secession.

Bibl.: *Ferdinand Hodler*, exhibit catalog, Petit Palais, Paris, 1983.

HOLST, Richard Nicolaus Roland
Amsterdam 1868 – Bloemendaal 1938

Holst, who received his training at the Amsterdam Academy, was influenced by Péladan. He made a large number of lithographs which drew their themes from Rossetti and Ricketts. He moved away from Symbolism shortly before the turn of the century and devoted himself thereafter to the decorative arts (murals for the Amsterdam Stock Exchange).

JOSEPHSON, Ernst
Stockholm 1851 – Stockholm 1906

After studying art in the leading European capitals, Josephson settled for some time in Brittany where he dabbled in spiritualism (attempting among other things to communicate with the spirit of his compatriot Swedenborg). He suffered from paranoia but was able to express his mystical hallucinations in a very free, almost Expressionist style.

Bibl.: *Lumières du Nord. La peinture scandinave 1885-1905*, exhibit catalog, Petit Palais, Paris, 1987.

KHNOPFF, Fernand
Grembergen-lez-Termonde 1858 – Brussels 1921

After attending the Academy of Fine Arts in Brussels, Khnopff came under the influence of Gustave Moreau and the Pre-Raphaelites (especially Burne-Jones). He participated in the Rose + Croix salons. His favorite themes, drawn from mythology and literature, are filled with female figures. His art had a considerable impact throughout Europe and was notably influential among the Viennese Secession artists.

Bibl.: R.-L. Delevoy, C. De Croës, G. Ollinger-Zinque, *Fernand Khnopff. Catalogue de l'œuvre*, Brussels, 1987.

KLIMT, Gustav
Vienna 1862 – Vienna 1918

Klimt began his career in the wake of Hans Makart (1840-1884), who was considered the great academic painter of his time. In 1897 Klimt took part in the founding of the Vienna Secession and became its first president. In 1900 his paintings for the main lecture hall at the University of Vienna caused an uproar because of their explicit eroticism. Klimt executed, in 1902, the Beethoven frieze for the Fourteenth Secession Exhibition. In 1904 he began working on the decorations for the Palais Stoclet in Brussels and undertook, in 1910, a series of canvases on the theme of life and death.

Bibl.: F. Novotny and J. Dobai, *Gustav Klimt*, Salzburg, 1975; J.-P. Bouillon, *Klimt: Beethoven*, Geneva, 1986.

KLINGER, Julius
Vienna 1876 – Vienna 1920

A painter, engraver, and graphic artist, Julius Klinger had ties with the Viennese Secession and illustrated the review *Ver Sacrum* and a book called *Sodom*. He also designed typographical characters.

Bibl.: M. Pabst, *L'art graphique à Vienne autour de 1900*, Paris & Munich, 1985.

KLINGER, Max
Leipzig 1857 – Grossjena 1920

The painter, engraver, and sculptor Max Klinger completed the academic training he had received in Berlin and Karlsruhe with sojourns in Brussels, Paris, and Rome. He admired Böcklin and Puvis de Chavannes. His interest in music inspired several suites of engravings (Brahms) and, above all, a statue of Beethoven which was the centerpiece of the 1904 Vienna Secession show. Deeply influenced by his readings in philosophy (Schopenhauer), Klinger executed a series of large canvases on religious and mythological subjects, which he treated in a syncretist spirit. His engraved oeuvre is substantial.

Bibl.: *Max Klinger, Wege zum Gesamtkunstwerke*, exhibit catalog, Roemer- und- Pelizaeus-Museum, Hildesheim, 1984.

KUBIN, Alfred
Leitmeritz 1877 – Wernstein-am-Inn 1959

As an adolescent prone to depression, Kubin discovered art while visiting the Alte Pinakothek in Munich and promptly enrolled in that city's Academy of Fine Arts. Deeply impressed by Max Klinger's engravings, he studied the graphic work of Goya, Ensor, Rops, Redon, and others, and began a career as a visionary illustrator and draftsman, mixing the burlesque with a sense of the tragic derived from Schopenhauer. He is the author of a Gothic novel, *Die andere Seite*, 1909.

Bibl.: *Alfred Kubin*, exhibit catalog, Musée-galerie de la Seita, Paris, 1988.

KUPKA, František
Opočno 1871 – Puteaux 1957

Kupka, who was initiated into spiritualism at a very early age, studied at the Vienna Academy, then moved to Paris where he supported himself doing illustrations for satirical reviews. His theosophical beliefs inspired him to paint in the Symbolist vein, and his research involving astral light led him, after 1910, to undertake increasingly abstract compositions.

Bibl.: *František Kupka, a Retrospective*, exhibit catalog, The Solomon R. Guggenheim Museum, New York 1975; *František Kupka (1871-1957) ou l'invention d'une abstraction*, exhibit catalog, Musée d'Art Moderne de la Ville de Paris, Paris, 1989-1990.

LACOMBE, Georges
Versailles 1868 – Versailles 1916

Brought into the Nabi group by Sérusier in 1892, Lacombe, a painter of mysterious Breton landscapes done in the Pont-Aven style, was known mainly for his wood carvings inspired by esoteric beliefs and influenced by Gauguin. After the turn of the century, under the influence of Van Rysselberghe, he embraced the Pointillist technique.

Bibl.: J. Ansieau, *"Deux sculptures de Georges Lacombe: Isis et le Christ,"* in *Revue du Louvre*, Paris, 4/1983.

LÉVY-DHURMER, Lucien
Algiers 1865 – Le Vésinet 1953

Lévy-Dhurmer, who began as a ceramist, was influenced by the Pre-Raphaelites and Italian art. His canvases and pastels often associate female faces or figures with poetic or musical themes (Beethoven, Debussy, Fauré). His vaporous touch draws on certain Pointillist elements.

Bibl.: *Autour de Lévy-Dhurmer. Visionnaires et Intimistes en 1900*, Grand Palais, Paris, 1973.

LIST, Wilhelm

Vienna 1864 – Vienna 1918

After studying art in Vienna, Munich, and Paris, List became one of the founding members of the Viennese Secession in 1897. A painter and lithographer, he was the driving force behind the Secession's review, *Ver Sacrum*, which he edited and to which he contributed numerous chromolithographs.

Bibl.: M. Pabst, *L'art graphique à Vienne autour de 1900*, Paris & Munich, 1985.

MACKINTOSH, Charles Rennie

Glasgow 1868 – London 1928

Before becoming the leader of one of the most important Art Nouveau movements in Britain, the Scottish architect and decorator Mackintosh, while still an architecture student at the Glasgow School of Art, painted a large number of mysterious watercolors steeped in the Pre-Raphaelite spirit and clearly influenced by Beardsley and Toorop. Mackintosh's paintings are also obviously related to the work of the Macdonald sisters: his wife Margaret (1865-1933), and Frances (1874-1921).

Bibl.: R. Billcliffe, *Mackintosh watercolours*, exhibit catalog, Glasgow Art Gallery, 1978.

MALCZEWSKI, Jacek

Radom 1854 – Cracow 1929

After studying art in Cracow, Malczewski completed his training in Paris and Munich. He later taught at the Cracow School of Fine Arts. His paintings, the themes of which are sometimes taken from Polish history, often depict a figure (perhaps the artist himself) on a country road encountering a young woman bearing a scythe—Death.

Bibl.: *Symbolism in Polish Painting 1890-1914*, exhibit catalog, The Detroit Institute of Art, Detroit, 1984.

MARCEL-BÉRONNEAU, Pierre

Bordeaux 1869 – La Seyne-sur-Mer 1937

A student of Gustave Moreau, Marcel-Béronneau contributed to the Rose + Croix salons. His favorite theme was that of the *femme fatale*: he painted countless Salomes, Judiths, and Sapphos. His superb craftsmanship and fondness for thick impasti and brilliant colors tend to make one forget the repetitiveness of his subject matter.

Bibl.: *Marcel-Béronneau, peintre symboliste*, exhibit catalog, Galerie A. Blondel, Paris, 1981.

MARCIUS-SIMONS, Pinckney (born Marius Antes Simons)

New York 1865 – Bayreuth 1909

Born in the United States but educated in Europe, Marcius-Simons exhibited at the Rose + Croix salons. A Wagner enthusiast, he painted numerous pictures based on the composer's music dramas (*Parsifal Tone*

Pictures) and worked as a decorator at the Festspielhaus at Bayreuth.

Bibl.: C.C. Eldredge, *American Imagination and Symbolist Painting*, New York, 1979.

MARÉES, Hans von

Elberfeld 1837 – Rome 1887

After studying art in Berlin and Munich, Hans von Marées moved to Italy. In 1873 he executed the frescos at the Stazione Zoologica in Naples. Unlike his fellow Deutsch-Römer artist Böcklin, and not unlike Puvis de Chavannes, he sought to express a vision of Arcadia where generations succeed each other harmoniously in a natural, paradisiac setting.

Bibl.: *Hans von Marées*, exhibit catalog, Neue Pinakothek, Munich, 1987-1988.

MARTIN, Henri

Toulouse 1860 – Paris 1943

Henri Martin painted large compositions in the manner of Puvis de Chavannes, using Neo-Impressionist techniques and drawing his subjects from the works of Dante and Baudelaire. His paintings were shown at the Rose + Croix salons and always attracted a great deal of notice. After 1900 he went back to painting idealized landscapes and executed murals for the Toulouse Capitol.

Bibl.: C. Coustols, *Henri Martin*, exhibit catalog, Palais des Arts, Toulouse, 1983.

MAURIN, Charles

Le Puy 1856 – Grasse 1914

A student at the Académie Julian and a friend of Vallotton and Toulouse-Lautrec, Maurin contributed Symbolist canvases on social themes to several of the Rose + Croix salons. He was also an interesting aquatint engraver.

Bibl.: *Charles Maurin*, exhibit catalog, Musée Crozatier, Le Puy, 1978.

MAXENCE, Edgard

Nantes 1871 – La Bernerie-en-Retz 1954

A student of Gustave Moreau, Maxence contributed idealist compositions, which usually had medieval settings, to the Rose + Croix salons. Prior to 1900 his works were distinguished by experiments with pigment which made his iconlike pictures a cross between painting and sculpture. After the turn of the century his Symbolism gained in decorativeness what it lost in profundity.

Bibl.: *Le symbolisme et la femme*, exhibit catalog, Paris/Toulon/Pau, 1986.

MEHOFFER, Jozef

Ropczyc 1869 – Wadowice 1946

A painter and mural decorator (especially of churches), Mehoffer lived in France and Switzerland after studying art in Cracow. He admired the works of

Puvis de Chavannes and Böcklin. His most significant project were his designs for the stained glass windows at the Cathedral of St-Nicholas in Fribourg, Switzerland.

Bibl.: *Symbolism in Polish Painting 1890-1914*, exhibit catalog, The Detroit Institute of Art, Detroit, 1984.

MELLERY, Xavier
Brussels 1845 – Brussels 1921

A member of the Groupe des XX and Fernand Khnopff's master, Mellery dreamt of decorating the chief monuments of Belgium's capital with huge frescos. These were never realized but the artist has left us gouache maquettes with gold and silver backgrounds. He was also an *intimiste* and painted a series of interior views of convents.

Bibl.: F.-C. Legrand, *Le symbolisme en Belgique*, Brussels, 1971.

MÉNARD, Emile-René
Paris 1862 – Paris 1930

Raised in a family that revered classical antiquity, Ménard painted mythological themes in the tradition of the historical landscape, seeking to render the timeless beauty of ancient Greek and Sicilian sites. His œuvre as a decorator belongs to the Puvis de Chavannes tradition.

Bibl.: A. Michel, *Peintures et pastels de René Ménard*, Paris, 1923.

MINNE, George
Gand 1866 – Laethem-Saint-Martin 1941

A friend of Maeterlinck, Minne began his career illustrating that poet's works. Deeply influenced by medieval art, he exhibited sculptures at the Salon des XX, representing emaciated and suffering figures, kneeling adolescents and relic bearers and, later, grieving mothers and Christs.

Bibl.: P. Baudson, *Constantin Meunier, George Minne*, exhibit catalog, Musées Royaux des Beaux-Arts, Brussels, 1969.

MONDRIAN, Piet
Amersfoort 1872 – New York 1944

Pieter Cornelis Mondriaan—the artist simplified his name when he moved to Paris—studied landscape painting at the Amsterdam Academy. He then met Toorop and, in 1909, became a theosophist and began to paint canvases with an esoteric content. Thereafter began a long period of pictorial researches in Paris, based on natural data and influenced by Cubism, which gradually led Mondrian to non-figurative painting, the theoretical basis of which he outlined in the art review *De Stijl*. He painted his first colored geometrical compositions in 1919. He settled in New York in 1940.

Bibl.: M. Seuphor, *Piet Mondrian, sa vie, son œuvre*, Paris, 1956; *Mondrian*, exhibit catalog, Staatsgalerie, Stuttgart, 1980.

MONTALD, Constant
Gand 1862 – Brussels 1944

Montald devoted most of his life to painting large canvases, idealist in inspiration, which were conceived as decorations for public buildings in Brussels (Musée d'Art ancien) and Paris (Faculté de Droit). He contributed works to the Salon d'Art Idéaliste organized by Delville and was a member of the Rose + Croix movement.

Bibl.: *Constant Montald. Une vie, une œuvre, une amitié, Emile Verhaeren*, exhibit catalog, Woluwe-Saint-Lambert, 1982.

MOREAU, Gustave
Paris 1826 – Paris 1898

Despite the training he received at the Ecole des Beaux-Arts in Paris, Moreau was especially sensitive to the influences of Delacroix, Chassériau and, somewhat later, the Italian Renaissance masters (Mantegna, Carpaccio, Michelangelo). He expressed his fantasies against backgrounds drawn from ancient myths and biblical stories. His painting is characterized by a rich colored texture and a constant search for harmonious arabesques. Toward the end of his life, Moreau was a remarkable teacher, and his students included Matisse and Rouault. He bequeathed his studio to the French state; it is now the Musée Gustave-Moreau in Paris.

Bibl.: P.-L. Mathieu, *Gustave Moreau, sa vie, son œuvre, catalogue raisonné de l'œuvre achevé*, Fribourg, 1976.

MOSSA, Gustav-Adolf
Nice 1883 – Nice 1971

Mossa, whose father was also an artist, came under the influence of the Quattrocento masters and was familiar with Gustave Moreau's work. A precocious artist thoroughly acquainted with Art Nouveau decors, he dealt in an original manner with all the favorite Symbolist themes, combining them humorously with private allusions to female perversity.

Bibl.: J.R. Soubiran, *Gustav-Adolf Mossa et les symboles*, exhibit catalog, Galerie des Ponchettes, Nice, 1978.

MUCHA, Alphonse
Ivancice 1860 – Prague 1939

Mucha started out as a stage designer in Vienna. Then, in 1888, after studying art at the Munich Academy, he moved to Paris and attended classes at the Académie Julian. An illustrator and lithographer, he gained celebrity with his posters for plays starring Sarah Bernhardt. He became one of the most prolific representatives of Parisian Art Nouveau. After 1900 he turned to mystical subjects which were more in keeping with his nature and, in his last years, executed vast decorative paintings which he conceived as epic celebrations of the great moments in the history of the Slavic nations.

Bibl.: *Mucha*, exhibit catalog, Grand Palais, Paris, 1980.

MUNCH, Edvard
Loten 1863 – Oslo 1944

Raised in a family marked by illness and death, Munch attended Bonnat's atelier in Paris between 1889 and 1891. He led the life of a Bohemian artist in Paris and Berlin and frequented literary circles in both cities. He undertook a series of paintings on the themes of life, love, and death, which he later exhibited under the title *The Frieze of Life*. He was also an engraver. In 1908 he received psychiatric treatment and thereafter retired to Norway. His works henceforth began to be accepted by the public and he was even given official commissions. The Edvard Munch Museum in Oslo now houses the works he bequeathed to that city.

Bibl.: A. Eggum, *Edvard Munch, peintures, esquisses, études*, Paris, 1983.

NERÉE TOT BABBERICH, Christoph Karel Henri de
Zevenaar 1880 – Todtmoos 1909

Obliged at the age of 20, for health reasons, to abandon the diplomatic career he had begun, de Nerée tot Babberich devoted his energies to poetry—composed in both French and Dutch—drawing, and watercolors, which he painted in a style reminiscent of Toorop and, mainly, Beardsley (whose life of illness resembled his own). After his death, his mother added delicate embroidery to some of his drawings, thus further accentuating their precious elegance.

Bibl.: *En wie, die midden tusschen de paardebloemen zit, beschouwt niet gaarne een exotische orchidee? 75 Tekeningen van Christoph Karel Henri de Nerée tot Babberich*, Gemeentemuseum Arnhem, 1986.

OSBERT, Alphonse
Paris 1857 – Paris 1939

Osbert, who studied at the Ecole des Beaux Arts in Paris, was influenced mainly by Puvis de Chavannes. He contributed to all the Rose+Croix salons and specialized throughout his life in visionary landscapes haunted by classical muses strolling in the twilight.

Bibl.: *Alphonse Osbert*, exhibit catalog, Ernst Barlach Haus, Hamburg, 1979.

PÉLADAN, Joséphin (called le Sâr)
Lyons 1858 – Neuilly 1918

Péladan, who was raised in a family that was drawn to the occult, began his career as a novelist and art critic, and was a determined opponent of Naturalism. After reviving the Rosicrucian Order with Stanislas de Guaïta, he broke with the latter in 1890 and founded a dissident group, l'Ordre de la Rose+Croix catholique, which aimed to organize art shows. Six Rose+Croix salons were held in Paris between 1892 and 1897, and the works of hundreds of artists drawn to Idealist art were exhibited. A devotee of Wagner and the Italian Renaissance masters, Péladan expounded his ideas in his art criticism, his theater, and in a cycle of novels called *La Décadence latine*.

Bibl.: R. Pincus-Witten, *Occult Symbolism in France. Joséphin Péladan and the Salons de la Rose+Croix*, New York & London, 1976.

PELLIZZA DA VOLPEDO, Giuseppe
Volpedo 1868 – Volpedo 1907

Studied art at the Brera Academy in Milan. Influenced by the Pre-Raphaelites and by Naturalist landscape painting. Adopted the Divisionist technique around 1892. His Symbolism was tinged with social considerations. He drew on the events of daily life but gave them a mystical dimension (e.g. the *Love in Life* triptych).

Bibl.: A. Scotti, *Pellizza da Volpedo. Catalogo generale*, Milan, 1988.

PICASSO Pablo
Málaga 1881 – Mougins 1973

As a young artist in Barcelona, Picasso was influenced by the interest in literary and pictorial Symbolism among the members of the Els Quatre Gats group. In the course of his numerous visits to Paris, he became acquainted with the paintings of Puvis de Chavannes, Carrière, Gauguin, and Munch. Badly shaken by the suicide of his friend Casagemas in 1901, he turned increasingly to the theme of man's fate. The canvases of this period are characterized by the predominance of blue, the color of melancholy, hence the name given to his early production: the Blue period.

Bibl.: *Der junge Picasso. Frühwerk und Blaue Periode*, exhibit catalog, Kunstmuseum, Berne, 1984.

PODKOWINSKI, Wladyslaw
Warsaw 1866 – Warsaw 1895

After studying art at the St-Petersburg Academy, Podkowinsky went to Paris in 1889 and discovered Impressionism—in particular Monet—which he later introduced to his own country. From 1892 on, he painted morbidly Symbolist compositions, the leading themes of which were woman, love, and death. He died of tuberculosis at the age of 39.

Bibl.: *Symbolism in Polish Painting 1890-1914*, exhibit catalog, The Detroit Institute of Art, Detroit, 1984.

POINT, Armand
Algiers 1860 – Naples 1932

A painter and goldsmith, Point was captivated by Florentine Renaissance art, studied its techniques closely, and drew on them in his own mythological compositions. Péladan and Puvis de Chavannes helped him to get launched. Point was one of the most acclaimed artists at the Rose+Croix salons. Following William Morris' example, he founded the Atelier de Haute-Claire at Marlotte, near Paris and, with a team of artist-craftsmen, produced art objects and jewelry worthy of a modern Benvenuto Cellini, to whom Péladan compared him.

PREVIATI, Gaetano
Ferrara 1852 – Lavagna 1920

Trained at the Brera Academy, Previati illustrated Poe's tales and showed his canvas *Motherhood* in Milan in 1891 and, the following year, at the Salon de la Rose + Croix in Paris. In 1907 his works were exhibited in a space billed the "Dream Room" at the Venice Biennale. One of the theorists of Divisionism as an expression of the spiritual energies of light and matter, his writings had a great impact on the Futurist artists Boccioni and Carrà.

Bibl.: *Gaetano Previati. Mostra antologica*, exhibit catalog, Palazzo dei Diamanti, Ferrara, 1969.

PUVIS DE CHAVANNES, Pierre
Lyons 1824 – Paris 1898

After attending several ateliers, notably those of Couture, Delacroix, and Chassériau, Puvis de Chavannes discovered the pre-Renaissance Italian fresco masters and was deeply impressed by their art. He executed large mural decorations for museums at Amiens, Marseilles, Lyons, and Rouen, and, more importantly, for public buildings in Paris (Sorbonne, Hôtel de Ville, Panthéon). Regarded at the end of the nineteenth century as the greatest independent artist of his era, he was internationally admired by young artists.

Bibl.: R.J. Wattenmaker, *Puvis de Chavannes and the Modern Tradition*, exhibit catalog, Art Gallery of Ontario, Toronto, 1975; *Puvis de Chavannes*, exhibit catalog, Grand Palais, Paris, 1976-1977.

RANSON, Paul Elie
Limoges 1861 – Paris 1909

A friend of Sérusier at the Académie Julian, Ranson was one of the first members of the Nabi group, and the most deeply committed to esoteric doctrines. He was keenly interested in the decorative arts (engraving, theater decors, tapestry). His pictorial œuvre is still little known and remains difficult to interpret. Shortly before his death, he founded a free academy where many of his Nabi friends came to teach.

Bibl.: *Paul Ranson*, exhibit catalog, Galleria del Levante, Milan, 1967-1968.

REDON, Odilon
Bordeaux 1840 – Paris 1916

Largely a self-taught painter and profoundly marked by the ideas held in the literary and musical circles he frequented, Redon published his first album of lithographs (*Dans le rêve*) in 1879. He contributed to the last group show of the Impressionists but found the latter "limited." Until 1890 he worked mainly in charcoal (calling his charcoal drawings, "blacks") and produced several series of engravings inspired by Poe, Goya, and Flaubert. Thereafter, he gradually began to use color and made remarkable pastels of fantastic themes, some of them derived from Moreau. He also produced lavishly colored paintings of flowers.

Bibl.: R. Bacou, *Odilon Redon*, Geneva, 1956, 2 vols.; *Odilon Redon*, exhibit catalog, Galerie des Beaux-Arts, Bordeaux, 1985.

RENAN, Ary Cornelis
Paris 1857 – Paris 1900

The son of the historian Ernest Renan, Ary Renan had a somewhat eclectic career as a painter, illustrator, poet (*Rêve d'artiste*), historian, and art critic. A friend of Puvis de Chavannes and Gustave Moreau—he was the latter's first biographer—he painted subjects inspired by ancient Greek and Roman myths.

Bibl.: G. Lacambre, *French Symbolist Painters*, exhibit catalog, Hayward Gallery, London, 1972.

RICKETTS, Charles
Geneva 1866 – London 1931

An aesthete *par excellence*, Ricketts, whose life is indissociable from that of his friend the painter Charles Shannon, was the best English draftsman after Beardsley. He was also a scholar, an art critic equally knowledgeable in Italian painting and the Far Eastern arts, an ardent collector, and an inventive stage designer. His best known works are his illustrations for Oscar Wilde's writings, which blend the twin influences of Rossetti and Gustave Moreau.

Bibl.: J. Darracott, *The world of Charles Ricketts*, London, 1980.

RODIN, Auguste
Paris 1840 – Meudon 1917

Rodin, who started out as a sculptor's rougher-out, was accused of molding his first works directly on the living model. Although self-taught and a virtual illiterate when he began, he was drawn to literary circles and became an enthusiastic reader of poetry. In 1880 he was awarded the commission for *The Gates of Hell*, a project which he worked on for many years and which gave rise to some of his most famous sculptures. Around the turn of the century his fame was international. Shortly before his death, he bequeathed the contents of his studio to the French nation, and the French government agreed to establish a Rodin museum in the sculptor's Paris town house.

Bibl.: A.-E. Elsen, *The Gates of Hell by Auguste Rodin*, Stanford, 1985; F.V. Grunfeld, *Rodin. A biography*, New York, 1986.

ROPS, Félicien
Namur 1833 – Essonnes 1898

Rops first brought notice to himself with his drawings for satirical magazines, then made a career mainly as an illustrator and engraver. He had close ties with literary circles, and in particular with Baudelaire. He ably exploited the sexual ambiguities inherent in the Symbolist repertoire and took pride in calling himself a "Satanic artist."

Bibl.: *Félicien Rops*, exhibit. catalog., Musées Royaux des Beaux-Arts, Brussels, 1985; R. Delevoy and G. Cuvelier, *Félicien Rops*, Lausanne, 1986.

ROSSETTI, Dante Gabriel
Londres 1828 – Birchington-on-Sea 1882

The son of an Italian immigrant who revered Dante, Rossetti was one of the founders of the Pre-Raphaelite Brotherhood and remained its most illustrious member. Equally gifted for poetry and painting, he was profoundly influenced by Italian art and by Dante's poems. His œuvre evokes woman to the point of being obsessive; his female figures are all either angels or demons. His life, love affairs, and flamboyant behavior make him a figure out of a romanticized biography.

Bibl.: V. Surtees, *The paintings and drawings of Dante Gabriel Rossetti. A Catalogue Raisonné*, Oxford, 1971, 2 vols.; J. de Langlade, *Dante Gabriel Rossetti*, Paris, 1985.

ROUAULT, Georges
Paris 1871 – Paris 1958

Rouault was Gustave Moreau's favorite pupil and was strongly influenced by that artist when he painted his first compositions with religious themes. He contributed to the last Rose + Croix salon in 1897. After 1900 he began to paint, in a manner close to Fauvism, scenes expressing man's fallen condition and his troubles on earth. Thereafter, both his painted and engraved œuvres were dominated by religious subjects.

Bibl.: B. Dorival and I. Rouault, *Rouault, l'œuvre peint*, Monaco, 1988, 2 vols.

RYDER, Albert Pinkham
New Bedford 1847 – Elmhurst 1917

Virtually self-taught and never in the mainstream of American art, Ryder lived as a recluse in New York City. A visionary artist, he drew his subjects from Shakespeare, Byron, Poe, and Wagner. His œuvre does not amount to more than 170 paintings, many of them small in size and characterized by contrasting zones of deep shadow and intense light. Ryder experimented with texture, trying to suggest the effect of musical waves. He is regarded as one of the precursors of American abstraction.

Bibl.: L. Goodrich, *Albert P. Ryder*, New York, 1959.

SARLUIS, Léonard
The Hague 1874 – Paris 1949

Of Dutch origin, Sarluis settled in Paris in 1894 and was popular in Rose + Croix circles, not only for his precocious talent but also for his good looks. He was hailed as a modern Leonardo—whose manner he copied. He illustrated the Bible but seems to have felt more in his element painting equivocal scenes of sporting androgynous youths.

Bibl.: *Kunstenaren der Idee. Symbolistische in Nederland, ca. 1880-1930*, exhibit catalog, Haags Gemeentemuseum, The Hague, 1978.

SARTORIO, Giulio Aristide
Rome 1860 – Rome 1932

Sartorio, the son of a sculptor, received a European training thanks to his numerous sojourns in Paris, London (where he studied the paintings of Rossetti and Burne-Jones), and Weimar (where he discovered Böcklin's work). He was a member of Gabriele d'Annunzio's circle and, after making a name for himself as one of the masters of the Roman school of painting, was appointed professor at the Roman Academy of Fine Arts and decorated the Italian Chamber of Deputies (1908-1912).

Bibl.: *Giulio Aristide Sartorio*, exhibit catalog, Accademia Nazionale di San Luca, Palazzo Carpegna, Rome, 1980.

SCHWABE, Carlos
Hamburg-Altona 1866 – Avon 1926

The designer of the poster for the first Rose + Croix salon (1892), Schwabe illustrated the writings of numerous literary Symbolists, as well as Zola's *Le Rêve*. He was strongly attracted by mystical subjects and expressed in his watercolors and canvases his ideal of virginal purity and his horror of death.

Bibl.: *Carlos Schwabe*, exhibit catalog, Musée d'art et d'histoire, Geneva, 1987-1988; J.-D. Jumeau-Lafond, "C. Schwabe, illustrateur symboliste du *Rêve* de Zola", in *Revue du Louvre*, Paris, 5-6/1987.

SEGANTINI, Giovanni
Arco di Trento 1858 – Maloja 1899

After studying art at the Brera Academy, Segantini started out painting rustic scenes somewhat after the manner of Millet. He then discovered Schopenhauer's writings and encountered Grubicy and, under their combined influence, turned to mystical subjects often inspired by Hinduism. His quest for solitude drove him to seek ever higher mountain vistas. He died while working on his *Tryptich of Nature*. The output of his last years can be seen at the Segantini Museum in St Moritz.

Bibl.: A.-P. Quinsac, *Segantini. Catalogo generale*, Milan, 1982, 2 vols.

SEGUIN, Armand
Paris 1869 – Châteauneuf-du-Faou 1903

Attended the Académie Julian in Paris and was a loyal and docile companion of Gauguin at Pont-Aven to the extent that the two artists' works have occasionally been confused. His engraved œuvre, which consists almost entirely of Breton scenes, is one of the best examples of the art of the Pont-Aven group. Suffering from depression and tuberculosis, Seguin spent his last years as a guest in Sérusier's home, where he died. His work was exhibited at the Le Barc de Boutteville gallery in 1895—the artist's only one-man show during his life time. Gauguin prefaced the catalog.

Bibl.: *Armand Seguin*, exhibit catalog, Musée de Pont-Aven, Pont-Aven, 1989.

SÉON, Alexandre
Chazelles-sur-Lyon 1855 – Paris 1917

Séon, a student and assistant of Puvis de Chavannes (notably for the Panthéon mural), contributed to several of the Rose + Croix salons and was Péladan's favorite portraitist, illustrating some of the Magus' novels. His painting was austere both in line and color: many of his canvases are limited to two or three dominant tones.

Bibl.: D. Montalant, "Alexandre Séon, peintre symboliste," in L'Œil, Lausanne, Sept. 1985.

SÉRUSIER, Paul
Paris 1864 – Morlaix 1927

In 1888 while still a student at the Académie Julian, Sérusier met Gauguin at Pont-Aven and painted *The Talisman*, a small Synthetist landscape, under his supervision. He handed on Gauguin's teachings to his comrades and founded the Nabi movement. Deeply interested in aesthetic theory, he studied, from 1896 on, the ideas of Father Desiderius at Beuron and sought to popularize the latter's "Holy Proportions" and "Golden Mean." He outlined his own ideas in his treatise *ABC de la peinture.*

Bibl.: M. Guicheteau, *Paul Sérusier*, Paris, 1976; C. Boyle-Turner, *Paul Sérusier*, Ann Arbor, 1983.

SIMBERG, Hugo
Hamina 1873 – Ahtäri 1917

A pupil of Gallen-Kallela in Finland, Simberg sojourned in London where he studied Burne-Jones' painting, medieval miniatures, and Hans Holbein's engravings. His artfully naive painting found its best expression in small, meticulous gouaches whose theme, more often than not, was death. Toward the end of the nineteenth century, Simberg went to Italy to study fresco painting and later executed the murals and stained glass windows for the Tampere cathedral in Finland.

Bibl.: *Lumière du Nord. La peinture scandinave 1885-1905*, exhibit catalog, Petit Palais, Paris, 1987.

SPILLIAERT, Léon
Ostend 1881 – Brussels 1946

A close friend of the poets Verhaeren and Maeterlinck, Spilliaert specialized in watercolors and pastels and drew his inspiration mainly from the desolate landscapes of his native Flanders.

Bibl.: F.-C. Legrand, *Léon Spilliaert*, exhibit catalog, Grand Palais, Paris, 1981.

STRINDBERG, August
Stockholm 1849 – Stockholm 1912

Not only was the great Swedish novelist and dramatist closely involved as an art critic with the artistic life of his times; he was also a visionary artist in his own right. He was friendly with Gauguin and, especially, Munch. Well versed in Swedenborg's writings, he frequented Péladan's Rosicrucian circle. In 1894 he wrote a theoretical text on painting in French, *Des arts nouveaux! ou le hasard dans la production artistique*, in which he undertook to demonstrate that painting, even landscape painting, is dominated by overwhelming creative energies.

Bibl.: *August Strindberg*, exhibit catalog, Rijksmuseum Van Gogh, Amsterdam, 1987.

STUCK, Franz von
Tettenweis 1863 – Munich 1928

Studied art in Munich, where he discovered the Pre-Raphaelites, Khnopff, and above all Böcklin, whose disciple he considered himself to be. A remarkably gifted draftsman, he contributed to an album of emblems and allegorical figures. Death and sin are the leading themes of his pictorial and sculptural oeuvre. In his lifetime he was regarded as the "prince of artists" and was knighted. He taught at the Munich Academy, where Klee and Kandinsky were students of his. He designed and decorated his Munich residence, now the Villa Stuck Museum, to provide a fitting setting for his works.

Bibl.: H. Voss, *Franz von Stuck, Werkkatalog der Gemälde*, Munich, 1973.

THORN PRIKKER, Johan
The Hague 1868 – Cologne 1932

Thorn Prikker, who received his training at the Hague Academy, exhibited with the Groupe des XX and was influenced by Toorop. Drawn to Pointillism, he used this technique to paint mystical canvases depicting Christ and the Virgin. He was able to put his research involving ornamental curved lines to good use when he was called to teach the applied arts (textiles, stained glass windows, frescos) at the Krefeld Kunstgewerbeschule in Germany.

Bibl.: *Johan Thorn Prikker. Werke bis 1910*, Kaiser Wilhelm Museum, Krefeld, 1982.

TOOROP, Jan Theodor
Poerworedjo 1858 – The Hague 1928

Born in Java, the Dutch artist Toorop was a founding member of the Groupe des XX (1888) and after discovering Seurat's Neo-Impressionism became a follower of the French artist. He came under the influence of Péladan's theories in 1891. His drawings and paintings express an elaborate, morbid Symbolism. He converted to Catholicism after 1900, went back to more traditional sources of inspiration, and took part in decorating a number of public buildings. He played an important role in popularizing Symbolism in Holland and Austria.

Bibl.: V. Hefting, *Jean Toorop. Impressionniste, Symboliste*, exhibit catalog, Netherlands Institute, Paris, 1977.

TRACHSEL, Albert
Nidau 1863 – Geneva 1929

After studying architecture in Zurich and Paris, Trachsel frequented the Parisian Symbolist circles and contributed a large number of drawings to the first Rose + Croix salon. Nicknamed the "Poe of architecture" by Vallotton, he composed an album of plates representing imaginary buildings *(Les Fêtes réelles,* 1897). After 1900 he painted dream visions inspired by nature (which he called *Paysages de rêve).*

Bibl. : *Albert Trachsel*, exhibit catalog, Musée d'art et d'histoire, Geneva, 1984-1985.

VALLOTTON, Félix
Lausanne 1865 – Paris 1925

Vallotton, who attended the Académie Julian in Paris, exhibited several woodcuts at the Rose + Croix salon of 1892 and joined the Nabi group in 1893, where he was known as the "foreign Nabi". His was not a metaphysical temperament and he was less interested in the Nabis's spiritual theories than in their flat decorative style. The subjects that claimed his attention had more to do with physical reality than with esoteric doctrines.

Bibl.: G. Busch, B. Dorival, P. Grainville, & D. Jakubec, *Félix Vallotton*, Paris, 1985.

VAN GOGH, Vincent
Groot-Zundert 1853 – Auvers-sur-Oise 1890

Van Gogh studied theology but realized in 1880 that he had an irresistible artistic calling and began working on his drawing while still in Holland. He settled in Paris in 1886 and discovered Impressionist painting. In 1888 he moved to Arles and invited Gauguin to join him there. Their joint stay ended with Van Gogh's mutilation of his own ear and his subsequent internment at Saint-Rémy (1889). He committed suicide at Auvers-sur-Oise in 1890. The only article devoted to his work during his life time was a review written by Albert Aurier, who classed him as a Symbolist.

Bibl.: R. Pickvance, *Van Gogh in Arles*, exhibit catalog, The Metropolitan Museum of Art, New York, 1984; R. Pickvance, *Van Gogh in Saint-Rémy and Auvers*, exhibit catalog, *ibidem*, 1986-1987.

VEDDER, Elihu
New York 1836 – Rome 1923

Vedder, who studied art in France, spent much of his life in Italy. He was close to the Pre-Raphaelites. He become a celebrity in 1884, thanks to his 56 illustrations for a deluxe edition of Omar Khayyám's *Rubáiyát*. The evocative power of these illustrations recalls Redons' drawings. A muralist as well, Vedder worked on a series of allegorical paintings for the foyer of the reading room at the Library of Congress in Washington.

Bibl.: *Perceptions and Evocations: The Art of Elihu Vedder*, National Collection of Fine Arts, Washington D.C., 1979.

VIGELAND, Gustav
Mandal 1869 – Oslo 1943

Trained as a sculptor in the classically-inspired style of Thorvaldsen, the Norwegian artist Vigeland discovered Rodin's work while visiting Paris, then went on to Italy to study Renaissance sculpture. At the beginning of the twentieth century, he undertook a monumental project for an Oslo city park: a granite fountain—to which he later added groups of figures—representing the Tree of Life and a 51-foot tall monolith consisting of human figures, rising from corpses at the base to a child at the summit.

Bibl.: *Gustav Vigeland*, exhibit catalog, Musée Rodin, Paris, 1981.

VRUBEL, Mikhail
Omsk 1856 – St. Petersburg 1910

Vrubel received his training at the St. Petersburg Academy and then went to Venice to study Byzantine art before returning to Russia to restore the frescos in the cathedral of Kiev. Lermontov's poem *The Demon* triggered his imagination and inspired the obsessive theme of the fallen angel which represented, in his eyes, the eternal striving of man's spirit. These exalted sentiments eventually led to insanity in 1902.

Bibl.: M. Guerman, *Mikhaïl Vroubel*, Leningrad, 1986.

WATTS, George Frederic
London 1817 – London 1904

Close to the Pre-Raphaelites and, like them, deeply influenced by Italian Renaissance art, albeit of a somewhat later period (Michelangelo, Tintoretto), Watts viewed his oeuvre as a pictorial lesson with which he intended to elevate the spectator's soul. He wanted his paintings to be shown in a "House of Life," and toward the end of his life gathered them together in a museum, The Watts Gallery, at Compton, near Guildford, Surrey.

Bibl.: J. Gage, *G.F. Watts. A Nineteenth Century Phenomenon*, exhibit catalog, The Whitechapel Art Gallery, London, 1974.

WEISS, Wojciech
Leorda 1875 – Cracow 1950

Weiss, who sojourned in France and Italy after studying art in Cracow, was influenced by the writer W. Przybyszewsky and, through him, discovered Goya, Rops, and Munch. Many of his canvases depict processions of nudes swept up in a bacchanalian dance. A sculptor and engraver as well as a painter, Weiss taught at the Cracow Academy.

Bibl.: *Symbolism in Polish Painting 1890-1914*, exhibit catalog, The Detroit Institute of Art, Detroit, 1984.

WELTI, Albert
Zurich 1862 – Bern 1912

Studied at the Munich Academy and was Böcklin's pupil. A painter and engraver, he sought to depict dreams and nightmares. He executed a series of etchings based on Wagnerian operas.

Bibl.: *Albert Welti im Kunsthaus Zürich*, Kunsthaus, Zurich, 1984.

WILLUMSEN, Jens Ferdinand
Copenhagen 1863 – Cannes 1958

In 1890 Willumsen met Gauguin, Bernard, and Sérusier in Brittany and was deeply influenced by the artistic credo the Pont-Aven group embraced. He was also interested in the decorative arts. He sought in his paintings to give a spiritual dimension to the mountain landscapes of Scandinavia and to show man's frailty and confusion before nature's forces.

Bibl.: *Lumières du Nord. La peinture scandinave 1885-1905*, exhibit catalog, Petit Palais, Paris, 1987.

GENERAL BIBLIOGRAPHY

Excluded from the list below are those monographs—reference works or exhibit catalogs—that already figure at the end of the biographical notices of individual artists.
We have organized our bibliography into two parts:
1) Reference works and articles devoted to symbolism, in alphabetical order according to the author.
2) Exhibit catalogs, in chronological order.

1. REFERENCE WORKS AND ARTICLES

AURIER G.-A., *Œuvres posthumes*, Paris, 1893.

BERNARD E., "Le symbolisme pictural 1886-1936", *Mercure de France*, Paris, 15 June 1936.

Lettres à Emile Bernard, Tonnerre, 1926.

BIRO A. and PASSERON R., *Dictionnaire général du Surréalisme et de ses environs*, Fribourg, 1982.

BOUILLON J.-P., *Journal de l'Art Nouveau 1870-1914*, Geneva, 1985.

BRAET H., *L'accueil fait au Symbolisme en Belgique 1885-1900*, Brussels, 1967.

BRETON A. and LEGRAND G., *L'art magique*, Paris, 1957.

BRETON A., *Le Surréalisme et la peinture*, Paris, 1965.

CARRÀ M., *Metaphysical Art*, London, 1971.

CASSOU J., *Encyclopédie du Symbolisme. Peinture, Gravure et Sculpture. Littérature. Musique*, Paris, 1979.

CHASSÉ C., *Le mouvement symboliste dans l'art du XIXᵉ siècle*, Paris, 1947.

CHASSÉ C., *Les Nabis et leur temps*, Paris, 1960.

CHRISTIAN J., *Symbolistes et décadents*, London - Paris, 1977.

DAGEN P., *La peinture en 1905. "L'enquête sur les tendances actuelles des arts plastiques" de Charles Morice*, Paris, 1986.

DAMIGELLA A.-M., *La pittura simbolista in Italia 1885-1900*, Turin, 1981.

DE LA MAZELIÈRE, *La peinture allemande au XIXᵉ siècle*, Paris, 1900.

DELEVOY R.-L., *Journal du Symbolisme*, Geneva, 1977.

DENIS M., *Théories (1890-1910) : du symbolisme et de Gauguin vers un nouvel ordre classique*, Paris, 1912.

DENIS M., *Journal (1884-1943)*, 3 vols., Paris, 1957-1959.

DORIVAL B., *Les étapes de la peinture française contemporaine*, 3 vols., Paris, 1943-1946.

FÉNÉON F., *Œuvres plus que complètes*, texts collected and presented by J. U. Halperin, 2 vols., Geneva - Paris, 1970.

FOCILLON H., *La peinture aux XIXᵉ et XXᵉ siècles. Du réalisme à nos jours*, Paris, 1928.

GIBSON M., *Les symbolistes*, Paris, 1984.

GOLDWATER R., *Symbolism*, New York, 1979.

GUILLERM J.-P., *Tombeau de Léonard de Vinci. Le peintre et ses tableaux dans l'écriture symboliste et décadente*, Lille, 1981.

HAUTECŒUR L., *Littérature et peinture en France du XVIIᵉ au XXᵉ siècle*, Paris, 1942.

HOFSTÄTTER H. H., *Geschichte der europäischen Jugendstilmalerei*, Cologne, 1963.

HOFSTÄTTER H. H., *Symbolismus und die Kunst der Jahrhundertwende*, Cologne, 1965.

HOFSTÄTTER H. H., *Idealismus und Symbolismus*, Vienna-Munich, 1972.

HUYGHE R. and RUDEL J., *L'art et le monde moderne*, 2 vols., Paris, 1969.

HUYGHE R., *La relève du réel. Impressionnisme. Symbolisme*, Paris, 1974.

JAROCINSKI S., *Debussy. Impressionnisme et symbolisme*, Paris, 1970.

JAWORSKA W., *Gauguin et l'Ecole de Pont-Aven*, Neuchâtel, 1971.

JULLIAN P., *Esthètes et magiciens*, Paris, 1969.

JULLIAN P., *Les Symbolistes*, Neuchâtel, 1973.

JULLIAN P., *Le mouvement des arts du romantisme au symbolisme*, Paris, 1979.

LEGRAND F.-C., *Le Symbolisme en Belgique*, Brussels, 1971.

LETHÈVE J., *Impressionnistes et symbolistes devant la presse*, Paris, 1959.

LETHÈVE J., "La connaissance des peintres préraphaélites anglais en France (1855-1900)," *Gazette des Beaux-Arts*, Paris, May-June 1959.

LUCIE-SMITH E., *Symbolist Art*, London, 1972.

MADSEN S. T., *Sources of Art Nouveau*, New York, 1956.

MADSEN S. T., *L'Art Nouveau*, Paris, 1967.

MASSON A., *L'allégorie*, Paris, 1974.

MAUNER G. A., *The Nabis: Their History and their Art*, New York - London, 1978.

MAURON C., *Van Gogh. Etudes psychocritiques*, Paris, 1976.

MELLERIO A., *Le mouvement idéaliste en peinture*, Paris, 1896.

MERCIER A., *Les sources ésotériques et occultes de la poésie symboliste. I – Le Symbolisme français*, Paris, 1969.

MICHAUD G., *Message poétique du symbolisme*, Paris, 1947.

MILNER J., *Symbolists and Decadents*, London, 1971.

MIRBEAU O., *Des artistes*, Paris, 1986 (re-edition).

PIERRE J., *André Breton et la peinture*, Lausanne, 1987.

PIERROT J., *L'imaginaire décadent*, Paris, 1977.

PINCUS-WITTEN R., *Occult Symbolism in France. Joséphin Péladan and the Salons de la Rose +Croix*, New York-London, 1976.

"Pont-Aven," *Bulletin des Amis du Musée de Rennes*, N° 2, Rennes, Summer 1978.

POUILLIART R., *Littérature française. Le Romantisme. III. 1869-1896*, Paris, 1968.

PRAZ M., *La chair, la mort et le diable. Le romantisme noir*, French translation, Paris, 1977.

QUINSAC A.-P., *La peinture divisionniste italienne. Origines et premiers développements. 1880-1895*, Paris, 1972.

REWALD J., *Le post-impressionnisme*, French translation, Paris, 1961-1988.

RITTER W., *Etudes d'art étranger*, Paris, 1906.

ROBERTS-JONES P., *La peinture irréaliste au XIXe siècle*, Fribourg, 1978.

ROSENBLUM R. and JANSON H. W., *Art of the Nineteenth Century. Painting and Sculpture*, London, 1984.

SCHMUTZLER R., *Art Nouveau*, New York, 1964.

SCHORSKE C. E., *Vienne fin de siècle. Politique et Culture*, French translation, Paris, 1983.

SÉRUSIER P., *ABC de la peinture*, Paris, 1943.

SIGNAC P., *D'Eugène Delacroix au néo-impressionnisme*, introduction and notes by F. Cachin, Paris, 1978.

SPAANSTRA-POLAK B., *Het Fin-de-Siècle in de Nederlandse Schilderkunst. De Symbolistische beweging*, Utrecht, 1955.

SPAANSTRA-POLAK B., *Le symbolisme*, Amsterdam, 1967.

THUILLIER J., *Peut-on parler d'une peinture "pompier"?*, Paris, 1984.

2. EXHIBIT CATALOGS

Cinquantenaire du Symbolisme, Bibliothèque Nationale, Paris, 1936.

Eugène Carrière et le symbolisme, Orangerie des Tuileries, Paris, 1949-1950.

Bonnard, Vuillard et les Nabis. 1888-1903, Musée National d'Art Moderne, Paris, 1955.

Les sources du XXe siècle. Les arts en Europe de 1884 à 1914, Musée National d'Art Moderne, Paris, 1960-1961.

Le groupe des XX et son temps, F.-C. Legrand, Musées Royaux des Beaux-Arts, Brussels; Rijksmuseum Kröller-Müller, Otterlo, 1962.

Les Salons de la Rose+Croix 1892-1897, R. Pincus-Witten, Piccadilly Gallery, London, 1968.

Esthètes et magiciens. Symbolistes des collections parisiennes, Musée Galliéra, Paris, 1970-1971.

Peintres de l'imaginaire. Symbolistes et surréalistes belges, Grand Palais, Paris, 1972.

French Symbolist Painters. Moreau, Puvis de Chavannes, Redon and their followers, Hayward Gallery, London; Walker Art Gallery, Liverpool, 1972.

Le Symbolisme en Europe, H. Hofstätter, G. Lacambre, F. Russoli, Musée Boymans-van Beuningen, Rotterdam; Musées Royaux des Beaux-Arts, Brussels; Staatliche Kunsthalle, Baden-Baden; Grand Palais, Paris, 1975-1976.

Art Nouveau. Belgium - France, Institute for the Arts, Rice University, Houston, 1976.

Kunstenaren der idee. Symbolistische tendenzen in Nederland, ca. 1880-1930, Haags Gemeentemuseum, The Hague, 1978.

L'Ecole de Pont-Aven dans les collections publiques et privées de Bretagne, Musée des Beaux-Arts, Quimper; Musée des Beaux-Arts, Rennes; Musée des Beaux-Arts, Nantes, 1978-1979.

American Imagination and Symbolist Painting, C. C. Eldredge, New York University, Grey Art Gallery and Study Center, 1979.

Post-impressionism. Cross-currents in European Painting, Royal Academy of Arts, London, 1979-1980.

Symbolism. Europe and America at the end of the Nineteenth Century, J. Kaplan, California State College Art Gallery, San Bernardino, 1980.

The Symbolist Aesthetic, The Museum of Modern Art, New York, 1980-1981.

L'éclatement de l'impressionnisme, Musée Départemental du Prieuré, Saint-Germain-en-Laye, 1982-1983.

Symbolisme en Belgique, Musée d'Art Moderne, Hyogo, 1983.

La Revue Blanche. Paris in the days of Post-impressionism and Symbolism, Wildenstein Gallery, New York, 1983.

Wagner et la France, M. Kahane and N. Wild, Théâtre National de l'Opéra, Paris, 1983.

Symbolism in Polish Painting 1890-1914, The Detroit Institute of Arts, Detroit, 1984.

The Pre-Raphaelites, The Tate Gallery, London, 1984.

Debussy e il simbolismo, Villa Medici, Rome, 1984.

Symboles et réalités. La peinture allemande. 1848-1905, Petit Palais, Paris, 1984-1985.

The Spiritual in Art: Abstract painting 1890-1985, County Museum of Art, Los Angeles, 1986.

Le Symbolisme et la femme, Mairie du IXe arrondissement, Paris; Musée des Beaux-Arts, Toulon; Musée des Beaux-Arts, Pau, 1986.

Lumières du Nord. La peinture scandinave. 1885-1905, Musée du Petit Palais, Paris, 1987.

Androgyn. Sehnsucht nach Vollkommenheit, Neuer Berliner Kunstverein, Berlin, 1987.

Salomé dans les collections françaises, Musée d'Art et d'Histoire, Saint-Denis, 1988.

Le Symbolisme dans les collections du Petit Palais, Paris, 1988.

A golden age: Art and Society in Hungary 1896-1914, Barbican Art Gallery, London, 1989.

The last Romantics, The Romantic tradition in British Art. Burne-Jones to Stanley Spencer, J. Christian, Barbican Art Gallery, London, 1989.

INDEX

LIST OF ILLUSTRATIONS

Note: In the following table the abbreviation RMN stands for Réunion des Musées Nationaux.

213

ACKNOWLEDGEMENTS

I would like to take this opportunity to express my deepest gratitude to the art historians, museum curators and private art collectors who generously assisted me throughout my research.

Jean Hirschen, who founded the Office du Livre, was the first to encourage me to undertake this work; his sudden death on 28 July 1987 sadly brought to a close a fine editorial collaboration with which I had been associated, as author, on three occasions since 1975.

Geneviève Lacambre, chief curator of the Musée d'Orsay and curator of the Musée Gustave Moreau since 1986, was the key figure behind the two most important exhibits devoted to symbolist painting. The author of the present work can attest to Ms. Lacambre's thorough understanding of the period.

Ian Millman, assistant professor at the Université de Paris V and author of a thesis on Georges de Feure, kindly made available his knowledge of the most recent studies of numerous artists.

Françoise Siess-Mathieu, my wife, helped me prepare the manuscript, put at my disposal a number of important documents she had collected concerning Péladan and the Rose + Croix, and finally was kind enough to reread the printer's proofs.

I would also like to express my gratitude to the following individuals for their suggestions and the warm welcome I received at their hands: Elisabeth and Clément Altarriba, Paris; Marie-Amélie Anquetil, curator of the Musée du Prieuré, Saint-Germain-en-Laye; Pierre Brochet, Paris; André Cariou, curator of the Musée des Beaux-Arts, Quimper; Christian von Holst, curator of the Staatsgalerie, Stuttgart; Bertrand Issaverdens, Seine-Port; Samuel Josefowitz, Lausanne; Jean-David Jumeau-Lafond, Paris; Ingrid de Kalbermatten, Fribourg; Rosy Kirsch, Paris; Paul Lang, Institut suisse pour l'étude de l'art, Zurich; Karine Malaterre, Bologna; Yukiko Oki, Tokyo; Françoise Paladilhe, Paris; Brigitte Ranson-Bitker, Paris; Anne Roquebert, researcher, Musée d'Orsay; Toni Stooss, curator of the Kunsthaus, Zurich; Marie-José Treichler, Fribourg.

Text and plates printed by
IRL Imprimeries Réunies Lausanne s.a.

Binding by
Schumacher S.A. Schmitten

Printed in Switzerland